William Peard

A Year of Liberty

Or, Salmon angling in Ireland, from February 1 to November 1

William Peard

A Year of Liberty
Or, Salmon angling in Ireland, from February 1 to November 1

ISBN/EAN: 9783337323257

Printed in Europe, USA, Canada, Australia, Japan

Cover: Foto ©ninafisch / pixelio.de

More available books at **www.hansebooks.com**

A YEAR OF LIBERTY;

OR,

SALMON ANGLING IN IRELAND

FROM

FEBRUARY 1 TO NOVEMBER 1.

BY

W. PEARD, M.D., LL.B.

LONDON:
HORACE COX, 346, STRAND, W.C.

1867.

PREFACE.

The "Year of Liberty," is as nearly as possible what the title imports—namely, a period of recreation after toil. During many entire seasons the Author, rod in hand, had rambled over the length and breadth of Ireland, seeing much and learning much, on all matters connected with his favourite sport. With the advantage of past experience, he again visited the island in 1865, pausing for a time at nearly all the first-class salmon rivers and lakes, arriving at each when in the highest order for angling. This plan often necessitated passing more than once through districts previously traversed, but as sport was the primary object of his visit, this was of little moment, for what was lost in order was more than compensated by success.

Whatever faults the work may possess, the writer at least lays claim to accuracy. That which he saw, he endeavoured to describe faithfully, and any reader who follows in his steps, and visits the various waters at the periods referred to, may safely calculate on sport.

It does not, however, necessarily follow that statements which were true in 1865, should be so in 1867, for the constant tendency of the annually increasing passion for angling, is to convert open into private waters. This spirit of exclusiveness prevails more in Scotland than in the sister kingdom, where, however, each year closes some station that was previously free to the wandering sportsman. The beneficial influence of the Fishery Act of 1861 is also fertile in changes; converting, rapidly and surely, bad streams into good ones. Everywhere through the land salmon are on the increase, not merely as regards numbers, but also as respects size, and in the few rivers where artificial propagation has been steadily and systematically followed that increase has been great indeed.

Whilst in Canada and the United States the king of fish is day by day becoming more scarce, in Great Britain it is growing more numerous.

Halcyon days are in store for the rising generation of anglers; and should one of these, faint and weary from the battle of life, stumble on this volume, then probably long forgotten, may he do as I have done, and gain new strength for the combat, through the healing influence of a second "YEAR OF LIBERTY."

W. P.

JUNE, 1867.

CONTENTS.

CHAPTER I.
Private and Confidential—Arrival at Lismore—Misgivings—Fish in the River—Scholar's Throw—Tendency of the Blackwater to get out of Order—"Show you the River, sir?"—The Bony Horse—Unexpected Fresh—A Walk in the Woods—Ara Glen—Operations Resumed—The Lessee—Sport for the Week—Expenses. 1

CHAPTER II.
Choice of a Profession—Spring Flies—The Round Hill—The Last Chance—The Finesk—The Valley of the Bride—At Home in the Evening—Awful Deficit, and the Occasion thereof 7

CHAPTER III.
Between Lismore and Fermoy—On to Killarney—Cost of Journey—The Flesk—Flies of the Neighbourhood—Trolling on Lough Guttane—Remarks—What might be done, and how to do it 12

CHAPTER IV.
Sporting Expenses—What they are, and what they might be—A Dry Sketch of the Lakes and Rivers of the District—Trolling for Salmon, or much Ado about Nothing—Cross-lines—Departure—The Laune—Killorglin to Carra 17

CHAPTER V.
Rosbeigh—The Beigh—Carra River—The Lake—"My Aunt's Legacy"—Glen Carra—The Great Unknown 21

CHAPTER VI.
Waterville—Concerning the Lake—How we got there and what we did ... 27

CHAPTER VII.

Waterville — Derrynane — Spring Equinox — Below Bridge — Lake in Summer—The Coach before the Horses—"Maiden Trout"—Qualms of Conscience—Experience 31

CHAPTER VIII.

I go, but under protest—Cummeragh River—Distant View of the Inny Lakes—Certain Local Matters the Reader ought to know—Ogham Inscriptions—Limerick—The Old Hookmaker—Doonass—How we got to Sligo 37

CHAPTER IX.

Our Hobbies—Morning Walk—Sligo—Mathew the Great—The Drought begins to tell—Waters of the Neighbourhood—Going a-fishing—Lough Gill—The Angler's Duty—Advice to a dear Countryman—Off for Lough Melvin 43

CHAPTER X.

Lough Melvin—A Week at Garrison—What the Drought did—Permission—Irish Follower—Advantages as a Station—Head Waters—Inhabitants of the Lake—The Great Middle Class—Trying our Luck—*De Omnibus Rebus*—Leaf from an Old MS.—We cry for Mercy. 48

CHAPTER XI.

Why certain People are neglected—The Lake—Islands—Woodcocks and Ducks—Trolling—Our Last Day—History of the Week—The Camp is broken up, and we march on Derry—Willie goes Home—Lough Swilly 54

CHAPTER XII.

What's in a Name?—Walking in the Mist, and Floundering in the Mud—A very rough Sketch of the Capabilities of Donegal—Not knowing, can't say—Lough Fern—Grand Day on the Leannan—Greenen Hill—Doings for the Week 60

CHAPTER XIII.

The Bush—Dulce Domum—From Derry to Portrush—What the Birds said—We sail Home, make Casting Lines and Flies, mend Rods, go to the River, and get paid for the Job—Pounds, Shillings, and Pence ... 67

CHAPTER XIV.

The Bush—From the Sea to the Leap—Rod-making—Headlands—We row up the Bann—Three Days consecutive Angling at Spring Tides—Laggandrade—Letter from Lismore—We go to Lough Neagh ... 73

CHAPTER XV.

In which there is not a Word about Salmon Fishing—Toom Bridge—Lough Neagh—Antrim—Two Days' Trouting—Business calls me to Dublin—Old Lodgings—Tackle Shops—The South Wall—We arrive at Mullingar—Fine Weather not ruinous to Belvidere—The Lake District 79

CHAPTER XVI.

He gets his Leg over the Traces—Mullingar—Its Market Population—Walk to the Lake—The size of its Fish as compared with those of Dereveragh and Lough Owel—The Blow Line—Mode of using it—We drift, and what we do—Cooking—A dead calm—Improving the Occasion—We talk Generalities, take to Roach Fishing, and determine to go to Dereveragh next Morning 87

CHAPTER XVII.

Contains nothing about the Killing, though a good deal concerning the Curing of Salmon—The Day ends better than it promised 93

CHAPTER XVIII.

We go to Castle Pollard—Fish Dereveragh for two Days—Return to Mullingar and Belvidere—Visit our old Acquaintance Lough Owel—And set out for Boyle 100

CHAPTER XIX.

Irish Ruins—Church Islands—Things in General—Boyle—Lough Gara—Lough Key—Lough Arrow—Prophetic of Good—We go to the Erne 108

CHAPTER XX.

The Erne - Early Morning—The Bridge—A " great' Misfortune—Subsequent Success—The Colonel discourses—Draughting under the Falls.. 116

CHAPTER XXI.

A Piscatorial Republic — " The Bank of Ireland " — Moss Row — The Captain's Throw—The Lost Gaff—" Luck's All " 125

CHAPTER XXII.

Ballyshannon—Salmon Leap—White Trout—Evening—The Grass Yard—How Pat was brought to Life—The Colonel Tries on his Boots, and John doth a Tale unfold 134

CHAPTER XXIII.

The Colonel takes Command of an Expedition—Through many Dangers we arrive safely at Beleek, and troll on the Lake for anything we can catch—After Mess the Crew cut their Sticks, but subsequently return to Duty—A desperate Character—Westward Ho! 141

CHAPTER XXIV.

Ballysidere—Its Fishery and Fishing 149

CHAPTER XXV.

Ballina—The Tideway 158

CHAPTER XXVI.

Ballina—The Scribe doth a Tale unfold—Up the River, with manifold Reminiscences of "Down the Water," illustrative of what may be done on the Moy under favourable Circumstances—Hypothesis 167

CHAPTER XXVII.

"Up the River"—Pontoon—Unexpected arrival of the Colonel—He discourses in the small hours—A week on Lough Conn—Departure for Galway 175

CHAPTER XXVIII.

Galway 186

CHAPTER XXIX.

Spiddal—Costello—Screebe—Furnace—Kilkerran Bay—Birterbury Bay—Roundstone—Ballinahinch—Clifden—View from Urrisbeg 195

CHAPTER XXX.

Early Morning—Up before the Sun—Autumn—The Evening fulfils its Promise—A Breeze—Journey to Kylemore—A Day on the Lake—Doings for the Week—Leenane—The Killeries—Delphi—The Errive—Drive to Westport—The Reek, and what we saw there—On to Newport 203

CHAPTER XXXI.

The Big House—Head-quarters at Newport—Advantages of our Position in Wet and Dry Weather—Newport River—Burrishoole, Tyrena—Pleasant Dreams—Michael O'Leary's Board—Early Start—An Inn amongst the Mountains—Breakfast—A Day after my own Heart, the Dawn of which is only shown in the present Chapter 213

CHAPTER XXXII.

A Day after my own Heart—Dinner by Proxy—The Spoils—Night—Pat redivivus 222

CHAPTER XXXIII.

After a lazy Day on the Banks of the Beltra, we become more lazy still; abandon our Duty in a shameful Manner, and go Sight-seeing to the Island of Achil 230

CHAPTER XXXIV.

Achil—Taken Captive—Western Village—New Style of Trolling—Inn Bill—Tyrena in "The Dry Season"—Father Ned—Perseverance—Erica Mediterranea—Carrig-a-Binniogh—A Quiet Evening—Under the Stars 237

CHAPTER XXXV.

Donegal—We lodge by the Castle—A Morning Walk to Mount Charles—The River—Strong Run after the Netting Season—The Blacksmith attends our Summons—A ministering Angel—Return in a Deluge, and, the lost One being found, the Bells are set a-ringing! 243

CHAPTER XXXVI.

Donegal—Lough Esk—A Journey through the Wilderness 254

CHAPTER XXXVII.

Gweedore—Poison Glen—Dunlewey Lakes—Arigle—Valley of the Claddy—Angling Regulations—"Waters of the Neighbourhood"—The Middle Lake—A Mountain Storm—Old Dan 262

CHAPTER XXXVIII.

Expectation—The Myrtle Grove—In at the Death—Ruined Cabin—An Impostor—Down to Bunbeg—Gweedore River, and how to get there—Mountain Lake—We set out on a long Journey, but say nothing about it 271

CHAPTER XXXIX.

Old Ground—The Major discourses about Prawns—Snipe-shooting—Autumn Surf—Old Gun—On the Mountain—Banks of the Cummeragh—My Friend's Yacht—We anchor the Horse, and launch forth on the Lower Lake—Black Trout—Upper Lough—Red Salmon—We leave off in the Dusk, and go home in the Dark 280

CHAPTER XL.

The last Act—The Inny in order—Disinterested Advice—The Major distinguishes himself—Grand Total—Homewards—De mortuis—The wind-up—Vale 286

APPENDIX.

A Tourist-Angler's Guide 292

A YEAR OF LIBERTY

ERRATA.

Page 7, line 1, for "profession," read "professional."
,, 48, ,, 6, omit the word "whose."
,, 97, ,, 2, for "constitutes," read "constitute."
,, 102, last line but one, for "produce," read "proceed."
,, 169, line 4, for "here," read "her."
,, 169, ,, 28, for "spite Tom's," read "spite of Tom's."
,, 172, ,, 9, for "that impression," read "some impression."
,, 190, ,, 14, for "ware," read "wares."
,, 208, ,, 27, for "in," read "into."
,, 222, ,, 4, for "in," read "into."
,, 227, ,, 4, for "strides, intent," read "strides. Intent."

close prisoner at home. The Salmon Act of 1862 was at length in full operation. "Queen's gaps" where no such royal roads previously existed, increased weekly close-time, together with the progressive demolition of "fixed engines," promised great things, as I lay awake on that blessed morning, thinking the dull dawn would never brighten into day. Though nearly dark, the sun was shining on a world of my own, for I was free—free to come; free to go; free to wander over delicious mountains, or rest by the sparkling river, and there drink in new life from the contemplation of an eternal youth, as fresh and bright as when the morning stars first sang together.

So many doubts and fears crowded the space between hope and fruition, that it seemed difficult to believe that the first day of my

CHAPTER XXXIX.

Old Ground—The Major discourses about Prawns—Snipe-shooting—Autumn Surf—Old Gun—On the Mountain—Banks of the Cummoragh—My Friend's Yacht—We anchor the Horse, and launch forth on the Lower Lake—Black Trout—Upper Lough—Red Salmon—We leave off in the Dusk, and go home in the Dark 280

A YEAR OF LIBERTY.

CHAPTER I.

Private and Confidential—Arrival at Lismore—Misgivings—Fish in the River—Scholar's Throw—Tendency of the Blackwater to get out of Order—"Show you the River, sir?"—The Bony Horse—Unexpected Fresh—A Walk in the Woods—Ara Glen—Operations Resumed—The Lessee—Sport for the Week—Expenses.

THERE was no happier man in Her Majesty's dominions than I, on the morning of January 30, 1865. During the previous sixteen years, I had passed fifteen entire angling seasons in Ireland; but in the last I had been less fortunate, circumstances having bound me a close prisoner at home. The Salmon Act of 1862 was at length in full operation. "Queen's gaps" where no such royal roads previously existed, increased weekly close-time, together with the progressive demolition of "fixed engines," promised great things, as I lay awake on that blessed morning, thinking the dull dawn would never brighten into day. Though nearly dark, the sun was shining on a world of my own, for I was free—free to come; free to go; free to wander over delicious mountains, or rest by the sparkling river, and there drink in new life from the contemplation of an eternal youth, as fresh and bright as when the morning stars first sang together.

So many doubts and fears crowded the space between hope and fruition, that it seemed difficult to believe that the first day of my year of liberty had actually come, and was no longer a portion of the uncertain future, but a present fact, a glorious reality.

With the *cause* of this happy consummation it is unnecessary to trouble the reader. After all, who cares what it may be? The other day my next-door neighbour ran away, and never told *me* the reason. Some men fly from their debts as birds before snow—one has been jilted, another runs from matrimony. Sickness, care, *ennui*, are all travellers; but I go without fear of duns or dishonour, whole in heart and sound of limb, and here stand in the street to watch for the 'bus, as happy and foolish as any man could wish to be.

As the reader will accompany us during the season, it is only fair to tell him something of his *compagnons du voyage*. The party consists of four persons—a lady and her maid, your humble servant and his man, who, besides being a master in all the mysteries of tackle, officiates as valet to please me, and does much amateur cooking to please himself.

In this practical age, as men care more for facts than fancies, it is only necessary to say we left home on the morning of January 30, and reached Lismore, *viâ* Bristol, Waterford, and Cahir, on the following evening. A few lights twinkled in the shops as we drove to our lodgings in the Mall, rejoicing not a little in the prospect of food, rest, and fire, after a journey of thirty-six hours. . . . And now, my dear sir, draw a chair to the side of this sparkling fire of turf and bogwood, for, as I hope to take you with me, it is only right to tell you my plans.

I propose, then, to visit most of the spring rivers and lakes in this beautiful land, passing from one to another as circumstances may render advisable, with the general design of working from the south, to the extreme north of the island. In the three or four weeks which divide the salmon from the grilse, I hope we shall enjoy many pleasant days with the trout; and from June, we shall hold a roving commission, hoist sail, and steer where water, wind, and weather promise most.

Punctually at seven on the following morning Willie brought hot water to my dressing-room—between the thumb and forefinger of his left hand was a fly ready for winging.

"You are early at work."

"Ned Ray has been here this half-hour, sir; we have been to the river, and our flies are rather large for the water."

I had studied the face before me years enough to read it with tolerable accuracy—there was something wrong. "Well, what *is* the matter?"

"I seen it this morning, and don't like it."

"Seen it—seen what? Where was it? What was it like? What on earth do you mean?"

"The pools, master—'twas the pools I seen, and they a'n't as they used to be."

"Nonsense, Willie; you know that twenty-eight stake-nets out of thirty are gone from the estuary—of course there must be double the number of fish; so make haste and get breakfast." We were soon out. The distance to the river, though only a few hundred yards, will yet afford time to say something of the fish before we get there. Besides clean and foul salmon, the Blackwater, now and for the next six or seven weeks, holds large numbers of fine fish, neither foul nor fair, coming up to spawn. These are of all shades—in short, they are exactly in the condition of those which you and I, to our shame be it said, killed in August and September last. So far as my experience goes, no other spring river in Ireland holds salmon at this season in a similar condition. In other waters an occasional gravid fish may be seen in March; here they are not the exception, but the rule, and are, at least below the weirs, invariably returned safe and sound from whence they came. Well, here we are at the end of the lane, and with wonderful unanimity, turn to the "Scholar's Throw," for its length the best piece of spring water in Ireland—such, at least, I have *hitherto* found it. Behind, the ground rises abruptly, clothed with brush and forest trees—a combination more charming to the artist than the angler—and here my attendant, two or three seasons since, attained considerable proficiency in the art of climbing, but subsequently lost it from want of practice.

B 2

All is soon ready; over the left shoulder flies the line, whilst the eye follows it amongst the branches, and then a turn of the wrist sends it light and true across the stream. At the fourth cast a fish rose. I hear the word "fresh" pronounced simultaneously by Messrs. Ned and Willie, the latter of whom, without a word, exchanges "the green" for "the grey."

Once more the fly skims over the water, a bright gleam marks the run, and the descending line tells me I am "fast" in my first fish for the season. A sharp round of ten minutes brings the fight to an end, and finds a nine-pounder, as bright as a new shilling, helpless in the net.

As "the Scholar" and your humble servant had not met for some time, we had no intention of parting so soon. We enjoyed his pleasant society for an hour or more; and then, as he only lent us one gravid fish, finding there was nothing more to be got out of him, we bade him good bye. For the remainder of the day we worked hard, now on this bank, now on that, without moving another salmon. I fear we all walked home silent and sulky.

On the following morning the air was mild and balmy, and I, at least, set out in hope of high achievements; but on reaching the river, which yesterday was so bright, we found it thick as pea-soup and yellow as a guinea. The Blackwater in its long course is joined by hundreds of mountain streams: heavy rain falling in the neighbourhood of one or more of these is sufficient to produce a fresh in the main river—not high, perhaps, but often indescribably dirty. With us, the moisture hardly sufficed to lay the dust. In short, the Blackwater is a carnally-minded stream, prone to break bounds and get into mischief, but slow to return to its happier state of goodness, purity, and order.

As nothing better may be done to-day, if the reader has no objection, we will "show him the river." About half a mile above the town stand the weirs, and from thence to the tideway the best angling has hitherto been found; *la crême de la crême* lies about midway between these points. We will take the casts in order, commencing with those on the south side—the "Scholar's Throw,"

"De Visnes' Stream," and the "Bull Sod;" on the north, Ex Hole, the Island, and De Visnes. All these are close to each other, and within three minutes' walk of the town. There are also good pools for a mile below; whilst between the bridge and the weirs, some weeks later, are three or four casts scarcely second to any on the Blackwater. Besides salmon, this river contains many inhabitants of a lower grade in fish society—some of them, indeed, being exceedingly low and vulgar. There are white trout, pike, perch, eels, gudgeon, brown trout, and flounders; and still one fish, "the Arab of the water," remains to be mentioned. There is little, of course, to be said in his praise, as he is carrion of the highest order; however, he will enter the estuary, whether we like him or not, in June and July, to spawn, but does not ascend much beyond the extreme tidal limit; he differs widely from the true alausa of the Severn, and is, I believe, identical with the twaite of that river. This naughty boy is only mentioned because he rises rather freely at a grilse-fly.

Owing to its width and general unsuitableness for wading, the Blackwater is not an easy river to fish successfully, but the rods employed are unusually long, and enable a skilful hand to deliver from twenty-five to thirty yards of line; but it is useless to-day, so we will extend our walk to the Castle grounds, through which the angler will have to pass on his way to the upper water.

The forest odours are already stealing through these beautiful woods. The bullfinch in his bridal jacket flits from spray to spray, and the woodrush spreads its shining and striated foliage as a carpet for our feet.

The present castle was founded in 1185 by John Earl of Morton; and its ruin and restoration through many bloody centuries would fill a volume. There it stands, on the verge of a precipitous cliff—below flows the river, far above the tops of the forest trees rise tower and battlement, and, from the terrace, the view over mountain and valley is exquisitely beautiful. In the shade of the ancient grove Raleigh perhaps once stood: here, too, Spenser may have dreamed, and peopled the solitude with naked kern and stalwart knight.

As the salmon-rod must rest for one day at least, we will take the reader to a charming little trout stream which crosses the high road, about two miles north-west of the town. It is the type and flower of mountain brooks, leaping in a series of noble cascades through a wooded ravine. Wonderfully wild and beautiful is Ara Glen, its sides clothed with oak and holly, pine and hazel. The winter floods have swept away the underwood, leaving sufficient space for a skilful angler. But little matters it what fly he throws, so it be small: light or dark, silk body or fur, each seems as good as the other and "perhaps better."

About the list of killed, the less said the better; for the season is early and the fish hardly yet in condition. Rather let me whisper that any performer as good as yourself, sir, for example, will not only bag here as many well-made "stumps of trout" as ever he killed in his life, but will moreover see a glen so weird, solitary, and beautiful, as shall take him half a lifetime to match.

The fresh cleared off sooner than we expected; in fact, it only lasted a couple of days. For the remainder of the week the weather was favourable, and the sport as bad as possible, the total for the six days being only two spring fish, five ascending ditto, and one brown trout about 3lb.

Before closing this chapter it is necessary to say that the first step to be taken by an angler on his arrival at Lismore is to write to the kind and courteous lessee for permission. This is rarely refused to a stranger, who is, however, expected to take care of such fish as he may kill, and hand them over to Old Shehan as soon as possible.

Ye potent spirits, £. s. and Co., what could we do without you? You certainly meddle awfully with our family affairs. You present the spoon which holds our first mouthful of pap; engross the marriage settlement, and hire the mourning-coach; keep us at home, or send us abroad, and fill our hearts with heaviness or our lips with laughter. I added up the waybill as I moralised, and found the journey cost exactly 2*l*. 1*s*. per head.

CHAPTER II.

Choice of a Profession—Spring Flies—The Round Hill—The Last Chance—The Finesk—The Valley of the Bride—At Home in the Evening—Awful Deficit, and the Occasion thereof.

A STRANGER'S first question to the waiter, on arriving at his hotel, probably is, "Who can show me the water?" and ten to one the luckless wanderer is saddled with some idle cousin or brother-in-law, who, in an easy obliging manner, eats and drinks all he can get, receives his money, and does nothing he undertook to do.

It may not, therefore, be out of place to speak of Ned Ray, than whom a more skilful fly-maker or a better fisherman never cast angle on the waters. Having spoken of honest Ned's manufacturing ability, we will show you two of his favourites.

No. 1.—Tip, gold thread and one turn of crimson seal; tail, topping with a few bright sprigs; body, green pig's-wool, two turns of crimson at the shoulders, ribbed with gold; legs, smoky blue hackle; jay shoulder; wing, mixed with plenty of bustard; horns, crimson; head, yellow seal; hook, O'Shaughnessy, Nos, 2, 3, 4.

No. 2.—Tip, silver thread and turn of blue seal; tail, topping and blue macaw; body, light grey donkey fur, well picked out; breast, two turns of blue seal; ribs, broad silver; legs, none; shoulder, jay; wing, a few bright sprigs, and two long feathers of the jungle cock; horns, blue; head, black; hook, O'Shaughnessy, Nos. 2, 3, 4, 5.

These flies are incomparably the best for the first three weeks of the season.

Never did kelpy haunt his favourite rill with greater constancy than I did the Blackwater. From morning till evening, all day and every day for the last week, the salmon have been attended with laudable perseverance. Had I stuck to business half as well my fortune would have been made long ago. Yesterday (Feb. 7) proved a blank, and to-day I have not yet seen a fish; the wind, too, has gone round to the south-west, and the clouds are gathering in heavy masses. Sulkily we returned through the castle grounds from the upper casts, Willie lagging behind despondingly with the rod. "Shall we give it up, or walk down to the Round Hill, and once more try the water from thence to the bridge?"

For once my faithful companion demurred. "Sure there was a power of rain overhead; of course the glass was falling; the wind had died away. Sorra a fish was there in the water, and if there was, there was not a ghost of a chance."

At this stage of the debate a policeman, for whom my attendant had conceived a violent friendship, passed, on his way to Cappoquin. The aspect of things grew brighter. Now, there was nothing like perseverance, so to the Round Hill we went. Over all the likely water at its base we fished with savage determination, but no success; pool after pool always the same—blank, blank, blank. At last we came to the lane. The wood round "the Scholar" looked awfully dismal. The rain was falling heavily, and every bush and tree had changed into a shower-bath. We had reeled in, and already taken a step or two up the hill, when better thoughts came to our aid, so we turned into the coppice. At the second cast I was fast in a good fish. Verily, these animals are a mystery. Had it not been for a wholesome fear of police, I should have shouted "Io triumphe!" as we marched up the Mall in the gloaming.

All night poured the rain, and in the morning Messrs. Willie and Ray were hard at work tying small flies, the "hare's-ear and yellow" being grudgingly supplied by my landlady's cat. As the Blackwater was impracticable, we were to turn our misfortunes to account, and take the Finesk at the fall of the fresh.

This pretty little stream, which crosses the road some distance beyond Cappoquin, has a high local reputation for the size and quality of its trout, but is useless to the angler, except at times like the present. Too much cumbered with alder, thorn, and hazel, it winds its way through meadows to the main river in alternate pools and shallows. In a few hours we killed about a dozen and a half of respectable fish in fair condition, and above a score of small ones.

What right or title I had to do these things, I know not. Mr. Ray, in glowing language, proposed the expedition, and I went with a hazy idea that something was wrong, and that I ought to have asked some one or other for that leave which is so seldom refused in this kindly land.

As our river is not yet in order, suppose we pay a visit to the Bride. The lady is capricious, and does not always smile when her suitors sigh; another offer can do no harm, so we will take the rod and try our fortune.

'The Vale of the Bride—were it not for the many Cromwellian fortresses scattered over it—has a strong English aspect. Familiar home names stare at us from shop fronts; drive in tax-carts; and own broad acres. Under the somewhat too vigorous administration of the Protector, much property changed hands, and the sagacious soldier rewarded those who served him. Neither life nor lands being too secure, each new possessor erected a square tower to remedy the difficulty, and add one charm more to the beautiful Bride. The river is of moderate size and unincumbered with wood. In the summer it holds grilse and white trout, at which time, it is only right to say, I never tried it. To-day the water proved in good order, and yielded us rather over two score trout, of all sizes, from ¾lb. to 3oz.

It was late when we left Tallow Bridge; and though the Blackwater cider needs no praise from me, I desire gratefully to record that a glass or two of that nectar made the long hill short and easy.

Home is a pleasant place. Within a stone's throw of my window stands the Cathedral, its square tower and lofty spire rising above the tall trees which surround it. The strains of the organ, touched by a hand of rare skill and taste, float through the room. In the old limes the rooks are picking and stealing, toiling and fighting, like so many featherless bipeds; and, heedless of the turmoil, two venerable birds, without household cares, discourse gravely and sedately. Are

they pitying some gay young reprobate as yet unconscious of the retribution that waits on naughty birds? or are they, as Longfellow sings—
> Talking about the farmer's crops?

At present I am not very well up in their language, but rather incline to the latter hypothesis.

But I must listen no longer, for we have dined already, and are going to pay a last visit to the river. In the little garden, Willie and Ned Ray, with rod and gaff, are chatting and smoking—so come with us; there is time to try Ex Hole and the Island before dusk. On with the boots, Willie, and do your best, whilst we light a post-prandial cigar and look on.

A light whistle announced good news. Man and rod might have formed a study—the one so erect, easy, and confident, the other so faultless in its perfect arch. We have scarce time to admire before we have cause to deplore, for the baffled angler is even now gathering up some sixty yards of slack line, taken in that fatal run—the first and the last.

The Island yet remains. Twice it has been carefully tried without a rise. Our third and last chance shall be with the orange grouse. Has the fly, or the witching hour, produced the change? A clean eleven-pounder has just been landed, and once more, about thirty yards below the rod, stands my honest servant on the watch that no salmon may turn at the fly unnoticed.

Simultaneously with his signal came a long drag on the line; swiftly and steadily the rod rose into position, and in thirty minutes the vanquished lay on the bank, not dead but done up. He proved a splendid ascending male, about 26lb., with a shoulder like a bull, and a hook as thick as a walking-stick. Tenderly we returned him to the water, and with very mixed feelings watched him sail slowly away. "What a fine ould ancient gladiator," sighed Ned. "Oh, master, what a kipper he'd have made," groaned Willie.

It is an awful thing to be called on to show one's accounts. The books of our firm reveal a terrible deficit. Well, if we must, we must. Clean fish, 5; ascending ditto, 6.

Our visit to Lismore is over. The three weeks spent here have been a dead failure, produced, strangely enough, by the improvements resulting from the Act of 1862, which, after careful examination, swept away the stake-nets from the estuary, and made a Queen's gap.

The reader will naturally say, all the salmon hitherto stopped by the twenty-eight defunct stake-nets must have come into the river, and nearly doubled the number of fish. Of course they came; but, alas! they did not take lodgings, but were, I regret to say, little better than tramps. Such is the fact; but it is not always easy to account for facts. Previous to this season the Blackwater, from the weirs to the tideway, was, in my opinion, if not the best, at least equal to any spring water in Ireland; and in support of this opinion I may mention that in one throw alone (the Scholar), net a hundred years ago, we landed sixty-two spring fish in little over ten consecutive weeks. It may be taken for granted that none of these sailed up to the weirs to ask if the door was open or shut, for ascending fish never return from the highest point they have reached, unless short of water. In fact, they lodged, not from necessity, but choice. And why have they not done so this season? Most probably because the increased flow of water, or alteration in the direction of the current, has pulled down their houses, without having yet found time to build new ones.

That the injury to this beautiful lower water is permanent I cannot believe. Let us hope that, like our navy, it is in a transition state, and will soon come out all the better for our glorious new fishery law. Of course, the upper waters have vastly improved, and the long-suffering proprietors at length enjoy their own. In the mean time we must wait, and I believe we shall not have to wait long before we see the lower pools regain their late excellence, and outdo their former great outdoings.

CHAPTER III.

Between Lismore and Fermoy—On to Killarney—Cost of Journey—The Flesk—Flies of the Neighbourhood—Trolling on Lough Guttane—Remarks —What might be done, and how to do it.

THE morning, on the 27th of February, was bright and breezy as we drove over the bridge of Lismore, on our way towards Fermoy. Here poor Ned was waiting to bid us adieu, and give Willie parting instructions. Far away, the Knockmel-dawn Mountains formed a background to the romantic glen, through which the Oun-na-Sheadh (a fair trout stream) brawls its way to join the main river at the bridge. It is a quarrelsome little water—as it ought to be, being born in Tipperary—and, on the smallest provocation, howls and shrieks and knocks the boulders about, in a way quite creditable to the county.

Between this point and Fermoy the Blackwater is a glorious stream, rolling on from broad pool to broader shallow, through English-looking meadows, and past English-looking houses, belonging to the resident gentry. Happy would it be for poor old Ireland if she had more of exactly the same pattern and quality. From the kindness of some of these gentlemen I obtained full angling powers, and shall stay two or three days at Fermoy to avail myself of their courtesy.

Few things are more agreeable than the first visit to a new river. Hope is our companion, and there is no end to the pictures imagination paints. The opening day on promising water is positively delightful—comparatively, doubly delightful to an obstinate pig, who for three weeks had been savagely working himself to death, in order to prove that he was right and everybody else wrong.

"Shall we begin here, Willie?"

My companion's mind, never very hopeful, was now quite out of tune. "Maybe, sir," was his cautious answer, in the most doleful of voices; "it can't be worse than where we came from."

The spot thus described was a splendid stream, ending in a pool, which, after dozing awhile, suddenly woke up, and, ashamed of being caught napping, hurried on its way with redoubled speed.

Presently there was a deep sluggish boil under the fly; we will rest him and cast below. There was another, and another. All our groanings and grumblings were forgotten. "Change the fly, Willie; we will try it down again;" and so we did, but only landed two old fish.

There were better things in store for us, as, before we left the water, three beautiful spring salmon were killed, one spawner landed, and I know not how many foul fish; these last keeping us through the day in a state of perpetual excitement. I thought of Mr. Ray's parting words, "Mind what I'm telling ye, your honour; they'll have the nice time entirely in county Cork."

The following day was much like the one which preceded it, quite as pleasant and nearly as busy. Unused, in a general way, to covet my neighbour's goods, I certainly then and there longed for the exclusive right of three or four miles of the Blackwater, somewhere about midway between Lismore and Fermoy.

We are now, as the reader knows, in the county of Cork. If he had read the following passage before his visit he would have believed he had gone somewhere else by mistake. Vast tracts of land are still unreclaimed—perhaps never can be reclaimed—yet the improvement of the last quarter of a century is marvellous indeed. "Prior to the year 1829 a great part of the north-west district of the county was almost inaccessible. This district, formed of a tract of 970 square miles, is comprised between the Shannon and the Blackwater, and up to the year 1822 contained no road passable for horsemen in wet weather. The entire district must have remained neglected by the hand of civilisation from the period at which its ancient proprietors, the later earls of Desmond, had been dispossessed of it in the reign of Elizabeth. The whole district contained but two resident landed proprietors, whose houses were distant thirty-eight and a half miles from each other. The inhabitants were poor and ignorant, and the inaccessible nature of the country made it the asylum of smugglers and outlaws."

Thank Heaven! none of these unpleasant gentry now haunt the environs of Mallow, which is a quiet peaceable place, celebrated for its tepid mineral waters. The walk to the springs is matter for a May morning. Health-giving fountains, lovely climate, capital fishing—what could a valetudinarian, piscatorially inclined, desire more?

The rail soon bore us to Killarney; a brief conversation with Mr. Callaghan McCarthy settled all necessary preliminaries, and in a few minutes more we were off to Fort William, half farm, half lodging house, with a very grand total of comfort. Do you think that all this steaming and driving is dear at 17s. 6d. per head?

The Flesk is full; and how different from the shallow stream which scarce fills half its bed in summer. The day is bitterly cold, the east wind striving, not in vain, to dissipate the caloric that wraps our bodies like a mantle.

Eight hours in the stern-sheets of a boat, watching for a run, is not to be thought of, with the thermometer three degrees above frost, and the wind as sharp as a razor; so this morning we will try the Flesk, which, through the kindness of Colonel Herbert, is open to all anglers who apply to him. Below our house is a beautiful cast, but we made nothing of it. For five hours we worked manfully over pool and rapid; not a fish was to be seen, and had it not been contrary to custom, we should have given it up in despair, and returned by the road from the bridge. What a different animal is man, with his stomach empty or full. At 2 p.m. we desponded; at 2.30 we lunched, and hope revived.

Cheerfully we lit a pipe, and leaned over the parapet, to mark a scene as stern and wild as ever Salvator painted. All parts of this district bear traces of the O'Donoghue; a hundred ruins record their feudal power, and here before me, near the bridge, stood Killaha, grey and savage, facing the wilderness of Glen Flesk, seeming still to keep guard over the vale below.

On the way home our work was as neatly executed as if instant payment were expected. At the eleventh hour it came.

A spirited rise in the "rough stream" broke the spell, and at the magical hour of sundown we were again successful. To land two good fish of 10lb. and 8lb. respectively, at the close of a day so inauspiciously commenced, was very conseling. In salmon angling perseverance is ever better than skill. He who keeps his fly longest in the water kills most; and to-day the happy consummation was due to dogged determination, which so often wrings victory from disaster.

The flies used in this neighbourhood are the ordinary claret, fiery brown, and olive, lightly dubbed, and lightly hackled. The only thing worth remark about them is, that they are invariably tied on hooks a size larger than would be employed by ninety-nine makers out of a hundred in the manufacture of an article of similar dimensions. It is many years since I first noticed this peculiarity, the advantages of which were so obvious that I at once adopted, and have never since abandoned, it.

A fly overtied never looks well, and rarely swims well; nor does it appear that the fish object to the Kerry plan. Doubtless the salmon sees nothing but the fly: his vision is bounded by the tip. Coveting the rose, he overlooks the thorn, like many a wise man. The professionals here understand their business thoroughly; but amongst them McCarthy enjoys a high reputation. Whosoever you select, keep him in his proper place. It will be true kindness, as well as sound policy.

On the shores of Lough Guttane stand two anglers, by the generous permission of Colonel Herbert; but alas! they have no bait, nor present means of procuring any, for the midge flies are left behind. Again and again every book and case has been carefully examined—not a hook in the most remote degree suitable is there. In sheer vexation, Willie stands sketching a fancy par on the lid of his tobacco-box with the end of a file. Necessity is the true source of inspiration. "Hand me a pin and the pliers." The head and point were soon off, and the requisite length of wire remained. A blow with a stone flattened one end, and with the file, point and barb were cut, in humble imitation of that king of hookmakers—O'Shaughnessy. Wax, silk, and hair were not wanting; a little extemporaneous dubbing from a Tweed jacket, and a few fibres from a drenched feather on the shore, did the rest, and sufficed to procure plenty of bait. But before we step into our boat, a word or two about the lake will not be out of place.

Lough Guttane, nearly six miles in circumference, rests in a hollow formed by the rocky and precipitous sides of Mangerton and Crohare—and between lies the desolate Glen Kippock. This sheet of water affords good trout-trolling in March, April, and May. Occasionally a twelve-pounder may be taken, but fish of 4lb. or 5lb. will generally be found on the *top* of the angler's basket. Any sportsman located in one of the cottages on the south shore (some of my friends have tried the plan, and found it answer) would undoubtedly kill, in the months before mentioned, an enormous weight of trout, some of them heavy fish; but whether any of the eighteen-pounders, of which I heard frequently, would figure in his list, seems less certain.

In my opinion Lough Owel, Lough Arrow, Dereverah, Carra, Lough Corrib, Lough Mask, and Lough Conn yield fish of a higher average.

Whilst visiting this district in former seasons, I occasionally devoted a day to Guttane, though never with any remarkable success. I am, however, bound to say I have often heard from undoubted authority of other anglers having enjoyed admirable sport.

Possibly the explanation of my failures may be found in the fact of my staying a long distance from the lake, and visiting it only when brought to a dead lock elsewhere. Nevertheless, I should not fear to locate myself during April and May on the south shore, in full expectation of good sport, brightened by some glorious days.

Round the lake, across the lake, backwards and forwards by the solitary islet, with its melancholy ruin, we pulled. A stiff north-west breeze and an ever-changing sky did all that winds and clouds could do. Guttane did not, however, respond very cordially, as our basket only contained thirteen fish, the heaviest 3lb., whilst two or three others ranged from $1\frac{1}{2}$lb. to 2lb.

CHAPTER IV.

Sporting Expenses—What they are, and what they might be—A Dry Sketch of the Lakes and Rivers of the District—Trolling for Salmon, or much ado about nothing—Cross-lines—Departure—The Laune—Killorglin to Carra.

FISHING, like other field sports, has its expenses, but to state these with any exactness is impossible, for one man will do as much with 50*l.* as another will with 100*l.* Every angler is intimate with one or other of the gentlemen selected as an illustration.

The Hon. Charles Fever hurries to a good station, buys a stock of flies sufficient to fill a portmanteau, and not succeeding at once, abuses the water and starts for another. Here he fails likewise, and again sets out in search of an Elysium where salmon can be taken without skill or perseverance. At length, purse or patience failing, he resigns the quest, votes salmon-angling a myth, and the whole thing a humbug. On the following day Mr. Steady arrives, gets into snug private quarters, makes himself at home, lands his hundred fish, returns triumphant, and declares the cost a mere bagatelle.

The professional attendant may be set down from 15*s.* to 20*s.* per week, and if a boat be required, from 20*s.* to 30*s.*; inn-bills about 10*s.* per day, and wine, ticket, and travelling charges *ad lib.* But should the angler arrange his plans judiciously, and make a happy selection of the district he intends to fish, his expenses would be very moderate, and for three pounds a week he might travel like a bagman—I mean, commercial ambassador—sport like a Nimrod, and live like a gentleman. As the waters round Killarney extend for many miles in lake and river, a few words respecting them may be useful. Into the lower and largest lake the Flesk debouches; at its north-west extremity the Laune carries off the surplus waters of the surrounding district, passing into the head of Dingle Bay at Killorglin. From this point the angling extends to the head of the

c

lakes in one direction, and in another for miles up the Flesk. As a rule, the lower lake offers the best sport in spring and summer, and during autumn spates, the Flesk. For beauty, the country is an Eden; but who dare describe what Macaulay has seen with a poet's eye, and touched with a painter's skill?

The lower lake, at this season, would afford noble sport, were it not for the cross-lines; as it is, the professionals have put fly-fishing nearly out of the question, so the stranger had better content himself with trolling.

At the present moment ten boats, and from twenty to thirty men, are diligently working five cross-lines. These on the lake are what "long-lines" are on the sea, and the owners, like other fishers, are earning their daily bread. Just now I heartily wish they were seeking it in any other way. It is difficult to say what a salmon can see so attractive in these diabolical inventions: come over him with long and light casting, make the fly swim deep and fair, and play never so seductively before his eyes, there he lies in stoical indifference. A couple of dozen flies, however, swimming, flying, bounding, and splashing over his head, banish all prudential considerations; they bewilder his judgment, and turn his brain. It is sad to think so dear a friend is only a frivolous weak-minded individual after all.

When we pushed off from the little pier at Ross Island, it was barely ten o'clock, yet our ancient mariner was somewhat testy. "Gentlemen," he said, "should come early if they wanted sport; them divils of cross-lines is raking the lake these two hours."

The wild woods, the fairy islets, green with holly, arbutus, and laurel, the sparkling water and delicious air, were all charming; and early in the day a run that sent the left-hand rod flying into the old man's lap, filled up the measure of our content. We lay on our oars to watch the struggle; but what chance has an unlucky fish in open water with three of O'Shaughnessy's hooks in his mouth? Our prize weighed nearly 13lb., being, I fancy, rather above the local average.

This success raised our hopes to an extravagant pitch. Round islands and over reefs we pulled with determined perseverance, but no further fortune; and when we stepped out of the boat our friend's parting words were emphatic: "Be early to-morrow, your honour; for your life be early!" The two following days we worked to the admiration of our energetic attendant; the reward, however, was by no means in the ratio of our deserts, as we landed only one small fish of 8lb., and an ill-conditioned trout of about half that weight.

The omission was, perhaps, culpable; but I breathed no benediction on the cross-lines.

To the best of my belief I have spoken justly, though not flatteringly, of the single rod fishing on the lake in spring. In summer the lines are popularly supposed to disappear; possibly they do, or perhaps they rise very early in the lovely mornings of June and July. Be this as it may, the single rod grilse-fishing is very fair, and the quarters, perhaps, more luxurious than any other in the island.

Beautiful Killarney, adieu! thy charms must no longer enthral me; yet where in nature shall I see a face like thine? Glorious are thy mountains, pellucid thy lakes, set with their fairy islets, draped in many colours, each one a marvel and a mystery. But, upon my life, I can't stand it. The lines are too mighty to be resisted; and as discretion is the better part of valour, we shall retreat to Lough Currane (better known as Waterville), and take the **Laune and Carra** by the way.

The road traversed by the mail-car follows the course of the Laune closely, at a likely part of which it pulls up, and leaves us to follow the river down to Killorglin. Not knowing the water, we worked over all the streams and pools that came in our way, asking questions when opportunity offered. This, though a pleasant mode, is seldom a profitable one, as much time is wasted on barren water. However, we rose two fish; that both were fresh I should be unwilling to assert, but the 7lb. salmon in the basket had, at any rate, a fine batch of parasites near the ventral fin.

In a former chapter I hinted at the advantage of selecting a central situation as a matter of economy. Killorglin is one of such, for east, west, and north are excellent waters. Through the village flows the Laune, always happily unconscious of fixed engines; and public conveyances pass every day, enabling a nomadic sportsman to reach any one of the number for half-a-crown. Salmon are taken in this river by drafting, but Monday belongs to the rod, and an angler would have reason to complain if he did not on that day "make a death."

Though never an intimate, the Laune is a very old acquaintance, and many a time in spring, summer, and autumn have we sauntered together for a pleasant hour. The general character of the river is particularly inviting; neither timber nor scrub offers any impediment. The water is rarely discoloured, and seldom low—characters common to all rivers which drain large lakes.

Castlepool and Garrynalanna!—it is pleasant even to write your names—and I inscribe them here just as Hodge or Joe might carve his sweetheart's name on tree or stile.

The tide met us about three miles and a half from Killorglin, so we put up the rod, and set off at a round pace, in hopes of gaining time to get a crust and an "air of the fire" before our party arrived. The Ventry Arms is comfortable, and the proprietor shows a due appreciation of visitors, by reserving five pools for their especial use and benefit. A stranger to the country would do well to make Killorglin his head-quarters.

Kerry, as its name implies, is pre-eminently a region of rock and water. Lough Currane, Lough Scall, Lough Carra, Guttane, the lakes of Killarney, and a host of others, whilst justifying the nomenclature, offer no common inducement to artist and angler.

Few waters in this county are closed to the wandering sportsman who asks permission; at least, I have found it so, and desire gratefully to acknowledge the many courtesies so often received.

To conduct the reader to all the streams in this district would be impossible; we will therefore, as we jog along to Lady Headley's, point out some of the best, premising that later in the season, when the grilse and trout arrive, we hope (remember we do not promise) to spend some pleasant days on two or three of them.

The rivers of Kerry are numerous, but of no great length. The

Maine debouches into the head of Dingle Bay, and offers excellent grilse fishing: it is *tolerably* independent of freshes—a great matter to an angler who has only a limited time. But few strangers find their way to Castlemaine, the stream of tourists flowing on to Carra, Waterville, and Glengariff. The Lee is a small river, rising a few miles east of Tralee, and happy is he who stands on its banks after a night's rain in July.

The Carra rises in the mountains of Dunkerron, passes through Glencarra, and, after forming an extensive lake, falls into Dingle Bay. The Fartagh and Inny rise in the Iveragh Mountains, and flow westward, the former into Valencia Harbour, the latter into Ballinaskelligs Bay. In this stream a friend killed twelve and fourteen salmon, on the two last days of a recent season, with his single rod.

The Roughty empties itself into the inner extremity of Kenmare River, into the northern side of which the Finihay, lesser Blackwater, and Sneem fall. Most of these are little to be depended on except in wet seasons, and, though admirable after rain, are apt sorely to try a gentleman whose time or patience is limited.

CHAPTER V.

Rosbeigh—The Boigh—Carra River—The Lake—"My Aunt's Legacy"—Glen Carra—The Great Unknown.

COMFORT and salmon-angling—fine mountain scenery and good living, are not necessarily united; but at the Headley Arms they are happily blended. The time was, and that not long ago, when a night's rest by a cabin fire, and a pot of potatoes, aided by the produce of his creel, occasionally served the sportsman for bed and board. But these days are passing away, and fair quarters are now to be found, where some years since no accommodation could be procured. Yet even now, on many mountain streams, so seducing in August and September, if the angler wishes to be near his water he must expect to rough it, nor hope to find all the blessings of Arcadia in a highland glen.

Suppose us now, however, at our comfortable breakfast in Lady Headley's Hotel. Above us towers a lofty hill, clad to the summit with larch and Scotch fir; round its base murmurs the little Beigh; from the window of our room Dingle Bay is seen in all its beauty, and in front, the road only separates the house from the heather, which stretches miles away, as far as the eye can follow it. In the winter the neighbourhood offers good duck and snipe shooting, and in summer, sea-fishing, boating, and bathing are perfect.

The angling is varied and extensive, and, from what I have seen at different times, by no means crowded—in fact, a man might work here for a week and meet no face, except his own, reflected in the grand mirror before him.

The lake is free; Mr. Winn rents a portion of the river near the bridge, and sub-lets it at thirty shillings per month for each rod. Mrs. Shea is, I believe, in treaty for that portion of the river extending from the lake to Mr. Winn's right; and Corney Clifford and young M'Carthy are the professionals.

The Beigh—it is but a brook—runs close by the house, and during autumn spates contains a capital assortment of trout, in size rather above the average of such waters. Many a happy, careless hour I have whiled away on its banks. Now, this little stream holds nothing but spent fish and brown trout, on which a good Catholic might dine any day in Lent, to the certain mortification of the flesh.

A walk of twenty minutes in an opposite direction brings us to Carrabridge. This water is said, and I believe with truth, to be one of the earliest in the county. In November, December, and January, clean fish enter in considerable numbers; and, as all impediments to their passage are then removed, they either settle in the upper pools, locate in the lake, or lodge in the Blackstones river. In the latter part of June come the grilse, which are soon followed by the trout— night fishing for which is much practised here in low water. These fish are, however, very small. There is some knack in casting after dark; the delivery must be particularly neat and clean, or the artist will speedily find himself in a fix, with very little chance of getting out of it. The lake holds brown trout of superior size and quality; and if, as Brother Michael maintains, "as is the redness, so is the goodness," they must be good indeed.

At the present season the angler has to make his election between the river and the lake—between the fly and the troll. Although often halting a short time at Rosbeigh, on my way to other stations, I had never remained except once, and then during the latter part of a season, about six years ago. True it is, every winter I vowed to try the Carra in the spring, but never kept that vow until now. My prime minister is violently anxious to try the fly, and, as he always gets his way, we shall make our *début* on the river as soon as breakfast is over.

For two entire days we flogged the uncomplaining Carra without success. The fine rocky pools doubtless held salmon, but we could make nothing of them, for, in sixteen hours' thrashing, we rose only two shy fish, nor am I sure that either of these were fresh.

The lake is a noble sheet of water, and right glad was I to stand on its shores. The wash of the waves on the strand sounded fresh and musical after the monotony of the last two days; and with the first roll of the boat half our vexations were forgotten.

The plan proposed was to pull in and out along the east and south sides, and then fish as much of the west as we could. When we reached the head of the lake we had three runs—all trout; and near the outfall of Blackstones a small fresh fish, under 8lb., was added to the stock: but, like good simple souls, we were easily pleased, and when the day was over, seven trout added to our salmon made us as happy as kings. The lakers were by no means large; the best only weighed $4\frac{1}{2}$lb., whilst the remaining half-dozen did not make collectively 8lb.

All the next day the rain fell heavily; to go out would have been worse than useless, so the hours were devoted to domestic felicity. My dear companion had been busy as a bee. Correspondence long in arrear had been written up. Embroidery, crochet, plain work—why, the quantity got through was tremendous. There was nothing more to do, so the stock-piece, which always seemed to take—crooning and purring over the quiet little events of the day—was forthwith put on the stage. Certainly it was very rude to sit in the window with one's back to a lady, but the truth is, I was engaged on a very interesting work of art.

"What are you doing?" at length observed my companion.

"Finishing a minnow."

"Will you please to let me see it?" in the sweetest of voices.

"With the greatest pleasure, as soon as completed. I am polishing off the marks of the file, and the rigging won't take half an hour."

The—what shall we call it?—the polite reply was so big that it nearly produced a spasm of the glottis. Our good little maid opened the door. "Please, ma'am, do you know anything about your spoon? I can't find it"—with a wicked glance towards the window. At that moment I knew exactly what a thief, in the hands of the police, feels when the stolen goods are in his pocket. "Is this it?" I faltered, producing the shaft of a small embossed silver article. On cross-examination I was obliged to confess that, wanting such an artificial bait for to-morrow, instead of taking a common one, I selected what suited me best, and that happened to be an uncommon one.

Vowing never to offend again, I promised all sorts of things—to send the mutilated article to town to be reproduced—to do—to do anything—everything.

Fortunately, the opposite "party" was as good and peaceable as wise. "You know you might have taken the teapot, had you wanted it; but *why would* you take my poor aunt's spoon?"

There was a delicious spring feeling in earth and air, in body and spirit, as we stepped out merrily for our boat. The rain of the previous day had filled the bog pools, and the small rills, not yet quite run down, were bearing their tribute of amber to the lake. The west wind was hurrying along, waking up the last of the clouds which slept on the hills; in short it was just the kind of day that you and I know and appreciate.

We commenced on the west shore, and did so little that we determined to cross to the opposite side. Paddling and chatting, we had done about half the distance, when a desperate run woke us up, only just in time to seize the butt as it was diving overboard. In the hurry, line and rod had been grasped together, and in a moment eight or ten feet of its length were dragged into the water; quick as light, however, the line was released, and away went the fish—down, down, down—as if he never intended to stop. Ten minutes, twenty, thirty passed, and still our friend was tugging away as hard as ever at the bottom of the lake. Willie, who in fifteen years, had seen too much to be surprised at anything, was at last growing curious. Laying the paddles over the gunwale, he crawled over the beams, gaff in hand. Another quarter of an hour passed, and then our fish, slowly yielding to the heavy strain, came gradually nearer the surface. Peering anxiously into the water, my companion leaned over the side; " He's uncommon short, sir," looking inquiringly at his master. The fish was now perfectly tractable, the line being rapidly gathered in and coiled on the beam, rip-rip-rip. I actually felt the gaff tearing its way out. The force brought the side more clearly into view; it was broad as a plank. Whish, whish, shrieked the wheel; there was a slight check and a snap; and that was all I ever saw of my stout friend and "my aunt's spoon."

My faithful servant cast one imploring glance at the master; his unlucky knee still nailed the line to the beam. In winter and rough weather, in heat and cold, he had served me with a love and fidelity seldom met with—never before had he made a mistake. " Cheer up, old friend—it was far more my fault than yours; we shall both be wiser another time."

Whether such a chance will ever recur remains to be seen—but to lose a lake trout from 18lb. to 20lb.—Bah! it gives me a pain in the præcordial region even to recall it. As if to make amends, fortune favoured us, for we carried home two fresh fish, 11lb. and 12½lb. respectively; together with fourteen trout, one of which was fine, and weighed 6lb.; the rest were small.

We have closed our account with Carra, and should have been

well pleased to have spent this our last day on the Blackstones; but it cannot be, as the sporting rights are reserved. In such cases I never give leave, except to an old friend; so, of course, never ask it.

A walk through Glen Carra, however, may not unprofitably occupy the time, for it possesses the gifts of grouse; spring and summer salmon; and for cocks, the covers of Lickeen are second to none in the kingdom. Situated in an extensive basin, the moors rise gradually to the summit of the mountains. On all sides the heather stretches for leagues, and were it not for the "big house," with a few scattered cabins near the bridge, the region might pass for a wilderness. Fancy a bright morning in February; the dead leaves filling the air with their odours as they crackle under your feet; the oak and holly scrub full of cocks, and many a bright-eyed salmon waiting your commands in the rocky pools of the Blackstones. I think we should then deem Lickeen sufficiently charming.

At no great distance up the valley lies an extensive lake, which a friend (one of the most accomplished sportsmen in the kingdom) assured me holds noble red trout. It had been the chief object of my walk to visit this water, but the time failed me. Hitherto it has, I believe, been very little fished, as the situation is so remote. I *think* Captain D—— told me, no boat but his own had ever floated on it.

Were I to become skipper of a curragh and master of a tent, I should like to launch the one and pitch the other on the shores of this solitary lake.

All the surrounding waters contain red trout, and here, doubtless, undisturbed for centuries, they have reached a good old age, and attained the maximum of size and dignity.

CHAPTER VI.

Waterville—Concerning the Lake—How we got there and what we did.

The mail-car from Killarney to Waterville stops daily at our door, and, barring accidents, will carry us this evening, the 13th of March, to the shores of Lough Currane. This sheet of water, ending at the west end of the village, is fed by the Cummeragh river, which flows from the smaller lakes of Derriana and Elaineane.

Lough Currane—justly celebrated, not only for its spring salmon, but for a run of trout greater, I believe, than any other open Elysium Piscatorum in Ireland—boasts two distinct seasons; the first from February to the end of May, the second from the middle of June to the end of October, during which latter period the upper waters are full of fish.

In the earlier months, for some unknown reason, the salmon, with *very* rare exceptions, refuse all lures except the troll, which, however, they take freely; but in May a change for the better comes over them, and they rise sportingly at the fly. Spring trout also, from 4lb. to 9lb., may be taken, but they are a wary race, which, having lived long in this deceitful world, profit by experience. Red trout are not only numerous, but fine, and in quality second only to those of Westmeath. During the trolling season they add a weighty item to the creel.

When I first visited Waterville, Jerry Quirk reigned in a grand Hibernian hotel at the eastern extremity of the village, where many a night I have gone to bed with the poker, as offering some slight protection against the said Jerry's nocturnal pleasantries. But this mode of exercising hospitality exists no longer, since Mr. Quirk emigrated to the States, where, for anything I know, he enlisted in M'Mahon's brigade, and there gained high renown for brewing whisky punch and breaking heads.

Her Majesty's Irish mail-cars, though always appearing to do great things in the way of speed, in reality do very little; so, though the distance to Waterville was not great, we took a considerable time to do it. Our steed was a representative animal, with a high irregular spinal ridge, a wonderful absence of flesh, and an eye in which fun, pluck, and devilment were happily blended, whilst the saucy toss of his head and general bearing said plainly, "Here we are, full of life, and up to anything."

The road ran over a dull waste of peat bogs, at this season flowerless and desolate, the black pools trembling as we drove along. Our conductor, however, took especial care that the silence should not be oppressive. "Ah, Barney, ye divil!" (to the vicious, rawboned horse) "ar'n't ye ashamed of yerself—whoop!—to keep her beautiful ladyship's honour here in the cowld? Get along wid ye, darlint" (with a gay good-humoured glance at our little maid from those sly, grey, inscrutable Kerry eyes). "And so yer honour is come again to the ould country for spourt. And it's lots of it ye'll have. There's lashings of fish in the lake; houl regiments of 'em. Sorra such a season ever there was."

This sort of thing used to charm me a few years ago, for I heard and believed, being thereby the gainer of many fallacious but pleasant hopes. Knowledge may be power, but it is not necessarily happiness. Now my humour had grown sceptical. I did not believe a word of it (Wisdom was wrong for once); so I chose to feel sure the speaker was talking bosh, and merely intended to say something pleasant.

I was glad to scent the peat smoke in the sweet evening air, as it showed we were near the end of our journey. Taken as a whole, the drive had been a success, the only accidents of the entire distance being one broken trace and a fracture of the hind leg of a luckless cur, who, in a fit of sudden insanity, challenged us to a race down hill; and so we came to the Lake Hotel, to supper and rest.

Dear old Waterville! in this cold March morning your mountains show as clear and lovely, and your bogs rather browner than when we parted. Perhaps, as regards complexion, you might say the same to me. I should not be hurt; truth, kindly spoken by lips we love, seldom does wound; and with you, old friend, I have passed so many happy months, that, though an unusually shy man, I do not blush to make the touching avowal—I love you.

We made quite a grand procession at starting. John marched first with the rods, followed by Tim bearing the net and gaff; next came Willie with the basket and bag—the former, as it contained raw materials for manufacture, always looked prettier on his shoulder; next in order was your humble servant; and last of all shambled the waiter, with a small stock of preventives against cold and hunger. Nor was our start on the lake less dignified; for Willie had extemporised two new cleats, and some thole-pins, so that we went off in great style with four oars, the old boat groaning and plunging forward like an overrun bison on the prairies.

I became acquainted with John something in this wise. A hundred years ago, let us say (one ought not to be personal), our professional anglers were rather naughty boys—picking up, retaining, and improving all the sad things so carelessly thrown away by certain fast young gentlemen I have in my eye. Now my friend John had rather an indifferent reputation in the village, being considered a poor mean-spirited fellow, who never drank whisky, nor figured in a faction fight; he was said, moreover, to be respectful and quiet, so I took him, many a day ago, and stuck to him. But, alas! John had two faults—firstly, being sometimes passive when he should have been active, and secondly, having a sad constitutional tendency to colic when the wind was ahead. Pulling a diminutive oar, he placed himself in the bow, and when abreast of Church Island calmly drew his paddle over the opposite gunwale, and produced his pouch.

"Here's for luck, y'r honour, and plinty of it;" but whether the latter clause was addressed to the pouch or myself seemed uncertain.

I feel rather unwilling to say anything about the tackle we are going to use—doubtless you know it as well as I do; but then, by a sort of *fictio legis*, I am bound to hold you do not—or what would be the use of my writing at all? Well, then, on this thread of single gut are two treble hooks (not over large) an inch and a half apart. Insert the end of the thread through the vent of the—we were going to say parr; but *that* could not be, as the law is dead against it—and bring it out at the mouth. This small piece of lead has, as you see, a brass pin at the bottom and a brass eye at the top; pass the free end of the gut through the eye, and bury the lead in the mouth of the bait; put a stitch through the loop, including the upper and lower jaw; then with the thumb and forefinger give the requisite curve, and the business is done. Before you drop it over the side, observe the length of the loop on the trace—tight fits do not answer for boat work on cold days in March.

As I said before, John stopped to light his pipe; the example was contagious, and, with incense reeking from four altars, and zealous invocations to Fortune, the baits were dropped into the water, and the first act on Lough Currane began.

We took two courses round Church Island, but did nothing, so we proceeded to call at the best lodges on the eastern shore, where our luck began to mend, and by three o'clock ten good trout were in the bag; but not a salmon, nor the sight of one. Another hour passed, and the faces of master and men grew longer and bluer. To add to our distress, John's symptoms pointed to a severe attack of colic. At this critical moment both rods were run simultaneously. There was no mistake about it; we were fast in two salmon.

I believe, on my honour, that a Waterville spring fish fights more desperately than any salmon of his weight elsewhere. In the present case they fully justified our good opinion. Two fish hooked at the same time require careful handling; and more than once, when they crossed, we were obliged to pass one rod over the other, and exchange, to avoid fouling. It cost us nearly half an hour before both were secured. New remedies are brought to light every day, but I first learned this afternoon that the struggles of an unlucky animal were a sovereign cure for colic.

In this benighted region, when a salmon dies, certain ceremonies are wont to be performed, the most imposing of which appears to be "the libation," or grace cup. Although stoutly resisting such heathen practices, on the present occasion I could hardly do so, as to-day partook of the nature of a festival, not wholly unlike the *dies festi*, on which Adams informs us " there was a general cessation of business."

When the funeral rites were duly solemnised, and the baits once more spinning over the quarters of the boat, it was getting late, and little chance of further sport remained. Still the spirits of my crew did not flag, so we worked steadily homewards, and thought ourselves very fortunate in landing another small fish of 8lb.

If in the morning John marched in the van like a hero to battle, you may be sure he held the post of honour when returning victorious.

At the landing-place bright eyes awaited our return. As a matter of course, my faithful follower walked up to his mistress.

"Come, Willie," she said, "turn out the bag. Ah! three nice fish—9lb., 11lb., and 8lb." And so ended our first day on Lough Currane.

CHAPTER VII.

Waterville—Derrynane—Spring Equinox—Below Bridge—Lake in Summer—The Coach before the Horses—" Maiden Trout "—Qualms of Conscience—Experience.

DURING the succeeding week the weather continued fine, and, for the season, reasonably mild; so our excursions on the lake met with no interruption, and we worked all day and every day with infinite gusto. The year was above the average, and the sport, for a moderate-minded man, excellent, our worst day being two clean fish, and our best five. If to this the usual quota of brown trout be added, I think we had sufficient reason to be satisfied, which, believe me, is not always the case with gentlemen who travel for amusement.

The principal scene of our week's happy toil was the eastern shore of the lake, including Cummeragh Bay; so to-day we will change our ground and visit the opposite side.

On the western shore the wild mountain range, extending from Derrynane, rises abruptly, forming a grand and beautiful setting to the silvery sheet below. But these mountains will never again echo to the joyous hallo or cheery horn of the great Dan. Why here, actually here, on his own happy hunting grounds, he is dead as a door-nail. Such is fame. What a change this peaceful wilderness must have been after the sweat and turmoil of "Conciliation Hall." Surely he must often have quitted his home with shaken purpose and sinking heart. Could he have gazed into the magic mirror below, and seen things as we see them to-day, he would have remained with his hounds when "Emancipation," the great monument of his life, had been built up, and rested on his fame.

We cannot start till the bait arrives. John, whose business it is to procure it, ought to have returned long ago. As he was nowhere in sight, I strolled to the bridge to look after him. Lo! there he was in all his glory. With his legs comfortably disposed on the shingle, and his back supported by a smooth boulder, the wretched man was fast asleep.

Across his knees lay the butt; his hands had relaxed their hold, and two-thirds of the rod lay quietly in the water—no, not quietly, for an unfortunate eel was tugging at it with all his might, begging the inexorable sleeper "to get up and take the nasty pin out of his throat, for it hurt him very much, and he was but a poor slimy fellow after all, and meant no harm in tasting what Misther John had so kindly placed at his disposal."

I felt seriously alarmed at this unexpected malady. I had learned how colic might be cured, but was fairly puzzled how to treat the present crisis. It would be unsafe even to trust him alone in future, as the poor fellow might, at any moment, fall into a state of coma.

The first thing, however, to be done was to rouse the sufferer, so

I administered a sharp counter-irritant on the spot, and then dosed him with good advice.

The oration was touching, and the pith of it was, that though perfect quiet was essential to the success of bottom-fishing in clear water, yet if I found him practising again in his sleep, he might go to ———. I fear I mentioned a gentleman with whom I earnestly hope poor John will never take service.

It was fully eleven o'clock when we set off, and as trout formed the main object of the expedition, we put out the baits as soon as we had shoved off. How pleasant it was, sweeping round the little bays, and doubling the rocky headlands, now playing a laker, and then listening to the innocent kindly chat of the boatmen. John, having no relapse since the morning, was rapidly recovering his spirits, and in full talk about "a mighty big fish he had once seen caught at the Old Ship." Poor Pat had never read the fable of the goose and the golden eggs, and, being only a simple uneducated fellow, did not perceive that if greedy proprietors and bad bog-trotting boys—in the dark ages, of course—had not so often interrupted Mrs. Salmon in her household duties in dark November nights, and slipped a neat wire grating over the eye of the cutts on Saturday evenings, or sometimes in a fresh, let the breast of the traps fall accidentally after dusk on Sundays, there might still have been a fish as big as he remembers to have seen. In this lake, as in all others, salmon either lodge on certain favourite shores or on rocky reefs, and towards some of these we were slowly making our way. A few fathoms to the south of an elevated rocky islet we had some pretty sport for an hour, landing five or six very nice lakers, and, returning by the Old Ship, ran the only salmon of the day. On feeling the hook our new acquaintance darted towards the boat, and then, with a vicious lash of his broad tail (which made an eddy like the sweep of an oar), plunged headlong downwards within a yard of us.

It was impossible to keep the rod in position, as the line would not run; so with three or four feet of the top under water, and the butt above my head, the reel all the time groaning as if very bad indeed, I let matters take their own course. It seemed as if the salmon had made a perpendicular run of fifty yards; whether he did, or only appeared to do so, I cannot tell. I remember having a vague idea that my hooks might be fast in an ancient relative of John's stout gentleman. However, he was a good fish, the best I killed during my stay, and weighed a little over 15lb.

The glass was falling when we left home, but we found it much lower on our return. The wind, too, was moaning and shrieking over the mountains, and soon after dark the rain came down as only Atlantic rain can do. There was no help for it—we were in for the equinox. and for the next day or two must give up all thoughts of the lake. It should not, however, be supposed that Currane is at all given to dirty tricks—on the contrary, by its inherent goodness it soon purifies the nasty things thrown into it, and only rises higher and purer from the attacks of its brawling and petulant tributaries.

A few seasons ago, the kind old lessee, with whom I shall never chat again, told me that in the spring, the river was full of a small silvery fish which he called "maiden trout." These were said to be brought down by the March and April spates. Whether this statement was critically exact I do not know; positively, I have no theory of my own on the subject; and being a member of the Society of Friends, have no intention of doing battle physically or intellectually on the question, and shall positively decline if summoned to "the field."

As this was about the time, we made a cast of trout flies, and strolled to the bridge. Before wetting the line I may as well say a few words about this river. From the bridge to the sea the distance may be two hundred and fifty or three hundred yards, the best portion being that nearest the beach. This is indeed worth visiting when the summer trout are in full run. Many a time have I stood by the old peat-stack watching these beautiful creatures glistening in the pool, turning first one silver side and then the other to the smooth sand—no doubt thinking it capital fun to feel the dear but troublesome friends they brought from the sea growing more sick and brown every hour in the fresh stream. I believe there are no better twenty yards of trout water in Ireland than that space above the shingles: there may be, I can only say I never found it.

Let no man visit Waterville in July with the hope of catching grilse. The lake is a trout lake, and nothing more. It is only fair, however, to say, that a friend, of whose skill and veracity I entertain a high opinion, dissents from this statement, and declares he has occasionally taken two or three peel in a single day on the lake. Of course this may always be on the cards; still the run of summer fish is far too small to offer a reasonable chance of anything worthy the name of sport.

In a previous visit we arrived early in June, and remained till the end of September, and in that time I never killed one, nor saw anyone else do so. On every breezy day, a red salmon or two would come at the fly, just to say, "How do you do?" and then, with a scornful wave of his tail, depart as free as he came. I mention these matters here, as we shall have no time to visit Currane in the summer, though, if we pass this way again during the late autumn rains, I hope to spend a day or two with my old friend the Inny, and also visit Lakes Derryana and Elaianane. These two musical words, are spelt, after the local pronunciation, and not according to the Ordnance survey. All this, however, is in advance of my subject, so we will try back, and look for our "maiden trout."

My old friend's statement, that the water at times like the present was full of these creatures, was soon shown to be correct. In the flat, between the bridge and the weirs, I killed a score and a half, and might have filled the basket had his theory been more conclusive. In short, I was suffering from an unwonted attack of conscience, and was tormented with frightful suspicions of murdering "water babies," wandering from home for the first time.

Do men ever profit by the experience of others? Not often, I fancy, though they may sometimes learn a lesson, when the good fairies are pinching them for their sins. Now, gentlemen, after these general moral observations, fancying myself once more seated in the professor's chair, I will finish my lecture with a story, every word of which is, however, true.

A long while ago, a sharp, active, good-humoured young fellow, an old schoolfellow of mine, made his first visit to this country. Of course he took his tackle with him, and the entire stock might have easily packed into his waistcoat pocket. His enemies asserted that he carried it in his aunt's snuff-box, but I solemnly assure you gentlemen, that this was scandal.

Well, to Ireland he came, and having some common sense, soon found that (piscatorially speaking) he knew nothing he ought to know. And how do you think he set about his education? Why, he went on his travels, and visited nearly every river and lake in the island.

On arriving at a new station, his first visit was to some professional, to whom he put such questions as these; "Have you any spring fish? At what time do the grilse arrive? Ditto white trout? What would you consider a good day's angling? Is leave to be bought, or had for the asking?" Being rather a modest young man, he did not put above a dozen or two questions besides. Our friend believed about half he heard (which, as you will remark, was a very liberal allowance), posted his books, and next set off for the river. Here he hooked the first unfortunate angler he saw, and put him through the same examination. If prosperous, he said as little as possible; did he fail, no terms were strong enough—"The river was a humbug; there was not a fish in it—never had been, he believed, nor ever would be." Here, again, our judicious traveller struck a balance, made up his notes, and hurried to the lessee, who, in turn, submitted to the infliction as best he might.

Thus he went on from day to day, raising all sorts of hopes in the minds of professionals, and boring innumerable other innocent people nearly to death. At length his journey brought him to Dublin, and by this time he knew a thing or two. So he bought three or four rods, lots of seals' furs, pig's wool, and no end of useful things; and having done all this, went calmly home with a quiet conscience, and waited, not too patiently, for the coming season;

then he returned, soon gained practical skill, got into good company, was often beaten but never disheartened, and during the next fourteen or fifteen years held up his head with the best, and made a bag as good as any of them.

In conclusion, gentlemen, let me commend our friend's example to your notice, and advise you to follow it.

CHAPTER VIII.

I go, but under protest—Cummeragh River—Distant View of the Inny Lakes—Certain Local Matters the Reader ought to know—Ogham Inscriptions—Limerick—The Old Hookmaker—Doonass—How we got to Sligo.

March 24.—Waterville.

YESTERDAY I promised to leave; to-day I vowed to depart; well, there is no faith in man. But, indeed and indeed, I will positively go to-morrow, though under protest. The lake promises excellent sport for the next month to come. Could I follow my own inclinations, not a step would I stir; but there you are, my dear friend, grimly shaking your paper-knife at a poor fellow, and saying in an awful voice, which makes me tremble all over: "Halloa, you sir, what are you loitering about for? Come, be quick, move on, do you hear?" Well, if we must, we must; but if all the bobbies in Christendom are after me, to-day I will go to Cummeragh.

There was rain yesterday in the mountains, and the water is of the true coffee colour; so, if there be but a couple of salmon in the river, we shall be pretty sure of one.

The Cummeragh, as I remarked in a former chapter, is the chief feeder of Currane. It is a short river, merely the connecting link between the lakes. The best part of it does not exceed a mile or a mile and a half, of which the first half is rocky, and the second a dismal swamp.

Tim, Willie, and I pulled to the head of the lake, drew the boat up, hid the oars, and commenced fishing with a fly, I will try to describe. Tip, silver twist; tag, golden-yellow seal; tail, topping, bustard, mallard, and ruff; body, brightest scarlet seal's fur ribbed with silver; shoulder, golden-yellow pig's wool and jay; hackle, scarlet; wing, two feathers of the jungle cock, rich but light sprigging, topping over all; horns very long, crimson macaw.

In the rocky pools of the lower part we had one shy rise, which I thought was made by a spent fish, the rather as I had landed one of these sick people just before. By and by we came to the dismal swamp, where for some distance the river was as dead as a canal, but not so wide—deep, and black as ink; but here, also, was the part where we expected to succeed.

After landing another spent fish and half a score of foul trout, we struck a ten-pounder and killed him.

I looked at Willie's face as he lifted our prize from the water, and should not have recognised it. The salmon ran gallantly first up and then down the river at a splendid pace; of course we followed in single file, up to our knees in slush, each man splashing his next neighbour as far as was possible, till both became a deep maroon colour. Had Tim and Willie been buried in the bog for a week, and then dug up, they could scarcely have been more perfectly cased with the solution of peat.

Finding we could do no more in this horrible hole, we rubbed ourselves as clean as we could with dry heather, and having thus completed our toilet, commenced fishing back to the boat, killing on the way the salmon I had risen some hours before, which proved a small fresh one of 7lb.

Many a time did we turn to look at the desolate Dunkerron mountains, the birthplace of the Inny, and the cradle of Derriana and Elaineane, and wonder whether Fortune or the rains would bring us to either, late in the coming autumn. I have often spoken of our boat and men; to-day they were paid; thirty shillings per week for all; but to this must be added whisky and lunch—such is the custom here.

Mr. J. P. Nunn, proprietor of the Lake Hotel, is willing and quite able to make his guests most comfortable at 9*l.* per month up to May. These terms may seem a little high, but we must bear in mind that, unless a man has the constitution of a buffalo, wet, cold, and hard work require comfort; that the season is very short, and the accommodation of such a house incalculable to the tourist.

The present lessee of the fishery, with the most far-seeing liberality, allows strangers to angle on the river below the weirs—in fact, he lays open to them his whole run of fish. All he asks in return is, that any early salmon taken by the rod shall be placed in the "pond," or, if retained, be paid for at market price. So he gives all that a true sportsman can desire, *freely,* and only requires that his property and interests may not suffer for his kindness.

Once more we are at Killorglin, on our way to Limerick *via* Killarney. Here I once asked a friend (a man of extraordinary singleness of purpose) whether he had seen this view, or examined that ruin. He replied, "I came to see salmon, not archæological curiosities." Many men, however, have many minds, and the reader might like to see some of these, though my friend did not.

The traces of antiquity scattered over the county are very numerous. I do not pretend to be deeply learned in such matters; nevertheless, if wearied by hard work, or brought to a stand by bad weather, I would pay a visit to the Ogham inscriptions, in the vicinity of Kilmelchedor Church, near Smerwick Harbour. Præ-Roman præ-Christian—older than history, older even than tradition—these inscribed stones have still the power to cast a strange spell on the beholder. I do not understand the characters, and doubt whether I should enjoy them half so much if I did. The key is said to be found, but to me this revivification of dead symbols seems unsatisfactory. Could we really get at the truth, what should we learn? Would these mystic lines speak of a life of triumph, or a death of fame; of love enjoyed, or affection slighted? Who can say? The characters, however, stand eloquent in silence. Well may we moralise with the banished duke—

> This is no flattery; these are counsellors
> That feelingly persuade me what I am.

Thanks to the rail, we are in Limerick. The new town has nothing remarkably new about it, and the old town on King's Island looks as dismal and dilapidated as if, since the days of Ptolemy, Dane and Norman, Edward Bruce and Ireton, William and Ginkel, had been battering at it all day long. Perhaps severe recent study had soured my temper, for I had just finished a huge tome touching the Shannon. The subject had there been considered in all its branches—historically, poetically, botanically, mythologically, traditionally, agriculturally, prophetically. It had been regarded as a means of traffic and a means of salmon. Start not, O reader! If I gained nothing else from the perusal, my own sufferings have at least taught me tenderness and compassion towards others. This morning, however, we feel so much better—so much less bilious, in fact—that we are able to invite our friends to a walking party to see a hook made, and if possible a 50lb. salmon killed, at Doonass.

Amongst all the innocent enjoyments this beautiful world affords, I know none comparable to the delight of a new place. The sun seems more bright, the air more charming, than elsewhere; and even common things are invested with new sensations—emphatically new, for there is nothing old or effete about them. Travelling, as a boy, was my passion; it is a passion still. It has never become flat, stale, or unprofitable; and all it ever was, it is now.

In this city there is much to see, much to please. The lace manufactory is well worth a visit. I am sure it was beautiful. I know it was dear. The quays, too, are full of life and novelty. The river had been most magnanimously forgiven, and we did all justice to its grandeur and beauty. Full of history (the guide-book was in our pocket) we strolled over King's Island, fully appreciating the present as compared with the past. Of course we went to the top of the Cathedral tower. Below lay the city, every street, lane, and court spread out like a map. Eastward the river came broad and shining to the sea; westward it still rolled on, widening as it went. The rich lowlands fell off on either side, leaving a broader channel, till the half-transparent mist so mingled land and water, that the eye strove in vain to decide where the meadows ended and the ocean reigned supreme. All this, and much more, we saw from the tower. Getting up was an easy affair, but coming down was altogether a new sensation. I would not wish my worst enemy a worse cramp. I could have outroared Caliban.

Before starting for Doonass we must pay a visit to O'Shaughnessy. A fortnight ago, sizes and pattern hooks had been sent to him, and the order must now be called for. If you never saw the process, listen, and learn how to make one. We climbed the rickety and dirty stairs, and in an upper room found the old artiste hard at work.

On a table before him lay several fine triangular files, a few pairs of pliers, a piece of boxwood, and a tray divided into compartments, containing small bars of Swedish iron, of sizes suitable for hooks of every number. Now he takes one of the bars and cuts out the barb; then turning the iron in his hand, shapes the back. Again he turns the half-finished hook, and carefully completes the barb, giving it a spherical point as fine as a darning needle. Lastly, he puts on his glasses, and carefully examines what has been done, adds a few finishing touches, and with the pliers gives the exact shape according to pattern, remarking, with a severe glance at the luckless innovator, "*Some* gentlemen are a little self-willed, and like to spoil a good thing by *their* improvements." Nothing now remains to be done but the tempering. I have used these hooks for many years, and have killed salmon with every size, the two largest and two smallest excepted; as one fracture only occurred, I feel bound to bear testimony to their excellence. The price is high, but when it is remembered they can be used season after season, in a series of new flies, they are cheap at any money.

Truly the Shannon is something like a river. "Its length and size are unexampled in any island in the world of similar extent." It rises in Lough Allen, runs a race of 240 miles, and is navigable for small craft till within a few miles of its source. Relatively to the magnitude of the country it enriches and beautifies, it seems like a giant born from a dwarf—like the dinornis compared with the egg from which it sprung. Large as it is, mighty as are its lakes, innumerable as are its tributaries, I fancy our good Salmon Act found it bad enough, The labyrinth of stake-nets in the lower river, draught-nets, burning, and angling, had cruelly injured poor Mr. Salmon's prospects. Now what the river can produce we shall see. In five years' time, I believe, if men have one grain of common sense, for every ten fish brought to market we shall have fifty, besides leaving pretty pickings for honest men.

There stands Castle Connell, nestling amidst demesnes and pleasure grounds, a very paradise for anglers. The glorious rapids, ever chanting the same sweet lay, sing to it night and day—now *piano*, now *forte*—till with the shout of ten thousand voices, they thunder over the "Leap of Doonass."

From its source to the sea the Shannon is said to have a fall of only 150 feet, more than half of which occurs between this place and the city. These beautiful casts being all in private hands, or leased, especially to the rod, you and I have nothing to do with them at present, beyond envying a gallant officer, an especial friend of some of my especial friends, labouring with his usual energy. We should have liked to have heard his recent experiences, but as it is quite as practicable to carry on a conversation across Niagara as across these rapids, we did not attempt it. We watched him for some time, but saw nothing of the fifty-pounder.

These rapids extend for miles, with here and there spots of surpassing excellence. What will they be in 1870?

We must leave Limerick and Mr. Cruise's comfortable hospitium early to-morrow, and try to find our way to Sligo, for we have much to do before the middle of May. I certainly could not make out our route satisfactorily that night. If the reader wishes to learn *exactly* how we got there the next day, I cannot tell him. At this moment I retain a general impression, that between going up and down, backwards and forwards, we wandered in an irregular manner over about half the island, and that is all I know about it.

CHAPTER IX.

Our Hobbies—Morning Walk—Sligo—Mathew the Great—The Drought begins to tell—Waters of the Neighbourhood—Going a-fishing—Lough Gill—The Angler's Duty—Advice to a dear Countryman—Off for Lough Melvin.

March 31.

EVERY man keeps a hobby—some men have a whole stableful—so I have as good a right to such an animal as my neighbour.

In all works on horsemanship, this humble quadruped is sadly neglected. No writer has yet thought it worth his while to devote even one chapter to its use and abuse, its treatment, management, or mismanagement. Some day, when I supply this deficiency in our literature, the following rules will be strongly laid down, and considerably amplified: ride your nag gently, and not too frequently; avoid splashing your neighbour, and never wilfully gallop over him.

Our present hobby is "peep-of-day." To compare one's rising with the sun would be absurd; moreover, it would be taking a monstrous liberty with that heavenly body. Fancy a poor wretch, one day strong and gay, the next sick and sad, challenging him who of old was worshipped as a god, to a race for the year. He would lose to a dead certainty. However, I always try to *imitate* his getting up as well as I may, and am now taking an early walk to the nearest high ground to see all I can. In the face of my own rules, my friend must not be worried into early rising; I can only give him an occasional hint, and set him a good example; one hour of sunrise such as this is worth half the day.

Far away to the west and the north, stretches the broad Atlantic, sparkling in the morning sun; below me is Sligo Bay and Harbour, through whose sandbanks and shoals a steamer is carefully threading her way. The town lies sleeping on the old waterworn level, and to the east is the lake, second only to Killarney in beauty. The sun looks full on the clear purple water, warming into life the insect world, and casting here and there a deep shadow from mountain or island. Water birds are chattering, making their morning toilet, and giving good morrow to each other; whilst many circles, widening as they go, show that the trout are at breakfast.

These are some of the things which can be seen in the morning, you lazy lie-abed. If you heard more, you would only yawn, turn on the other side, and bid me begone. But to you who possess a kindred taste, I will say—stop, stop, or my hobby will be ridden to death.

I walked home through the thriving, well-built country town, but looked in vain for some monument recording Father Mathew's labours and the public appreciation of them. Here, if anywhere, one might have expected to see "a statue of gold on a pillar of porphyry" raised in his honour; but no such thing. The good father preached here the great crusade of 1840; nearly two-thirds of the Catholic population flocked to his standard, took oaths of service and fidelity, and—better still—kept them. What easy work Peter the Hermit had, compared with Mathew the Great! The former had only to launch semi-barbarians (fond of fighting for the mere pleasure of the thing, and doubly fond when there was anything to be got by it) against better men than themselves; but our gallant soldier had to fight against habit and inclination, confirmed by older habits and inclinations in father and grandfather, back to the days of Noah. Good man, true priest, he has long gone to his rest. No cross on his breast, no palm in his hand, show that he reached the Golden City. No matter:

> His bones are dust, his good sword is rust,
> But his soul is with the saints, we trust.

The first thing I saw on entering the street where our hotel stood was a short, stout fellow in close conference with Willie, who, the next instant, dived into the passage. He had secured a boatman, and was gone to boil the inevitable egg, which he not only *would* dress, but bring up, to the great scandal and wrath of all waiters.

Lough Gill runs through the town by a narrowing creek, called the river Garvogue; here, an hour later, we embarked, and rowed away to the broader reaches above, passing a long line of poor cabins. In all old towns, poverty dwells by the water, and Sligo is quite in the fashion.

The drought which distinguished the present season began now to make its effects felt, in the temperature and lowness of the rivers. These effects, however, must, of course, be greatly modified by local peculiarities. Streams with a large outfall will feel it least. So far as spring angling is concerned, the early run of fish (before February 1) is certain to give a reasonable stock to the rivers, and the high water and freshes of that and the succeeding month will, in nine seasons out of ten, constantly add to the stock.

Should such a river flow from a lake, the want of water will not be felt as an inconvenience, the fish being certain to run into it, and consequently a long spell of dry weather will interfere less with angling in spring than in summer. Nevertheless, a drought is our greatest enemy, except perhaps in such rivers as the Erne and Blackwater below the weirs, where it must be greater than I have ever seen it, to injure sport materially.

In Lough Melvin, which will be our next station, its effects must be more felt, for although the Bundoran river—the little Drowse—(the word is spelt as pronounced), enters the sea in a narrow and sufficient stream, yet, as it approaches the lake, the shallows in dry weather are so low, as to offer an almost impassable barrier to the farther advance of the salmon. In such circumstances they have no alternative but to drop back into the deeps above the village, lie like logs at the bottom, and pray to Jupiter for rain.

Instead of dragging out the reader this morning, to see only perhaps one or two fish killed, it appears more advisable to devote as much of this paper as possible to a description of the waters of the neighbourhood, and thus give him the means of performing this most agreeable part of an angler's business for himself.

Sligo forms excellent head-quarters for the tourist. He may take his ease at his inn, or, if economically disposed, can secure comfortable lodgings and make himself at home. This is my plan, whenever such a plan is possible. Then the lake is at the door, and this is no small advantage.

Five miles west of the town is the village of Ballysadere, through which flows a river of the same name. This stream is formed by the union of the river Awinmore and the Unshin or Arrow, near the town of Collooney, and falling over a ledge of rocks, which crosses its entire bed, thunders into Ardnaglass harbour. Here the angler may look for sport in the late spring and summer freshes.

What shall we say of Lough Arrow? Why, simply this: that the man who cannot be satisfied with this sport in April and May, either with fly or troll, and will not laud it to the skies in June, when the green drakes hover over it like a cloud, must indeed be hard to please.

Lough Tult, imbedded amid precipices, abounds with trout; Lough Easkey and Lough Glencar well deserve a visit. If to these attractions be added the fact that he is on the high road to the Drowse, Lough Melvin, and the glorious Erne, I think the tourist will admit that Sligo forms a centre of operations not to be despised.

Should our friend be a botanist, Benbulben will cheer him: if he be painter or poet, he will feel a still deeper delight on the breezy summit of that noble mountain; and, on his way home, should he pace the ruined cloisters of the fine old Dominican abbey, I doubt not he will return a better and a happier man.

We have reached Lough Gill at last, and are gliding along its southern and most beautiful shore. If the lake looked lovely in the early morning, it looked not less lovely now, as we stole over its curling waters, between islands of all sizes, beautiful with rock and wood and shadow.

The lake, though by no means in the first rank for size, is yet six miles in length by two in breadth, and boasts twenty islands, the largest of which (Church Island) reckons 42 acres, and Cottage Island 14 acres; both are inhabited, which must prove of immense importance to the hungry angler. Our broad-shouldered guide declared the fly to be "the thing wherewith to catch the conscience of the king," so we tried the scarlet, donkey, parson, green, olive, claret, and fiery-brown—and did nothing.

As each was shown in turn for his approbation, the stout man shook his head oracularly, and observed, "It *might* do, yer honour," intimating clearly that in his opinion, unless the salmon were hopelessly lunatic, not a tail should we see, and I am bound to say he was right.

Perhaps thinking our obstinacy sufficiently punished, the honest fellow drew out from the depths of his coat pocket an ancient and tattered song book, from between the leaves of which he produced a ragged and faded fly, of no definite colour, having very much the appearance of a decayed gentleman who had known better days, and to this I added a pair of dark small flies. After this our fortune in some sort began to mend, and we soon killed a nice dish of trout; still not a salmon could we see. In this extremity, Willie proposed a spoon and minnow, which were presently spinning over each quarter of the boat.

Passing Culmore Point we had a smart run. The fish felt light—too light, I thought, for a salmon, though the boatman of course was positive, as boatmen should be. Whatever he was, he gave us the slip; but to this day, no doubt, Mr. Gallagher maintains that, "Bedad, the obstinate gintleman hooked a splendid salmon wid a spoon off that Pint—divil a lie I'm telling ye." Presently, however, near Church Island, we did hook a salmon. There was no doubt about it this time, for in five-and-twenty minutes we had the satisfaction to see a neat thirteen-pounder crimped, "making the green one red," as he soaked and stiffened over our stern.

What would it avail to say that we gave the lake little rest—that Dromohair, Connormore Stone, The Ridge, Pigeon Point, The Hollow, Culmore Point, O'Rorke's Castle. The Shell-house Shore, Church Island, and Castle Point, were tried again, and again? Few readers would be much the wiser, and when they visit the lake I promise that Pat Gallagher shall faithfully exhibit them all.

After working steadily for the next five days, sometimes with salmon and trout flies, at other times with the troll, we bagged six more fresh fish and about forty small lake trout. The salmon were of fair average size, from 8lb. to 11lb., none coming up to our number one.

A gentleman's first duty is to ask permission. I avoid names, since even those whose whose daily acts to strangers are all kindness might not desire such publicity. I may mention, however, that application to the courteous owners of Newton Manor, Hazlewood, Killery, and Claveragh House will make the angler a freeman of the lake. My dear friend and countryman, the recipient of such liberality, when you go home I hope you won't put bad boys in the stocks for looking after your roach and dace.

At the end of our week we packed up, and drove merrily away for Lough Melvin. Before evening we sat down to dinner in the unpretending hospitium of Garrison; watched the sun go down too large and red for our wishes, yet went to bed to dream of fresh triumphs on new fields.

CHAPTER X.

Lough Melvin—A Week at Garrison—What the Drought did—Permission—Irish Follower—Advantages as a Station—Head Waters—Inhabitants of the Lake—The Great Middle Class—Trying our Luck—*De Omnibus Rebus*—Leaf from an old MS.—We cry for Mercy.

April 3.

IF A MAN could ever hope to find Peace in this troublesome world, he might reasonably expect to meet that sweet saint somewhere about Garrison. Preaching night and day, the gentle lake is for ever and for ever giving good advice, mingling with our waking thoughts and slumberous fancies. The mountains are like sober "friends in council," and the islands ought to have at least one hermit, to preach a homily, *De solitudine*.

The power to wander over this beautiful world, with free limbs and a light heart, is an inexpressible delight. It seems to bring back the innocent patriarchal days, when the strife and turmoil of busy life were well nigh unknown, and now, after the lapse of thousands of years, men still turn to the old nomadic life, as to a normal state ; and in after years remember their too brief wanderings as the brightest period of their existence.

William Scott, the straightforward and intelligent proprietor of the hotel, shook his head mournfully, when consulted as to our prospects. The drought formed the burden of his song—in fact, made up the greater part of it, and, like the ancient chorus, he denounced all kinds of disagreeable things. "Of course the first run," he said, " was safe and snug enough ; the high waters of February had increased the stock ; nevertheless he wished them fresher and in better spirits; for his part, he liked to see the crathers fierce as blazes—tearing away like mad ; but there was no help for it, and gintlemen must do the best they could." Then came the argument. Latterly, few or no fish were able to pass the shallows on the upper portion of the River Drowse ; in short, the supply was cut off, and we were likely to be starved out. However, there was balm in Gilead, for we, being early in the field, might hope to fatten where later comers would run short.

On the evening of our arrival we found letters containing most kind permission from the three noblemen and gentlemen to whom the shores of the lake belong, which, we may add, is never refused to strangers who apply for it. Moreover, Archy Cathcart and his mate were selected as our boatmen, at the reasonable rate of 24s. per week, and hardier fellows or more zealous anglers it would be difficult to find.

Your Irish attendant is a man *sui generis ;* at least, there is nothing like him in our own land. Compare him with an English gamekeeper—be that functionary land rat or water rat—Pat is as much like him in body and mind as he is in dress, and in this particular there is no great degree of comparison. Our well-fed friend in neat velveteen, gaiters, and boots, stalks solemnly after you, as though he had reluctantly made up his mind to do a disagreeable duty. He shows not the smallest interest or pleasure in the business—neither exults at your success nor commiserates your failure, and pockets his half guinea with a silent touch of his hat and an aspect of being the most ill-used man in Christendom.

Now look on this picture of rags, hearty interest, indefatigable zeal, and active good humour, all for two shillings a day. If he cannot show you sport (and you may take your corporal oath he has done his best), he will tell you what might, could, would, should, or ought to be done—some of it truth, more, probably truth embellished. But with all his failings—and poor Pat is only a man after all—he is the best and pleasantest attendant, through heat or cold, hunger or thirst, in good fortune or evil fortune, that can be found out of his own tight little island.

With your florin in his hand, he bids "yer honor the best of sleap," says something hopeful about to-morrow, and with his duddeen in his mouth, and very little under his waistcoat, talks by his bit of smouldering turf for the hour together of what you did, he did, and they did.

Archy and his mate have been standing this half-hour under the windows with rods and gaff. There, too, is Willie, critically inspecting the boat, hammer and bradawl in hand; one of his eccentricities being a delusion (of course it *was* a delusion) that all the craft which float on Irish lakes required repairs, and that it was his special mission to execute the same.

As a station Garrison is perfect, all the best casts being close at hand. No comfort can compensate for want of proximity, and here the one and the other go hand in hand.

I have little to say about "the waters of the neighbourhood," as they have scarcely any connection with the angler, if we except the river Drowse, the outlet of the lake.

Loughs Macnean and Melvin stretch along the north-eastern boundary of the county of Leitrim, separating it from Fermanagh, in which, however, they may be said to lie partly. These lakes are connected by the Kilcoo river, and, with Macnean, form the head waters and chief breeding grounds of the district. I never fished either, as they were not in order during any of my visits, but believe they are of very small account till the late autumn freshes; at all events the Kilcoo can hardly be of importance until the grilse arrive in July, nor even then, except after heavy rains. Lough Macnean is a good-sized piece of water, having a circumference of ten or eleven miles.

Spring salmon, like early spring flowers, are only to be found in favoured localities, Lough Melvin being, of course, one of these. Besides the *Salmo Salar*, the lake contains other inhabitants. Not to mention "the swinish multitude," such as eels, perch, and the like, it boasts (over and above the aristocratic visitors drawn hither for change of scene and air) a large number of resident gentry, of three orders—the great laker, gillaroo, and brown trout. There is also said to be another class, shy, modest, and retiring, by no means easily brought under public notice, the pullan, or fresh-water herring. These fish, I was informed, are tolerably abundant here, and in Lough Neagh, and are only taken by netting. To the best of my belief, the large lake trout are not trolled for with any system or perseverance; still they are not unfrequently taken in a chance kind of way, as the angler who is not too lazy to change the fly for the troll, passes from one side of the lake to the other. Should any one, however, diligently cultivate the acquaintance of this great middle class, I doubt not he would gather round him a very numerous circle. That they run large here is certain, for I *saw* one in the hands of a Ballyshannon professional, which he told me was 17lb., and I am sure he *was that* weight, *if not more*.

The gillaroo rise well at the fly, but are far smaller than the preceding. I do not remember ever seeing one exceeding 4lb. Highly favoured are these creatures, combining as they do beauty with goodness; then, they may eat what they choose! They might begin with fish, and end with pastry and cheese, without being the worse for it. Oh that excellent gizzard of theirs; as a digestive apparatus, it could convert tenpenny nails into chyle.

But it is time to leave off "talking shop," and be up and doing, for a west wind is curling the lake, and the boatmen, together with our prime minister, are waiting on the strand, doubtless wondering what has come over "the master."

We pulled direct to one of the best casts—the high rocky bluff on the eastern extremity of the lake—where we remained for some hours trying it over and over with fresh changes, and were not dissatisfied with hooking two fish, one of which was landed, and weighed a little under 10lb.

Shifting the ground, we continued our pleasant toil by the rushes under the Priest's house, and then round the pretty bay immediately above. These throws (the best on the lake) proving blank, we stretched over to the north side, and, keeping slow way on the boat, fished the rocky shore as we proceeded.

Finding the fly unavailing, the troll was set to work, and as we came abreast of a bold bluff, half a mile or so below Bilbury Island, had the good fortune to run and kill a small salmon of $6\frac{1}{2}$lb. From the island we worked our way home with small flies, taking three or four gillaroo, and a score of pretty little brown trout. This, as far as salmon were concerned, proved the best day of our week's sojourn. Instead of wearying the reader with hopes disappointed or toil rewarded, it will be better to speak of matters more generally, and thus enable him to gain a few facts for his own use. Lough Melvin is by no means the worst of Irish waters; the station is convenient, and the salmon and grilse fishing generally good. The spring fish run from 7lb. to 11lb., though of course these figures are not to be taken *absolutely*, as larger and smaller are occasionally killed. The gillaroo, if nothing better is to be done, are always to be taken on any day suitable for angling; and systematic trolling would produce good results, as I hope to show; and for smaller game, the shores yield plenty of bog-trout, and, to the best of my belief, charr. In the *spring* and summer there is something to be done in the lower part of the Drowse; and during the late *autumn* spates, excellent sport with salmon, grilse, and gillaroo is to be found.

Not a hundred years ago, after, as I thought, winding up the season in the Rosses, we chanced to reach Bundoran on the 1st of

October, intending to botanise from thence to Benbulben. But it happened that the little river was clearing, after prolonged rains; the lake was high, and of course so was the Drowse. Under these circumstances, if another rare specimen had never been added to my *hortus siccus*, I should not have cared. So I unpacked a rod, engaged an old fellow as guide, whom I subsequently learned was *the* very worst in all Ireland, and set off for Mellinaleck Bridge. There was, at that state of water, a lovely stream just below the bridge, where we commenced with an olive; half-way down, I found him, and a capital salmon he was. From thence we worked *up* the water. Before evening, the basket contained three stout fish, two grilse, thirteen gillaroo, some brown trout, and, if my memory is correct, two or three white trout.

This leaf from an old MS. may serve as an illustration of the remark that during the late autumn spates good sport may be had on the Drowse. I do not pretend to be an authority on this subject, as my experience is too limited. I only visited the river once or twice in each of the many happy seasons spent on the Erne, seasons which have a pleasant place in my memory, recalling many kindnesses and many friends. I feel bound, however, to say, that the visits above referred to seldom proved satisfactory; perhaps they were ill-timed; perhaps all my luck had ended with the first speculation; there ought, however, to have been ample compensation, as I figured in "somebody's" black books a long time after, and was always considered a defaulter from the tranquil pursuit of botany and the picturesque.

In the next chapter we shall go back to the lake and narrate our small experience of the *Salmo famosus*. I hope, however, no very learned person will expose me for calling the large trout of Lough Melvin "names;" I care little what their scientific appellation may be; ignorance profound as mine is hardly worth so large a waste of wisdom.

CHAPTER XI.

Why certain People are neglected—The Lake—Islands—Woodcocks and Ducks—Trolling—Our Last Day—History of the Week—The Camp is broken up, and we march on Derry—Willie goes Home—Lough Swilly.

April 7.

I WISH to know how you, sir, would like to be called "fierce," "lusty," "cruel," "crust," "surly," "insolent," "huffish," and "headstrong;" yet all these comfortable words belong to the adjective Ferox, and my friends in the lake object to such language, and beg me to say so. To remark to one of these gentlemen who had just made his best bow on the floor of my boat, "I rejoice sincerely to see you, Mr. S. Ferox," would doubtless be equally correct and equally insulting. "Do as you would be done by" is a favourite maxim of mine: unfortunately, memory is defective, and it goes out of one's head sometimes when it should not.

The reason these fine fish are not more looked after is this—the society they move in is too good for them.

If you said to me, "Look, there is President Johnson, and the gentleman half a pace behind him is his secretary, Captain Bobadil, a man who *must* have distinguished himself at the bloody battle of Tiptree Farm, had he not been knocked down, out of hand as it were, by a nigger at the commencement of the fight"—if you said this, I should pull off my hat, do homage to a great and self-built man, and probably forget all about the pseudo-general half a pace behind. No doubt Captain B. *is* a sparkling luminary, but then unfortunately he is too near the sun.

In fact, he is remarkably like our poor friend Splendidus. I see, my dear sir, a very proper amount of virtuous indignation on your handsome countenance at this hero-worship; yet, if you were at Lough Melvin, I'll be bound you would say, " Hang your trout, and hurroo for the salmon." But no, you could not be vulgar. *You* would lay a hand on your waistcoat, and murmur softly—" Believe me, my dear Mrs. Salmon, yours faithfully, till death. . . . ."

And quite right too. But most vows are conditional. For the last four days I have fished—*slaved* would be more correct—from 9 a.m. to 7 p.m., with certainly not ten minutes' rest, and for these forty misspent hours have only two fish to show. Well, there is no knowing what a man may do when he is vexed. I *am* vexed, and shall go trouting. This was resolved on last night, but there was a little difficulty about bait, which we overcame in this wise. Archy and I set out in the twilight to look for a boy, and soon found one. The negotiation was left in his hands : " Arrah, Patsy," to a shoeless mass of rags, " come here. Is it a throut ye'd know, if ye seen it— as long as this ?" Here Archy marked the exact length of the animal required, with the end of his pipe, on the knuckle of his forefinger. Patsy felt hurt by the implied doubt, so he did not answer, except by grinning from ear to ear. "Hurry, ye young villin; hurry off wid ye at the fust light, and be shure ye come back before the master's up ; sorra a cross ye'll get else, and Holy Peter, won't I lash ye; mind, I'm telling." At the conclusion of these energetic instructions, Patsy made his bow and departed, to meditate on the doctrine of rewards and punishments so forcibly laid down.

The young scapegrace returned in time to win his sixpence, and escape a "lashing" and brought twelve or thirteen baits, so with these we started. . . . . The reader knows, of course, he is at Lough Melvin, but, from any description of mine, he has not " the least idea in life " what sort of place that may be, except a kind of debatable water between the counties Leitrim and Fermanagh.

Wonderfully lovely is the lake with its sparkling wavelets breaking in the sunshine, and its islands tinted with the green and pink, grey and yellow, of the coming spring. How charming these little worlds look in the undress of this morning of their immortal lives ; nor is space wanting, for our lake is rather more than seven miles long by three broad. Of course it is not a first-class water, for, compared with its neighbour Lough Erne, with Lough Neagh, Lough Corrib, and Lough Mask, it is but a baby—even as Gulliver amongst the Brobdignags. Nevertheless I wished it no larger this morning.

The plan proposed was to pull in and out along the east and north shores, and "do" the island on our way back. Now this arrangement had one or two advantages—first, we should go over all the best salmon lodges, and by keeping well on their outer edges were as likely as elsewhere to find Splendidus at home ; and next, by dodging off the Fermanagh side, our baits would be trailed over all the ground which promised best.

Near the Point we soon had a run. The fish felt heavy on the rod, but, after two or three weighty lunges, broke away. Of course, it was *my* fault; it always is the angler's fault in the eyes of his zealous attendant. "Fortune had deserted us that day for good and all." "Not a taste of luck should we have; not the least in life— and him the first!"

The prophecy proved false, as abreast of "the rushes," rather outside the cast, we had a second run, and landed a fine stout trout of 6lb. This was quick work, and promised well for our last day. The blind goddess, however, deserted us for the time, leaving us to prove by perseverance that we deserved her favours. In the middle of the lake, when the sun was far in the west, we again got a run. This time Willie laid his pipe carefully between the knees of the boat, as if he thought it might be some time before he wanted it again.

In pure love and charity we had shipped a new hand, who expressed himself "kilt entirely" by setting potatoes. Nobody wanted him; but I was unwilling to refuse the poor fellow a day's amusement. He was the queerest, most tattered, and most impulsive party ever seen. Watching the fish like a hawk—himself nearly as wild—he sprang on the beam just in time to catch a glimpse of Splendidus, as he reeled over on the surface at least fifty yards off, in a very intoxicated manner.

"Holy Mary! what a baste. Hand us the gaff—quick there ! Is it deaf that ye are ?"

With freezing dignity, without moving a muscle, the gentleman thus addressed made answer :

"I land for the master!"

No whit affronted, the excitable party by this time was about on a new tack.

"Hark till it!" meaning perhaps the wheel; "he's at it agin, as mad as blazes; hurroo, hurroo! Nicholas mend him." Whether this devout ejaculation had any effect on his wild courses, or whether he was done in the regular way, seems uncertain; at any rate, it was the last despairing rush, and when he again rose near us, on a short taut line, Willie executed him *secundum artem*, with a sidelong glance at his master, which seemed to say, "I've got him *this* time, though I did make a bungle at Carra."

That there were scores of stouter individuals in the lake cannot be doubted, yet the present one gave 10½lb. on Salter's balance.

Nor was Fortune yet weary of us, for she gave us another three-and-a-half-pounder, and a small recently-run salmon of 7lb. Thus ended our week at Garrison; five fish and two good lakers were not much to boast of—may I never do worse.

The cock shooting in the Marquis of Ely's islands is something marvellous to Saxon minds. The ducks are now building or laying; household cares probably keep them at home, for we see little of them. In July and August, however, the long strings of babies paddling about after their mammas show there is no fear of the race dying out.

That stupid almanac says it is Friday, April 7th. My ticket for the Bush commences on the 15th, but do what I will it is impossible to be there on that day. There is Lough Fern for a week; then two or three days will be lost on the way; however, we shall reach Derry to-morrow by noon, and crossing Lough Swilly gain Rathmelton before night, and no man can do more.

Brave old Derry! seated on your hill, and crowned with your grey cathedral spire, you look like a queen—and a very sensible queen, too. There is no nonsense or frivolity about you. You have accepted your position, and feel that even Gosnell and Co. cannot make old men or old cities young or new. Rowland's Kalydor cannot preserve our bloom and smoothness. "The United Service" will not give to hair youthful gloss or beauty; the wrinkles are there; and for old cities the only cosmetics are fire and powder, too costly for general use.

Londonderry has strong claims on the stranger, and as you and I have a reputation for paying our debts, we will stroll round the ramparts, which, in fact, will be giving an I O U for the amount. I wish my tailor's little bill were as easily disposed of.

Externally, at least, the walls of Derry are as sound as when Hamilton, defeated and disheartened, fell back towards Strabane. Doubtless the good citizens are proud of their city, and take all care of their time-honoured ramparts. Had there been rents in the old garment, so carefully were they darned that I could not find them out. Here, in the principal battery, stands a handsome pillar crowned with a statue of the dauntless Rector of Donaghmore, and below are the old guns his hands pointed so often against the foe; his especial pet, "roaring Meg," seeming still able to shout as defiantly as ever. But ladies, we have heard, are adepts in getting up; so perhaps "Meg" is neither so sound nor young as she looked.

It is a spirit-stirring place, this old battery, for here, in the pleasant month of April, commenced a sensation drama, which has enjoyed a long run, even till to-day. Faint with famine, weary with wounds and watching, dwindled to a handful, the defenders of the maiden city stood where I now stand. in an evening of July. wildly looking for succour long delayed. The sermon was over; not one of your fifteen-minute affairs, but a good old-fashioned article, with its "twenty-thirdly," "lastly," "to conclude," and the "yet one word more"—these stout hearts liked such things, and found they could fight their daily battles all the better for them;—well, the sermon was over, and the congregation, with haggard faces and tottering steps, but with spirits unsubdued, remembered that by no art could even their loathsome food hold out two days more. The tide was at the flood; it was now or never. On comes the *Mountjoy*, Micaiah Browning, himself a "Derry boy," at the wheel. Will chain and boom at Culmore stand the charge? For an instant the smoke of the guns hides the headmost ship, it clears, and blank despair darkens those famished faces, as the vessel reels back from the barrier. But another, with a freshening breeze, and the last of the flood, comes on gallantly. Will she, too, fail? No; the stranded leader has done her work, and that wild shout, "We are saved," tells the triumph.

The tide flows as far as Strabane, through a rich, reedy, alluvial flat, so sleepy and quiet that an alligator or hippopotamus dozing on the mud would hardly be out of place. The rivers Finn and Mourne flow into it at Lifford, and ought to be capital angling streams. I never fished either the one or the other.

Below Culmore point, Lough Foyle spreads out her waters gloriously. On the western shore, the Innishowen mountains (whose inhabitants formerly drank their corn instead of eating it) rise in magnificent confusion almost from the water's edge. Handsome villas speak well for honest Derry. Fast little cutters, gay with bunting, flit over the tide, and at the mouth of the lough, where the entrance is scarcely wider than half rifle range, stand the ruins of Green Castle, once an important place, now solitary and deserted, but very beautiful. Dear old ruins, from which I can see my own cottage, near the Giant's Causeway. Well, home is home, after all—if you don't have too much of it.

We shall go to Rathmelton with a diminished party, as Willie leaves us here to fit out our little schooner, and see that she looks her best when we arrive. The Pet is the pride of his heart, and he is chief mate. I do not like to part with him, even for a day; something is always wanting, which no one else can do as well. Man and boy, we have roamed about the world many a year together.

Well, faithful friend, good bye. The poor fellow looks as if he had a bad cold, for his eyes—we must not disgrace his manhood, as he wears a beard—they are usually weak at such times; and so it came to pass that we trotted off towards Lough Swilly rather dolefully.

This noble sheet of water always strikes me as inexpressibly solitary and desolate. Large enough to hold all the war fleets of the world, if they would only agree to live peaceably together, its present navy boasts only a few fishing-boats, hauled on the strand, some half-dozen hookers, and now and then a schooner bringing Scotch coal and carrying back Irish meal. As soon as the stranger lands on the western or Donegal shore a marked change for the worse is everywhere apparent. The land is more peaty and wet, the farms are small and poor; in fact, from hence to Donegal, *viâ* Gweedore, Glenties, Guibarra, and Ardara—three sufficiently long summer days' journeys—the whole country is made up of mountains, morass, lakes, rivers, and bog. Man seems merely allowed to exist, so ungenial is the soil, so capricious the climate. We must not abuse it, however, as we have spent many, many happy months in the district, and intend to visit it again in the coming autumn. If the climate be inhospitable, it seems to have ripened all hospitable virtues, for the fairest land under the sun cannot show warmer hearts than are there to be found. Dear friends, believe me, your kindness is fresh in my memory.

This chapter is as long as the road, but, thank heaven! here is Rathmelton.

CHAPTER XII.

What's in a Name?—Walking in the Mist, and Floundering in the Mud—A very rough Sketch of the Capabilities of Donegal—Not knowing, can't say—Lough Fern—Grand day on the Leannan—Greenon Hill—Doings for the Week.

Friday, April 14.

WHAT'S in a name? has been asked on very high authority. The answer is, that it depends entirely on circumstances.

If a pair of bright eyes, with lips to match, said, "Ah, you rogue," even a gentleman from Galway would hardly think of calling out the brother; but "Ah, you rogue; here, policeman, take this fellow in charge, my pocket is picked," would bear quite a different value, and place a strain on your Christian charity sufficiently strong to test its quality.

Now, they tell me Rathmelton is a town. I should not have thought so, since it does not look at all like one; but then, you know, it depends on circumstances, for a village in any other country would be a capital city in Donegal, and a Donegal village in another land would be a—a curiosity.

For an idler, Rathmelton would prove a first-rate station. The man does not live who could stand at that inn-door for one morning watching the rain-drops gather on the eaves, with now and then the excitement of a draggle-tailed cock slinking under a cart, and trying in vain to look comfortable. The laziest Saxon on earth would seize his rod and sally forth in the drizzle, as I did.

Donegal is a remarkable county in the matter of rain. Should a cloud from the Atlantic hold but a quart of water, this favoured region is sure to get a pint of it. In point of fact, it has "first choice," and, as the wind blows from the west for nearly half the year, that "first choice" is worth something. A man in a dropsy is always drinking; this land is anasarcous, and does the same.

In most of these papers I have endeavoured to give some account of the streams of the neighbourhood; but Heaven help the man who undertakes the waters of this county. Why, it is all water, except some parts, which are a mixture of water and vegetable mould in about equal proportions. All the anglers in Britain might here have a station apiece, if they wished it; there need be no jealousy, gentlemen, I assure you. For several years past I have spent a portion of each autumn in this thirsty land, but know no more of the lakes immediately beyond my route than I did years ago. As his car rolls along through heathery wastes, pieces of water of all sizes meet the traveller's gaze, laying solitary, tempting, and deserted. The majority of these have, probably, never been fished, unless by some chance grouse shooter or a peasant in the vicinity. If the length of the line between Rathmelton and Gweedore, and thence to Donegal, be considered, the number of these lakes is great indeed,

From the summit of Muckish, as far as the eye can range, silver pools dot the brown expanse. Mountain streams connect many of these with the sea, and probably afford a passage for salmon to reach their lonely winter quarters. That many of these lakes hold large red trout, I know; what the majority are worth I do not know; but if local accounts are to be trusted, the sport in the north, west, and south of this country must be excellent. Some ardent spirit, stimulated by the difficulty of the enterprise, will doubtless start up and astonish the world piscatorial with his discoveries; but such an explorer should possess a rare combination of gifts. *Imprimis*, a waterproof skin, like a seal, or one of Mr. Cording's best boots; *secundo*, a stomach that can digest anything, or thrive on nothing; *tertio*—but a truce to nonsense. This country I believe contains lake treasures unknown to the outside world. They are awfully out of the way; in countless cases too remote from anything deserving the name of accommodation, to be available except to the neighbouring cottar, who, being destitute of a boat, can only paddle about on the margin.

What Lord George Hill's country was some years ago, anyone who reads "Facts from Gweedore" may see. No roads, no resting-place; only a few panes of glass in the whole barony, one or two flannel petticoats amongst all the ladies, and so on. It is now some years since I read the pamphlet referred to, but the facts are much as I have stated them. At that time nothing but a seagull or a wild duck could have visited the district and made himself at home.

What that region *was*—before the good man who tried to cultivate the soil and those who dwelt on it—other parts of the country are *now*, wild, desolate, and inaccessible; but, as we shall see more of it in September, enough has been said for the present.

We have been flying over the country as if an excursion-ticket were in our pocket, whereas a *tour de ma chambre* would have been better; so perhaps the reader will please to remember we only arrived last night at Rathmelton.

This frontier town of Donegal dozes away its existence on the banks of the river Leannan. The seedy, disconsolate aspect of the place would lead a stranger to imagine it had taken to drinking and lost all self-respect. . . . Before a box had been taken off the car last night my host informed me, " there had not been a drop of rain for the past five weeks, and the river was as low as it could be." He repeated the same statement this morning, though the draggle-tailed cock at the door flatly contradicted him. Drizzle in Rathmelton must be a synonym for fine weather. This, however, was a matter of little moment, as here the salmon ascend to the lake at a very early period—all through the winter, in fact—at which season, at least in Donegal, there is sure to be no lack of moisture.

After an early breakfast we set off for Lough Fern, following the course of the Leannan along a shallow boggy depression, which here passes for a valley, in which I believe conscientiously every species of juncus figured by Hooker find a "local habitation," if not a name. A short drive brought us to the cottage of the resident professor, when, leaving our horse happy in munching some sour hay, we walked to the lake, baled out the boat, and commenced operations with two trout and one salmon-fly. Round the sedges, at the south-south-west extremity, we fished, rising and hooking respectable trout at short intervals, changing the trail again and again without changing our fortune. The guide paddled and paddled in ghost-like silence, which was only broken by my inquiring "What was to be done next?" Resting on his oars with the aspect of a deeply injured man, he observed, "it would have been as well to have consulted him sooner," and next pulled from his pocket an article, the prevailing hue of which was whitey brown, the gut and hook thereto belonging being sufficient to fill an angler with despair. Madame, with great zeal, instantly commenced what she had the assurance to call an improvement on the pattern; with which, alas! it was destined never to be compared, as before its completion a fine fish carried off the antique, to some subaqueous museum. I *might* have said with Paulina—

> What's gone, and what's past help,
> Should be past grief;

though I fear I did not utter anything half so reasonable.

Silent Charon was unmoved, even by the loss of his property. Whether the abnormal spell of sunshine and dry weather had withered his spirits, whether that morning he had been requested to pay a "thrifle on account of rint," or whether a solitary life had impaired the flexibility of his vocal organs, is uncertain. It might have been either, neither, or a little of each; but whatever the cause, our pulling machine no more resembled an ordinary Celtic boatman, than a modern perfumer in Regent-street resembles Da Ponte's Figaro.

"The improvement" did not for some time mend our broken fortunes, but at length, as we neared the upper end of the water, a deep eddying swirl gave promise of better things. What children we are, when a bubble on the surface of a small boggy lake can set our hearts beating, and make us oblivious of cold, hunger, and disappointment! A fiery brown, and next an olive, were offered and sullenly rejected; then came the rising fly. A bright flash through the rippling water acknowledged the attention. For an instant the line is strained, by compression between the hand and the butt, and then "away for life he springs." The prolonged screech of the wheel bespoke an able and vigorous adversary. Now to the bottom, right below the boat, he dives; then once more tries his speed. The line, with wonderful velocity assuming the horizontal, shows what is coming. Low stoops the rod, just in time to meet as desperate a leap, in the direct course of his headlong race, as ever salmon achieved. The guide casts a quick glance upwards at the rod; its curve satisfies him that nothing has given way, and now on one palm, now on the other, he tests the sharpness of the gaff. The examination seems satisfactory, for with a grim smile he lays the weapon across his knees, ready for instant use, and proceeds to light a pipe, his glance never for a moment quitting the spot at which the line cut the surface of the lake. Shorter grow the runs; the airy somersaults are now exchanged for feeble plunges; a few minutes more, and we are admiring the first prize drawn from Lough Fern.

The shores of the lake offered no temptations to wander away in search of the picturesque, so we stuck to business with considerable perseverance, and by "closing time" had every reason to be satisfied with the amount of patronage bestowed on us. In the till we found two score of trout and a salmon of 14lb.

Many reasons combine to render Lough Fern an *aqua incognita* to the sporting world. It lies in a remote part of the country, which, possessing few attractions, is not often visited by tourists. The art of puffing seems little understood in honest Donegal, and the sport is best in spring, when boat-fishing is rather cold, uncomfortable work. Moreover, the quarters, though sufficient, are not splendid; the town is poor and uninviting, and, on market-days, may my good genius preserve me from Rathmelton. Nevertheless, if a man desires to kill salmon, let him go to Lough Fern in the spring.

Yesterday, as we drove to the lake, along the banks of the river, I noticed some deepish stretches of water, and this morning there was a fine south-easterly breeze. On mentioning my intention to the landlord, he shrugged his shoulders, saying, "if exercise were necessary, I could not do better; but as for catching anything, the road was as good as the river." On close inspection, it did not look so promising as from a greater distance; nothing but small flies would do, and as none of the requisite size were in the book, we manufactured a dark claret, with orange tips, black hackle, jay shoulder and mallard wing, on a medium grilse hook. Whenever a cloud came over the sun, I worked as men do whose time is limited. When the sky was all blue, I set to at the junci, with every chance of making a good bag. Were the family tree at hand, on some important branch unquestionably the honoured name of Porcas would be seen. What a fool was I to go on such an errand! What an obstinate pig, to remain against conviction! Yet on the whole, perhaps, it was not an unsuccessful day. In the morning, the tail of my self-conceit was over my back; in the evening it was so tight between my legs as to impede locomotion; but I brought back a basketful of good resolutions, much respect for local opinions, and an appetite that would have done credit to a wolf.

We remained here a week, fishing for six days, in which time we bagged eight good-sized salmon, and about half a hundredweight of trout.

In bidding adieu to Lough Fern, the reader takes his leave of the last of the spring lakes which lay in our proposed route. Hitherto the drought had injured us but little; in the coming summer, however, the evil will be found great, so great indeed as to make the season quite an exceptional one. It seems wiser, therefore, to represent the sport such as it really is in average seasons; this plan will also be more instructive to the stranger, as well as more generally correct. I have avoided all "tall talking" about large bags, and have purposely painted that part of my pictures in very sober colours indeed.

Well, then, we have taken our leave of spring lakes, but before we part, the reader will yet float on three or four summer seas, and how different will he find them! Instead of cutting wind and driving rain, there will be flowers and rustling trees, the song of birds, balmy airs, and islands whose delicious beauty would have made the poets of old days fix on them as the abodes of the blessed. These bright days and pleasant things will all come in time; at present the car is at the door, and we are bound once more for Derry, *viâ* Greenon Hill.

Along the shores of Lough Swilly and over heathery swells we roll, till before us stands the mountain, on the summit of which is the Grianan of Aileach, the most remarkable piece of antiquity in Donegal. Here was the palace of the northern Irish kings, from the most remote antiquity down to the twelfth century; and what a picture of the time does this place afford. Fancy his Majesty Donnell Mac Loughlin, the last monarch of Ulster, by right of his august title, taking up his quarters for the night on the lee side of the Cyclopean wall, "which served him for parlour, for bedroom, for kitchen and all." This *al fresco* sort of thing might do very well in the Friendly Islands; but his majesty and court must have had a damp time of it on Greenon Hill. In the "Memoirs of the Ordnance Survey of Ireland," there is a minute description of this interesting ruin, together with an ancient poem, which bears undoubted evidence of having been written before A.D. 1101.

The view from the summit is exquisite—over lough and heath, mountains, and the broad Atlantic. It comes back to me now in its wondrous beauty, as fresh and bright as when I turned my steps down the hill to mount the car, and continue my journey to Derry.

CHAPTER XIII.

The Bush—Dulce Domum—From Derry to Portrush—What the Birds said—We sail Home, make Casting Lines and Flies, mend Rods, go to the River, and get paid for the Job—Pounds, Shillings, and Pence.

Friday, April 21.

MEN seldom love but once in their lives; that is, love really and truly in the most exalted sense of the word. There are of course no end of shams and make-believes, to which all kinds of fine names are given, but these are counterfeits, and won't wash.

Now as with persons, so is it with places. We have all "a first love." It may be some country village where our childhood was passed, and where our mother lived; it may be at home, it may be abroad; mountain, valley, or stream, may be the charmer; but somewhere or other, to all men there is one spot dearer than all others in the world. I know there is to me, and thither I am flying.

All the stations hitherto visited have been favourites; but what are they to Ballantrae? We are speeding along the shores of Derry Lough, and each moment some well-remembered object comes into view. On the left the Inishowen Mountains rise peak above peak. Yonder glides the swift river steamer, from Green Castle to the Maiden City. The curlews, the graceful cranes, the little clouds of sandpipers, all seem to cry "Welcome home, welcome home!"

The matchless strand of Magilligan, where we have so often trawled, lies sleeping in the sunshine; there is Down Hill, and here is the Bann, one of the monster rivers of the dear little island, flowing broad and majestic through Coleraine, "famed for lovely Kitty," as poor Thackeray sang. A few minutes more, and the scream of the engine announces our arrival at the Portrush station.

Foremost amongst the little crowd stands a neat figure in white canvas shoes, blue trousers, blue jersey, and white hat, on the band of which, in gilt letters, is the word "Pet." Very busy is he with the luggage, handing out of the van (such liberties are allowed in the north) boxes, portmanteau, carpet bag, and rod case, to arms eager and willing to receive them. Many a hand, hard and brown with honest seafaring toil, was outstretched to welcome us. Dear honest fellows! little had I ever done to gain their kindly hearts—now and then a dose, advice, or a lecture, with which last a dram was usually ordered, to take away any unpleasant flavour. Had there been a dozen trunks, instead of the five or six vanishing out of the station, there would have been a hand for each.

Carrying the cloaks, the chief mate was in close attendance on his mistress; and what a running fire of hurried questions and replies.

"How is the dog? Was Jenny M'Cafferty's leg better?" Everything on board the *Pet* was, of course, as it should be—perfect. In a whisper: "How was the master's cat; was the stump healed?" Three parts of his tail, I heard afterwards, had been cut off in a rabbit trap; but this was a profound secret, not to be revealed till the last moment. "The river must be very low," &c., &c.

The baggage was on board when we arrived at the landing-place. The commissariat, for once in the history of nations, was up to the front, and very satisfactory it looked, in the shape of a hind quarter of beef, wrapped in something that appeared wonderfully like a sheet; together with a couple of hampers containing various fluids. Good eating, it is said, requires good drinking.

To carry animal food with us was a necessity, for the Bushmills cows, though excellent animals in their way, have one remarkable and very disagreeable peculiarity—the horns are the tenderest part. I do not believe, on my honour, a tiger could digest beef such as that pleasant town produces.

The ladies—of course in a hurry—stepped into the punt, and were incontinently sculled on board; then the beef, bottles, and skipper pushed off.

How beautiful the graceful little schooner looked, as she lay at anchor; her long sharp wave bow cleaving the green swells as they rolled towards the strand. The mainsail was set—a few pulls at the hawser—"She's over the kedge, sir." "Up with the jib, then." The main sheet is eased off, the fore sheet hauled to windward, her head pays off; in comes the anchor, and the little craft gathers way; the thickening eddies at her heel show increasing speed, and, with the foresail set, she bounded close-hauled down the sound of the Skerries, at a good eight knots and something over.

A boy just out of school, a bird in full song, are held to be emblems of happiness; but neither bird nor boy was half so joyous as the skipper. The very touch of the tiller seemed like the kindly greeting of a friend; with childish pleasure his eye ran over the snowy canvas, noted the spars, and the rigging tight and true; then watched the foam which marked her path, as his favourite, bowing easily to every freshening gust, sped along like an arrow. The strand (whose old brown face the playful waves are decking with a snowy beard) is past. There are the chalky cliffs—"the white rocks"—full of galleries, halls, and pillared chambers, into which the breakers, like lusty revellers, are reeling, to shout and sing the livelong night.

As we open "our bay" the cottage is hailed with a shout; in two stretches the little *Pet* gained her moorings; one touch of the helm, and her head is in the wind; down come the sails; her way lessens and lessens; and then she is at rest under our windows.

I now found time to ask the chief mate about our fishing prospects. "There were lots of fish in the river," he said, "but the present warm bright weather precluded all chance of catching them; the glass and barometer, too, were very high, and promised to continue so." Now this state of affairs did not suit the Bush, that excellent lady being rather choice in the matter of weather; nothing pleases her except the united homage of wind and clouds. *Then* there is no end of her goodness.

Our stock of tackle consisted only of six or eight flies—none suitable for the water—and one casting line, which had seen service at the Cummeragh, Lough Gill, and Lough Fern. In fact, the season's fly-fishing was only now about to commence, and we had everything to get ready. We never keep old stock, so next morning were wonderfully busy. The first things to be made were half a dozen single and two or three treble casting lines, and this is the way we proceeded. Eight or nine threads of gut were selected with some attention to graduation; these were thrown into a basin of tepid water. Then a similar number were chosen, and *rolled* up to keep them distinct; then another and another lot, all fastened up in a different way. By this time the first were ready for use. At the end of each thread a small loop was made, the spare parts clipped off, and the strands laid one after the other on the table. When all were thus prepared, the line was finished by each loop being passed into the next.

So this first part of our business was done. For "the trebles" we set to work in a different manner. First, three suitable pieces of gut were knotted together at one end and thrown into water; then other lots followed, till sufficient were collected to make a total of 6ft. One set was now taken out, and fastened through the knot by a pin to the table. Between the thumb and fore finger one strand is slightly twisted and laid over the next, which in turn receives a few twists; the third undergoes the same treatment, and so the first stage is completed. The same manipulation continued to the end of the threads, finishes the first length; and by degrees the whole were made, spliced, varnished with copal, and hung on pins to dry. Before going to bed a dozen and a half of flies, on medium grilse hooks, were finished; and thus an impracticable day was turned to account. The following morning was as unfavourable as the preceding, so all the rods were overhauled and put into working order. Some day, when there is nothing else to be done, we will show how easy it is to *make* one. Something may be learned from all this detail. Single lines made as above described are stronger than any others—the goodness of the gut being equal—and are quite as neat in the water. In the ordinary method knots mean weakness; here the strength is uniform. This mode *may* be common, but, to the best of my belief, I never saw a line of this kind except on my own rod. The finer the gut, the more necessary to employ every aid to give it strength. By following this course many a fine fish is secured which would otherwise be lost. There is no law in operation to make it penal for a salmon to take even the smallest trout fly; last season I landed one of $17\frac{1}{2}$lb. on an O'Shaughnessy one size above the smallest, the casting line being the finest gut procurable. In the case of the trebles we have endeavoured to show they can be made without a machine. The less unnecessary baggage a tourist has to carry the better. He *must* take his fingers with him, and may as well make them useful,

The third morning after our arrival the quiet of the cottage was rudely dispelled; cups and saucers clinked up and down the stairs; the poker in the little breakfast room had an insane desire to make war on the coals; there was whispering, and the sound of feet. I wanted to sleep. I could only turn from side to side and groan in despair. This did not suit the conspirators. "Hurry, Mary, wid the tea; the master will be raging mad this minit if he hasn't his wather." Here the hall door swung open; I knew the keen whistling blast right well. "By Jove, the wind is north, and lots of it." You may believe breakfast that morning was a short ceremony; in less than half an hour we were tearing along the road for the Bridge Pool. This wind is the best that can blow for the Bush; the long broad sheet of water, from the old bridge to the Carry, was sparkling with ten thousand crisping wavelets. In less than a quarter of an hour after our arrival a beautiful ten-pounder lay crimped on the grass; another soon followed, and near the bottom of the pool a third came to hand. "Change the fly, Willis; we will try it again." This time, however, we did nothing; more correctly, worse than nothing, as we hooked a nice fish and lost him. Then it was time to move on. The Lilacs were too low; next in order is the "turn hole," the lower part of which lay in the full sweep of the wind, and seemed full of promise. Nevertheless, we passed four flies over that cast in vain. Now we reach Clatty Hole. Three parts of this long reach were also too low, but still there remained ten or twelve yards of excellent water. Here we succeeded again, landing our fourth fish. Next in merit to the Bridge Pool is Island Fad; but here the river makes a sudden bend to the west, so the north wind did not avail. The Colonel's Lodge was in a similar evil case, and we speed on to Skelly's Lower Holm. Over this the keen breeze blew fresh and fair, and, as we expected, another salmon was added to the basket, which, however, long since too heavy, had been left behind; so, "being added to the basket" was a figure of speech, importing that the last captive was bound head and tail, and thus carried. The Brambly Corner, the Ford, and "the Stone Throw," were all in excellent order, but not in a charitable mood. The day was wearing late. Should we go home? No, by no means; so we trudged back to the bridge, and fished all the pools down without moving another fish. The last cast on the river was the lower island, and here, after much flogging, we whipped up another twelve-pounder and killed. The six fish weighed 67lb.; the smallest 9lb., the largest 15lb.

It was late when we reached the cottage, but not too late to exhibit our prizes on the grass-plat. "You would have done better had you stuck to the old river, instead of running half over the country," observed Madame; and I was much of the same opinion.

Nothing has been said regarding pecuniary terms on this river. The omission is intentional, as I have no warrant for promising that the price of one year will be the price of another. As a general rule, the market has an upward tendency. Whether it has reached its highest quotation may be a matter of doubt. Our glorious fishery law, by improving second and third-rate streams, will, I believe, lessen the angling value of those whose reputation has hitherto been of the highest. This silence on the money question is no injury to the reader, who, by applying to my old and valued friend the lessee, may learn all he wishes to know ; and I will venture to promise that the reply he receives shall be as courteous, as straightforward, and explicit.

CHAPTER XIV.

The Bush—From the Sea to the Leap—Rod-making—Headlands—We row up the Bann—Three Days consecutive Angling at Spring Tides—Laggandrade —Letter from Lismore—We go to Lough Neagh.

Saturday, April 29.

RISING at the foot of Knocklayd Mountain, the Bush pursues first a westerly and subsequently a northerly course ; visiting one or two small hamlets it passes Bushmills, and enters the sea close to the little village of Port Ballantrae. Owing to natural and artificial causes, this river holds a large quantity of water, and is probably, for its size, less dependent on rain than any stream in the three kingdoms. For a considerable portion of its course the Bush passes through a flat marshy valley, and then thunders over a cascade, known locally as "the Leap." From thence to the sea, a distance of about two miles, are several weirs, which prevent the water falling below a certain level. Let there be clouds, and wind from the north, north-west, or west (if rain, all the better), and I will ensure the angler sport, be the drought what it may. Warm, bright, and still weather put an absolute stop to fishing in this stream. Of course if a man wants exercise he may thrash away, but by so doing he spoils his chance ; it would be better to practise gymnastics anywhere than on the still, unruffled pools of the Bush. The fish get sick of the flies as you, without appetite, would of panada or jelly. If a lion is wanted to roar outrageously at feeding-time, let his beef be a novelty.

After the change recorded in the last chapter the weather became " too bright, too blue " for our purpose ; to-day forms no exception.

so we will walk the river from the sea to the Leap and carry a rod *pro formâ*.

Over the firm strand flows the Bush, and just above high-water mark is Welland's Pool. Ah me! if I had as many guineas in my purse as I have landed salmon from this spot it would be far heavier than it is. Next come the Upper and Lower Islands. These are but indifferent lodges, yet always worth a trial with the wind in the north. "The Throat," "The Stone Throw," and "The Ford," are continuous, each nearly commencing at the point where the other ends. "The Brambly Corner" is excellent for 15ft. or 16ft.; also "The Holms," upper and lower. The latter is very good in high water or a sharp breeze. "MacLoughlan's Ford" seems shallow, but is a very pretty run. Now, flourish trumpets, for here is "Island Fad," a long reach of dead water. It is hard to name the best part, where all is good. "The Clatty Hole," "The Turn," and "The Lilacs," bring us to the "Bridge Pool," the best stretch in the river. Above the little town of Bushmills are "Jamie's Dam," "Laggandrade," "Langtange," and "The Leap."

Here we will pause and put on the casting line, for the sun, hitherto cloudless, has sunk behind the wooded heights which at this point surround the stream, whilst a light easterly air, the only one which strikes, gains strength as the heat declines. In the rocky and foaming basin under the cascade, we killed a fourteen-pounder, and in the neck of Laggandrade landed another fish of less weight. Such unexpected good fortune rarely falls to mortal lot.

As we shall want a very light rod for green-drake fishing, we will devote this glorious day to making it. Nothing can be more easy or simple than the whole affair. This slender bit of lancewood, about 1ft. in length, is reduced to the size required. A few strokes with a plane form a $3\frac{1}{2}$-inch splice; then another and another similar piece is treated in like manner, and glued. The lower part of the joint is formed from one length of seasoned hickory, sufficient to make the whole 6ft., for the article we are working at is to be 18ft. in three parts. Next, another piece of hickory of the required length is put under the plane, and brought down to its due proportion. Here, too, a long splice is cut, and glued to the first part. The spring, straightness, and balance are now carefully examined, and any fault corrected. Lastly, the butt is made from clean ash, and glued. The rod being now roughed out, we will next suppose it perfect, so we put on the slides for the wheel.

The finishing is done by rasp and glass-paper. We must now stain—shall it be yellow or black ? If the former, the wood must be brushed over with diluted nitric acid, and heat applied. If the latter be preferred, treat the parts with a strong solution of nitrate of silver, and afterwards with hydro-sulphuret of ammonia. Glass-paper is again wanted, and now our work is smooth as ivory, and round as a ruler. We have spent so much time on the job, that it is not worth our while to omit French polishing. Rings are put on, and top splices finished. The lapping must be perfectly smooth and even. Copal varnish for the silk, and a lignum vitæ button, the size of a five-shilling piece, for a rest, and you have an article our friend in Jermyn-street need not blush to own.

The coast scenery round the cottage is perhaps the most beautiful in Ireland. Within half an hour's stroll is the Giant's Causeway. The mountain cliffs of basalt extend for miles, terminating at Fairhead; and happy is the man who has yet to see for the first time the glorious beauty of that scene, extending far and wide over land and water, mountain and island, bays, harbours, and hamlets, beautiful in detail, and as a whole almost without a rival.

As everybody has at least half a dozen stereoscopic views of the Causeway, we will climb the Giant's path, and walk along the furze-clad headlands, which, in my humble opinion, are worth all the Hexagons in the world. I felt disappointed on first seeing this wonderful piece of crystallization, and the feeling has never left me; compared with everything around, it seems insignificant. Well, there is here beauty to please every taste ; but the breezy mountain rocks for me. Shall I tell you what may be seen from their summits? Far away to the north, clear, blue, and beautiful, lay the Hebrides, the sun shining brightly on the cliffs of Islay, whilst the peaks of Jura mingle with the clouds. At our feet the Causeway slopes gently into the ocean, beneath whose clear blue waters the columns can be seen trending off in the direction of Staffa; and the restless heaving Atlantic stretches away, away, bearing many a homeward sail down the Sound. So close, that it seems but a step, is the rocky isle of Rathlin, still haunted by traditions of the Bruce. To the north-east bonny Scotland shows fair and clear, whilst the glorious columnar rocks sweep in graceful curves to Bengore-head. What poor words of mine can paint their beauty of form, their infinite variety of colour, from layers of ochre, earths, and lichens? They must be seen, not told. To the south-west, bright reaches of strand, basaltic rocks, peaceful Lough Foyle, and the Donegal highlands, complete the view; whilst landwards, the storm-beaten fields and wastes of Antrim roll, swell above swell, to join the lofty range, of which Knocklayd is the king.

All this is very fine—quite touching; but what has it to do with fishing? Nothing—nothing at all. But, my dear friend, we can't have everything we want in this life. We can't make clouds, or bring wind and rain. Look at my diary: "Monday, blazing hot. Tuesday, ditto ditto. Wednesday, worse than ever." Well, take comfort; the glass is falling, and to morrow is the first of the springs; so if we have any luck, there will be sport yet before the week is over.

Barometer still falling, but not a cloud in the sky or an air on the water. Nothing can be done here, so we will go to Coleraine and take a look at the Bann.

On this noble stream there is a boat club, and a good one too. What a treat to set foot in a light wherry and feel one of Searle's oars in your hand. With the sunshine glittering through the woods on either side, and gilding the windows of many a villa, we steamed up a river, wide as the Thames at Hammersmith, with a head water like an inland sea. At present we will confine ourselves to the Bann, as we hope to be tossing on Lough Neagh within five days. The water from the sea to the weirs at Castle Roe is free to all rods; above, it is rented by a club, the terms of which are very moderate. The run of salmon is late, and little can be done till June; the trout, however, afford excellent sport. and range from 2lb. to 9lb. Hauling our boat at the weirs, we launched her again, and pursued our way towards Kilrea. Here and there on the broad bosom of the too tranquil stream we met a cot, holding an angler or two, some of whom had five or six trout. They were remarkably well-made fish, but I do not remember seeing one above 4lb., whilst the great majority did not exceed 2½lb. The day, however, was as unfavourable as could well be imagined. All parties, if agreeing in nothing else, seemed unanimous in the opinion that the Board of Works, whilst improving the navigation, had injured the fishing by removing or altering the fords; nor could I learn that a single salmon had yet been taken by the rod. In point of size, the fish rank next to those of the Erne and Shannon. Taking a hasty lunch, we pulled down the river at our best pace, and were just in time to catch the mail car back to Bushmills. . . . . The glasses kept their promise, for on the following morning the sky was covered with misty clouds. There was a smir of rain, too, and a soft west wind faintly ruffled Island Fad as we slipped on "the scarlet." Cast after cast fell light and true, but not a fish stirred. The soldier gave place to "the silver body," which in turn yielded to the "golden olive;" next came "the parson," but he preached in vain; and last of all a small dark claret was tried, with which, in about three hours, four salmon were landed. The upper pools lay still and unruffled. The west wind could do nothing for them, so we followed the stream down to the Stone and the Throat, where, after doing all we knew for four hours, we succeeded in killing two fish more. Thus ended the day, which was highly satisfactory, considering the small amount of air. The next that followed seemed far more promising. There was a spanking west wind over Island Fad and the lower water. We went to work early, but did nothing till after four o'clock, when we rose five salmon, killing three of 8lb., 10lb., and 10½lb. respectively.

And now our last day has come, and with it clouds and a keen small north-east breeze. No questions were asked; no consultation was needed; Laggandrade was our mark, and to Laggandrade we came.

This long deep sheet of water is the beau ideal of a "lodge." On all sides rise black basaltic rocks, clothed with tall furze, all golden with ten thousand blossoms, whilst bluebells and primroses make the dark glen glitter like a garden. The river here is wide, and, as may be imagined, the angling difficult, for each cast must be parallel to the bank, and sent by a turn of the wrist in the direction required. At the neck of the pool huge boulders rear their bald heads, among which I rose, hooked, and lost two fish. A few yards below lays a flat rock just submerged: here the sport was admirable, as in the shortest time that such a thing could be done, three salmon were landed and a fourth bungled. Over the rest of the throw the fish rose at intervals till evening; two more were pricked, and three played close up to the gaff and lost, at which you may be sure fearful growls were uttered; nor were we consoled by the seven salmon, which made our backs ache horribly before they were laid out for inspection on the grass plat of the cottage.

Cruel fate had still something in store for us, as the evening mail brought a letter from a friend at Lismore, an admirable angler, and a gentleman whose word is better than the bond of most other men. It ran as follows:—

"My dear old fellow,—You ask me what we are doing here. *Here*, where you vowed to astonish the natives, and where you certainly distinguished yourself in a remarkable way during the late blessed month of February, we are doing nothing; but didn't I tell you they would have a glorious time of it in co. Cork? Between this place and Mallow the river swarms with fish, the best streams are very strictly preserved. Cross-fishing is practised to a large extent, and some weeks *the average has been so much as fourteen salmon per day to each rod* on some of the flats near Fermoy. I only give you this information from hearsay, but I consider it reliable. Some of the stands are rented from the farmers on the banks, and on others, the holders employ men for cross-fishing as a matter of profit."

Hang the letter. It was gall and wormwood. Fancy twenty-eight salmon per day to a cross-line. Why, it would at least equal twelve or thirteen to the fair angler; and such fish. Unwillingly I left the Blackwater, and would have remained, had not inexorable fate driven me half over the island. But, if I live till next spring, see if I don't rent what my friend calls "a stand." Lucky dogs are the rising generation; they will skim the cream without the trouble of milking the cow.

Early to-morrow we go to Toom Bridge, for a few days' fly-fishing, but without the smallest expectation of slaying any of the mighty men of Lough Neagh. Neither do we propose *to show* this vast water. As well might Mr. Cook undertake to "make up" his happy family of tourists, in the geography, statistics, history, botany, and conchology of the entire Mediterranean seaboard, between Saturday and Monday, as I to conduct the angler round the coasts of this inland sea in a paper 18 inches by 3. No comprehensive picture can here be painted—only "a bit" from the north-north-west corner. A sketch, however, may sometimes give a good notion of the subject, like one of Mrs. Snarley's "hints," or Maurice Ritch's immortal "lines."

CHAPTER XV.

In which there is not a word about Salmon Fishing—Toom Bridge—Lough Neagh—Antrim—Two Days' Trouting—Business calls me to Dublin—Old Lodgings—Tackle Shops—The South Wall—We arrive at Mullingar—Fine Weather not ruinous to Belvidere—The Lake District.

May 8.

How are the mighty fallen! Where is Babylon the Great? Hiding under a few mounds of earth and sand, of bricks, bitumen, and pottery, till some Layard takes to digging, and sends home a bull or a sphinx, a tea-cup or a tobacco-pipe—when the learned with one voice exclaim, "Wonderful—wonderful! this dead nation knew China and Virginia—*ecce signum*: from this cup they quaffed: from this tube they smoked; lo! there is nothing new under the sun." Long ago Tyre laid aside her purple and soft vestments, her jewels and golden wine cups—yet she does to dry nets upon; and Carthage would have been forgotten, had not a love-sick queen required "a local habitation" for her name. Thus are the mighty fallen; and can Antrim keep her feet? Poor, dirty, tattered old dame! yet she was a sovereign once, till the quiet, orderly republico-aristocratic Belfast took the crown from her brows, and employed, I must say, the usurpation nobly.

Fancy this long row of cabins—with here and there a wretched huckster, selling everything on the earth and under the earth, in a space 9ft. by 7ft., sending two members to Parliament! Your splendid premises, Mr. O'Dogherty, and yours, Mr. M'Manus, are of course excepted. Then, too, she had a mayor, who was admiral over hundreds of miles of coast, and rode in plate and mail, like a good knight as he doubtless was, to collect his dues and astonish the natives. But, apart from history, Antrim has a special charm for me.

How well I remember my last visit, when you, dear lady, in hat plume and riding whip, walked by my side with a step more light, free, and elastic than ever trod on earth. Do *you* remember, brightest and pleasantest of companions? For the sake of those days I will visit the "Round Tower," if only to stand where we stood, and once more make the Past present; after which we will swallow our grief at the "Antrim Arms," even as you did the fine lake trout, by way of a light refection before dinner. Dear old happy days! Ah! Time, you are a sad thief. I wish from my heart the autocrat of Bow-street would stop your proceedings, and sign a warrant for your committal *usque ad æternum*.

Did you ever see a round tower? Here is one, perfect as the day on which it was finished. But who shaped this graceful needle?— for what purpose was it erected? Ah, there you are with your questions, Mr. Brown. On my word of honour, I know no more than the chairman of the Pre-Mediæval Society in Piccadilly. In a legendary land like this it must be old indeed to have outlived tradition. There *must* have been a sanctity about these mystic towers, since no ingenious monk ever hatched a new old chronicle to tell us all about them. The one before me is 95ft. high, and scarcely greater in circumference than the trunk of many an old oak. These things are pleasant to look on, perhaps all the more pleasant for our ignorance.

We have come a little out of our way in order to row back to the "O'Neil Arms," at Toom Bridge, on this fine Saturday afternoon. Willie has been left behind to lay up the *Pet*, and his sister remains to take care of him, with special orders to bring him on to Mullingar by the 8th. So the scribe and his fair companion strolled to the side of "Six Mile Water," took boat, and pushed off upon the broad bosom of the lake.

On the shore we had often been; on the water, never. Some chapters back, when citing several spots where larger trout were to be found than in Lough Guttane, I omitted Lough Neagh, which holds better fish than any other in Ireland.

On my first visit to Antrim, I had a very natural wish to see what the lake produced, and called on a professional for information, who promised to gratify my curiosity as soon as he could. Late one evening he came—it was after dinner, and a pullan had formed part of it, which fish you should know bears a very drowsy reputation. Now whether it was that fresh-water herring or a twenty-mile walk, I cannot undertake to determine, but certainly no young gentleman was ever more awfully sleepy. Hardly awake when we reached the cottage. I yawned out "Where is *the* trout?" "Your honour is standing on the same." The floor was thickly covered with flags and rushes, which, when partially removed, showed a sight that made me broad awake in a moment. *There* were fish of 4lb., 8lb., 12lb., 15lb. in dozens and dozens. That night my nervous system received a shock so severe, that I did not get over it for a week. How plainly that night comes back to me now! A thin stripling—the farthing candle—my poor comrade—the wretched hut—the flags and rushes—the dead bodies laid out in decent order, like heroes after a "stricken field"—you must admit the sight was very touching.

Not being anxious to gain a reputation for "tall talking," it is right to say that at this time I was not a very correct judge of weight; besides, my head was off, and the light bad. Nevertheless,

I remember *perfectly* my companion telling me that in the previous season a trout weighing 31lb. had been sent as an offering to Shunes Castle. It is hardly necessary to say this nice little lot had been netted for the Belfast market.

To-day the lake was without a ripple; the highlands of the opposite coast looked as mountains look from the sea, faint and far off; and well they might, for this vast sheet of water is two or three and twenty miles long, and nearly half as much in breadth. It is said to be little less than the Lake of Geneva, and with this exception is only exceeded in Europe by Ladoga in Russia, and Vener in Sweden.

The shores, though flat, looked very lovely in the misty light of a scorching sun. The rich woods of Lord Massereene, and the grounds of Shunes Castle, were all in keeping with the scene, so peaceful, that it seemed like an idle legend to tell how the good old earl, shot to death by the rebels, was borne through these grounds to take a last brief possession of all that an hour before was his. So we chatted and floated lazily along, our boatmen taking their time, like the ducks and coots, who hardly thought it worth while to hurry themselves on our account.

Our host at the O'Neil Arms, well skilled in the gentle craft, gave a cheering account of our prospects; engaged Edward Mac Ilroy as the best guide; and added, that if we did not kill 20lb. on Monday, we ought so to do. With the fly, the largest fish are of course rarely attainable; the troll would, I feel sure, reveal greater mysteries.

Mr. Mac Ilroy was punctual as the clock, and discoursed at length on the merits of the cross line "at say." "Wasn't there room for all? and shure, gintlemen here should do as they plased." Had he affirmed there were whales in this Mediterranean, perhaps I might have believed him; at all events, the space was large enough.

The usual style of lake angling was the order of the day—a pair of flies, sometimes three—claret, fiery-brown, orange, black and olive; quite the ordinary mode of doing business.

The breakwater was first to be tried, and as there was plenty of wind, our chance was good. All change is agreeable, even if it be from better to worse; so we set to in high hope and spirits. "There's a rise; I doubt your honour didn't see him." His honour had seen him, and struck as hard as Mr. Mac Ilroy himself would have done at some dearly-beloved neighbour in a scrimmage—so hard, indeed, as to leave half the light casting-line in his mouth. The damage was soon repaired, and at it we went again. "There's another." This time it was all right. How stoutly these Lough Neagh men fight—it cost full ten minutes to get a 2½lb. fish into the net—certainly the sport here is very pretty. Now we got a small one of 12oz. or 14oz.; by and by, another of three times that weight; and by dinner time had nearly satisfied the expectations of the chief of the O'Neil Arms. Perhaps the reader would like to see the slain. Well, here they are: 3½lb., 3lb., 2¼lb., 2lb., 2lb., 2lb., 2lb., ¾lb.

Let no stranger pass Toom Bridge in the season without trying his fortune. The following day we were not quite so successful, yet we got one four-pounder, and five or six more from 2lb. to ¾lb.

I had for some days been expecting a summons to Dublin on business, which might detain us a few days in the capital. This evening it came, and we started in an hour after; slept in Belfast, and reached Gresham's in good time. Happily, the cause of the visit was a pleasant one—merely to receive a small legacy of 50*l*. All old towns look especially interesting by night; but, owing to the extent of the squares, the remarkable beauty of the public buildings, and the crowded quays, Dublin is particularly charming. Strolling down Sackville-street, after a friend's good dinner and better wine, I felt to the full how beautiful the old city was. The moon was high, and shed a glory on the noble column of the Hero of Trafalgar. The Post-office, the river, the Bank of Ireland, and the College, each and all looked their best. Stephen's-green and Merrion-square showed all their charms, whilst the witching light concealed some of their defects. So near was it, that I could not choose but turn to the left, into Erne-street, to look at the place in which was passed the most miserable year of my life. There it was. Even the kind moon would do nothing to cheer it, although she smiled benignly on its opposite neighbour. Shall I ever forget that great gaunt room on the second floor, where I had come to study medicine in the early winter of 1849 ? How vividly that first day came back to me now ! For the previous year I had been free as a bird ; *then* I could only brood over lost liberty and present drudgery. What was the price of a donkey-cart and tinker's stock-in-trade ? With this at least one could wander at will. Or a pedlar's pack ? that might do—anything seemed better than the present lot. That day two books had been purchased—the nucleus of a future library: " Quain's Anatomy," and " Muller's Physiology"—comfortable little works of about 1000 pages each, large 8vo. The miserable pseudo-physician did not know a muscle from a tendon, the *os frontis* from the occipital bone. Unable to comprehend a single line, he learned ten pages by rote, laid aside the book, and meditated a last pipe and a pan of charcoal. In occasional hours of moodiness, that horrible room has often appeared before me. Now, having paid it a visit, I hope the ghost has been laid for ever.

Of Dublin we shall say nothing; of its beautiful surroundings, little. The Wicklow mountains, the Dargle, Killiney Bay, and Howth, have been described a thousand times already ; moreover, we are out of spirits, like Kingsley's lobster ; my Fifty is already in course of transmutation, for here is the door of a poplin manufactory in the Liberties.

This part of the city is to Dublin what St. Giles's is to London ; yet some of the streets are wide and the houses large, and probably knew much better days " when George the First was king." One of these we entered. The stairs were carpeted with venerable dust ; unmolested spiders' tapestry dimmed the windows; the looms seemed of the rudest kind ; yet here were produced the fabrics which queens are proud to wear, and tourists unwilling to buy.

My old acquaintance, Mrs. M., presented me with a bundle of " thrum silk"—for fly tying purposes the best material ever produced, as it can be employed nearly as fine as the thread the spiders were weaving, and, doubled or trebled, proves equal to any work an angler requires.

A stranger strolling along the quays east of Carlisle Bridge feels at once he is in a land piscatorial. The number and excellence of the tackle shops is extraordinary. From Martyn Kelley's, at the corner of Sackville-street, up to the Four Courts, on either bank of the Liffey, an angler can hardly go wrong in search of good things.

Poor Ettingsall's place knew him no more; the shutters were up, and the old house wore a mournful and desolate aspect. I trust the good fairies have taken my old friend to Shiny Wall, a place where honest anglers may hope to rest when their work is done.

The Dublin gut always struck me as remarkably good and cheap; for dyed hackles, seals' fur, and such like, this is the market for the world.

Our last day shall be spent on the South Wall—a humble name for a great work. Everyone has heard of the beauty of the bay; and this pier runs far out into its centre—17,754ft.—commanding one of the finest views in the world. It was built for the purpose of increasing the current, and so to enable the Liffey to do its own scavenger work. Nearly half-way down this vast mole is "the Pigeon-house," no longer a packet-station, but a great artillery depôt. Passing through small mountains of shot, and guns lying peaceably side by side, we reach the longer and outer portion, at the end of which stands the lighthouse. How fresh the sea-breeze felt after the breath of the great city!

Yonder lays the ragged hill of Howth; there Kingston and its noble harbour. Cutters and schooners, barks and steamers, were beating in or running out with the last quarter of flood. Behind lay the great Babel, still and quiet under its canopy of smoke; the infinite variety of the Wicklow mountains completing the picture.

Let no stranger depart without seeing what I have feebly tried to paint. He is safe to be sent to gaols, hospitals, squares, cathedrals, and penitentiaries; but if he desires to gain a just idea of Dublin and its lovely surroundings, let him take my advice and come hither.

It is only a short run by rail to Mullingar, on the platform of which two smiling faces greeted us. Little Mary had taken a lodging, and Willie had engaged a boat; the fly was "up," and all promised fair for the morrow.

The Green Drake lakes are arranged into two great groups in the counties Westmeath and Sligo. In the former are Belvidere, Lough Owel, and Dereveragh, *cum multis aliis*; in the latter, Loughs Arrow and Gara, and in Roscommon, Lough Ken. It is not asserted that these are the sole waters on which the fly appears—very far from it; but only that they hold a prominent place. For the Sligo lakes Boyle may be considered a central station; for Belvidere and Lough Owel, our present quarters; for Dereveragh and the more northern ones, Castle Pollard; not that either Boyle or Mullingar are in close proximity to their respective waters, for Belvidere, on which the fly rises soonest, is above two miles from the town, and Lough Owel, on which the drake appears latest, is still farther off. This, however, is of small importance, as early fishing is useless, our fair friends not being up and dressed for the fluttering, flirting business of the day, before 10 a.m. Nor am I prepared to say the distance is accurately stated, though I have walked it morning and evening some score of times—at any rate, the stroll is a pleasant one on a bright morning in the merry month of May.

Here, fine weather will not ruin us; nay, more, in some sort, it may do us good, by bringing us larger flights of the beautiful creatures on whom our sport depends.

The mode of angling with the "blow line" is so delicate, natural, and deadly, that the trout have no means of judging between what is digestible and what injurious. Even you, my dear sir, if six inches under water, taking your morning meal, would be quite as likely to select the wrong dish as the right one.

CHAPTER XVI.

He gets his leg over the traces—Mullingar—Its market population—Walk to the Lake—The size of its fish as compared with those of Dereveragh and Lough Owel—The blow line—Mode of using it—We drift, and what we do—Cooking—A dead calm—Improving the occasion—We talk generalities, take to roach fishing, and determine to go to Dereveragh next morning.

Tuesday, May 16.

THE scribe and his friends have now travelled together from extreme south to extreme north, and thence half-way down the eastern side of the island, yet "never a word" has been said about the health, bodily and mental, of the country. Silence more often proceeds from indifference than reticence, yet Heaven knows indifference has nothing to do with my silence.

But I am bound to "a speciality," and fear, if my tongue is not always in the water, there will be a fearful shout, "The dog is mad! mad dog!—mad dog!—hang him, drown him, stab him. shoot him!" Still to-day, as half his work is done, the animal feels disposed for a run, and will range a little wide, if the whole "field" cries out "'ware fence."

"Ireland, considered Morally, Socially, and Politically"—this title looks awfully heavy—"A Brief History of Erin, from the Days of Japhet to the Days of Julius Cæsar." I fear the public won't stand it. In these light sketches there is no room for vexed questions, nor has your scribe the least notion of sticking himself in the mud, if he knows it.

Great has been the improvement in this kindly country within the last fifteen years. Poverty and ignorance, wretched wages, bad tenures, and worse tenements, at that time had reduced her to a melancholy condition. Thank God, these are matters of history; and each year now adds to the material prosperity of the people. We have better houses and superior food; wages are more than doubled, tailors have become a necessity, education has made great strides, the wild rollicking days are gone, a more healthy working spirit has taken their place, and sobriety, order, and industry can not only look up, but even walk about without fear of being knocked on the head. To say there is not still much want and misery would be absurd; but Rome was not built in a day, nor can the most Utopian political economist reasonably expect in a few years to turn poor Ireland into a first-class European swell. Still there is a vast improvement everywhere and in all things; even when we get up our little drama of treason, the actors are poor and below their parts, and the company uncommonly short-handed. Undoubtedly the mother of our adoption has recently been a little indisposed with a slight attack of Fenian fever; but there is something hopeful even here, for had not the old dame been sounder in wind and limb than heretofore, she would have been uncommonly ill, with a frightful amount of constitutional disturbance. This malady has tested her strength, and proved her sound at bottom. Long may she continue to grow better and stronger, more happy, and more wise!

In small Irish towns there is always a chronic eruption of market folk, and this morning the street was vocal with the quacking of juvenile ducks, and a constant inquiry from pretty peasant lips, "Is it eggs ye are looking for?" Every place does its own business in its own way. Here one man drives a solitary little pig to the fair, and wastes the whole day looking after him; another pushes a calf along, born since midnight, yet evidently bound for the butcher; whilst a third sits leisurely down on a bale of home-made freize, and waits patiently for an offer. Along the side-walks coarse delf and crockery arranged themselves barricade-wise; cabbages, rough smith's work, and manifold varieties of the lollipop species making the market complete. Through all this we made our way, and padded along the white and dusty road towards the lake.

Though not yet "in the leafy month of June," Belvidere presented as pretty a piece of greenery as need be. The low rich shores were fringed with fine trees nearly to their edge; cows stood amongst the sedges gazing sleepily at their own shadows; and the birds—a countless choir—were in full rivalry, each one telling his tale of love.

The first thing to be done was to collect sufficient bait for the day. Basket in hand, our boatman walked up to some small alder bushes, and began to select the flies which sat in hundreds on the leaves. Those rough fingers of his, how delicately they lifted the beautiful creatures, depositing the brightest-coloured ones each after each under the lid of his little wicker cage; then we sat down under a tree to arrange the tackle. The small hook was neatly tied to a strand of the finest gut, which in turn was fastened to one end of a skein of floss silk, the other being carefully spliced to the light running line. There was nothing more to be done on shore, so we pushed off, rowed well to windward, and commenced our first drift.

There is some little skill required in this mode of fishing. The fly must *sit* naturally on the water; the long sail of soft silk, bellying out before the wind, *should* keep the gut perpendicularly *above* the fly; not an inch of tackle ought to be in the water. Supposing matters to be managed according to description, the fly sailing along fourteen or fifteen yards in advance of the boat, whilst neither sound nor motion gives warning even to the most wary old stager—I say, all things being *secundem artem*—poor trouty has no standard whereby to detect the thief from the true man.

"Dear oh! dear oh-o-o! Was there ever the like?" This doleful soliloquy caused me to look towards the bow; there sat Willie (he had asked for a holiday), his rod straight upright, with the straw-coloured floss floating in the wind, without fly, hook, or gut. The disconcerted professor had one weakness—he was vain of his skill: it was necessary, therefore, to account for the accident.

"Master," he said, with true northern solemnity, "the gut's rotten; you should look to yourn."

A quarter of an hour after this there was a light splash; this time the weed was sound. The game little fish, barely $1\frac{1}{2}$lb., fought to the last, and could not be persuaded to enter the net till quite helpless. This, our first prize, at once attracted attention by its great beauty. Belly and sides were of the richest golden hue, and if we add that the greatest possible breadth and depth were combined with the least possible length, the reader will have a fair idea of a Belvidere trout in May. Then the stern got a little job; by and by bow was again fortunate; and so we fished and floated, every now and then pulling to windward for a fresh drift. About half-past two an excellent "rise" came over the lake; opposite a low-wooded point on the eastern shore I struck a fish, evidently a good one, and in a second after Willie's turn came. The difficulty was to prevent fouling; so long as skill could do it, they were kept apart; but after ten or twelve minutes' manœuvring, a cross became inevitable. One fish was raised as much as the delicate tackle would afford; rods were exchanged, and the danger was over; but half an hour expired before both were on board, and they proved by far the best we took in Belvidere during our stay, the pair weighing nothing less than 10lb. Soon after this success the "rise" fell off, and before five o'clock had ceased. But we had not yet done with the trout, as the *chef* requested permission, or rather announced his intention of dressing a fish dinner for "the mistress." About seven p.m. getting savagely hungry, the cook's proceedings became of considerable interest. Before the fire, on a spit, one of the big ones was roasting, and at the moment of my entrance was being basted lavishly with butter, without the least regard to the price of that article. In a kettle on the hob, the other was boiling in water, judiciously flavoured with salt and chili vinegar; on the gridiron a two-pounder, split with masterly smoothness, was done to a turn. Though not fond of fish, and hating fish dinners, it was impossible to deny that the *chef's* performance was admirable, and that for colour and flavour a Belvidere trout is a marvellous dainty. So at least thought the cook, who that night went to bed at an early hour, much indisposed—the prominent symptoms being nausea and suffocation.

At the usual hour we were again by the side of the lake; not a breath of air stirred its glassy surface; but as wind and water are uncertain to a proverb, we gathered bait, pulled into the widest part, and waited patiently for what might happen. Nothing, however, occurred to better our condition, so having beached the boat, we lay down under a tree to lunch. Had a Cuyp or Sidney Cooper been there, he might have stocked his portfolio for life. How exquisite were the colours,

> By Nature's own sweet and cunning hand laid on!

how deep the tranquil enjoyment of such a time and place! Does this feeling arise from the possession of simple habits and tastes, mere idleness, or dislike of restraint; or is it that, getting out of the world, we get out of nine-tenths of the annoyances, vexations, shines, rows, scrimmages, and infernal hullabaloos that sour our tempers and bring on the gout?

Perhaps a little of each made up the sum of lazy delight with which I flung myself down in the fragrant fern, and listened to the drowsy song of ten thousand gnats, and the more drowsy hum of my companions.

Several boats were floating idly on the lake, at least half of which contained one or more of our countrymen, with whom Mullingar is a favourite haunt. No doubt it is an excellent quarter, though personally I should prefer the quieter waters of Sligo and Roscommon, and make Boyle head-quarters during the too brief reign of the Drake.

The trout in all the lakes differ widely from each other, in colour, size, and shape. Let us compare for a moment those of the water before us with the denizens of Dereveragh and Lough Owel. The fish of Belvidere are smaller than those of Dereveragh, which in turn are less than those of Lough Owel, but in my judgment they excel all others in form and flavour. In the clear springs of Lough Owel the trout are silvery and very fine; one weighing $12\frac{1}{2}$lb. being killed in our boat, as will be shown hereafter, and another as large—or larger—as was asserted by competent authority—hooked and lost. In Dereveragh 4lb., 5lb., 6lb., and 7lb. are figures not uncommon, and in colour and proportion they hold a medium position as compared with their kinsfolk in the two lakes so frequently mentioned, being less brilliant than the one, and less heavy than the other.

All this time we were lolling lazily in the sweet green fern, whilst the gnats sang to the accompaniment of Willie's bagpipe; but now another sound, compounded of sucking, sighing, and splashing, made itself heard among the sedges. Curious to see what was the matter, I walked quietly to the margin; there hundreds of roach were swallowing the Mayflies, gobbling the caddis, and amusing themselves in various ways, every now and then flying off at a tangent as a perch sailed past, with his bright mischievous eye, and spears set ready for battle. A trace was rigged for bottom-fishing by the time our quiet steady guide had scratched up some worms, with which we stepped into the boat, and pushed a few fathoms from the shore, leaving Willie, who had a mortal aversion to the whole family of the Lumbrici, to do as he pleased. Twick, twick, twick—first enters a small perch, next a smaller, then a fine one over a pound. The deserted professor, too, thought it worth his while to be up and doing. Roach were a new study, and he set to work zealously, in order to improve the occasion, by dapping or sinking and drawing with the Drake. His acquisition of knowledge was rapid; every two or three minutes a silvery flash showed how well he was getting on. A couple of hours at this style of thing was enough to give a dinner to twelve little boys, at a rate of eight per head. This lavish extravagance brought its own punishment; henceforward we were regularly waylaid on our return by the entire youthful population, who seemed to consider your scribe as a keeper who was bound to supply "the house." Ambushes were artfully constructed in unexpected places, and on several occasions happy was I to escape utter spoliation. In these moments of peril, our boatman was a host in himself—a finer or more sturdy fellow you could not find between the Land's End and Cape Wrath. He spoke honestly, reasoned correctly, wrote a fair hand, and, what is more, spelt well—an accomplishment by no means necessarily attendant on caligraphy. He was not one of your plastic Larrys or Micks drawn by writers of funny Irish stories; he was something much better—a brave, straightforward man, and, I believe, a fair specimen of his time and class; if so, the land has reason to be proud of her sons. The witty, careless, improvident animal, who makes you laugh in books, or grins and roars his brief hour behind the footlights, is not generally met with in common life. Among the car drivers of Dublin, Cork, and Waterford he is still to be seen, as also among the guides and boatmen of Killarney. With these the science of chaff is partly traditional, partly acquired; they are actors, and, like other performers, earn a salary in the ratio of their merits.

The glorious sun went to bed with a very red face : the clouds, his gentlemen ushers, clad in crimson, bowed low in the west, and the night was warm and calm—from all which signs any baby could tell you how small was the chance of wind on the morrow. So before "turning in," we decided on an early start for Castle Pollard, and hope to find a change for the better when we return.

CHAPTER XVII.

Contains nothing about the Killing, though a good deal concerning the Curing of Salmon—The Day ends better than it promised.

May 17.

L'HOMME propose, Dieu dispose. We are but poor creatures. Last night it was determined to make an early start for Castle Pollard; this morning a crushing sick headache put such a move altogether out of the question. Fortunately, my present disagreeable inmate seldom pays me a visit; but even twice in the year is more often than I wish to see him. Of course he will keep me at home all day. Well, if he does, we'll be even with him, and dish up a blue pill and a black draught, instead of soup and fish. What a bore it is to be laid up in a country town! I have sent out to forage for books, and the messenger brings back an ancient number of the *Gentleman's Magazine*, with the martyrdom of St. Anthony, of some place which did not exactly appear, the title-page being considerably the worse for wear. Since there is nothing to read, we must try to write. What shall it be? May we assert "the waters of the United Kingdom are capable of producing a weight of animal food equal to the land?" The very thing: such a theme will do exactly, as it will not take us much out of the road we are bound to travel.

Some years since this text was one on which I often held forth, till at length my small congregation would stand it no longer. The hearers, less polite than sincere said, "Come now, old fellow, don't bore us any more; we all know there are a good many things which ought to be, and are not, and this amongst the number." Occasionally I took up my parable, but it would not do, for my friends, driven to frenzy, were becoming dangerous. Silenced, but not convinced, I held my tongue and retained my opinion. Fortunately, these insane animals are the other side of the water now, so I am safe, and need not fear either horns or hoofs. Well, then, our waters ought to yield as much good food as the land—how shall we set about their cultivation? The farmer's maxim is, "he is the best beast which attains the largest quantity of flesh and fat with the least food in the shortest time." Now, the salmon fits into this definition of "the best beast" exactly, for he costs his owner not a penny for provender: of course he must be taken care of, but the outlay is nothing in the ratio of the profit. It is not all aqueous farms, however, that can be thus stocked. Those only which have a reasonably good outlet can be so dealt with; other waters must be filled as the Acclimatisation Society deem best; I hope they won't insist on too many *Siluri*.

What a comfort it is for a poor fellow to find a great man patting his hobby. Now a very great man, in his book on the salmon, writes, "The weight of 'fish' produced by the Spey is equal to the weight of mutton annually yielded to the butcher by each of several of the smaller counties." If the Spey supplies the mutton, would not the other rivers and lakes more than make up the beef, veal, and pork? Of course they would, for in this calculation the king of fishes is alone taken into account; and it must be remembered that the water, unlike the land, can bear two crops at one and the same time. Even his worst enemies cannot charge him with stealing the bread from the mouths of any of his relations. They (unnatural beasts as they are) eat up as many of the children belonging to our harmless silvery friends as they can catch; but poor Salmo does not retaliate—he humbly asks to come with his wife during the period of her lying-in, promising to return to the great city from whence he came on the first convenient opportunity. In due time his children follow, grow to be men and women, and do as their forefathers did. But here we meet a difficulty, "the half-and-half theory," which arises out of the question. "At what age do the parr put on their gala dress and set out on their travels?" One man, after diligent investigation, finds they migrate at one year; another, after equally praiseworthy labour, learns that they depart at two. Something is to be advanced in support of each opinion; so, by way of smoothing down contending parties, a peaceable Christian observes, "Well, well, it doesn't signify much—you need not quarrel about it; some shall go this year and some the next." All the little boys and girls in my street (your pardon, my children—young ladies and gentlemen) number, perhaps, two hundred. When one hundred of these at twelve or thirteen years become adepts in geography and Greek, music and the fine arts, plain work and etiquette, and are, in fact, really fit for the serious business of life, whilst the other hundred are dressing dolls and playing marbles—when I see this unusual state of things, then, and not till then, will I believe the "half-and-half theory." Nature is guided by one invariable law. All my young ducks are feathered about the same time. Our dear mother does not ordinarily work by miracles, and it would be miraculous indeed if half the parr in any river, exposed to the same temperature, born about the same time, and fed with the same food, were to dress like young beaux and go forth into the world, whilst the other half were content to stay at home in the nursery. Would it not be better to suppose even the ablest observers in error, than to adopt an opinion which requires for its support a violation of well-known natural laws? But all this has little to do with our thesis. The rivers will not give us their beef and mutton till cultivated, and talking will not stock them. There has been too much of this already. Theory is an excellent thing in its place, but, if exceeding due limit, it fetters practice; in which case philosophy does more harm than good. A gamekeeper might not be able to say *exactly* how many cocks are required for a given number of hen pheasants, in order to produce the best results; yet, if the coverts were unstocked till the question was settled, we should be obliged to pay more than 7s. 6d. a brace for our birds.*

Let each owner of a river set to work himself, instead of watching how some more enterprising neighbour fares with *his* undertaking; then theory will soon be corrected by practice; out of work will come experience, and from experience knowledge. The whole thing lies in a nutshell. Stock the rivers—there are plenty of ways in which it can be done; let a sufficient number of fish pass up to the spawning beds; take care of them when there; and see that the little ones are not hurt as they toddle downstairs in search of the hall door, and from thence into the high road of nations. When this is done I think it will be found that the parr enter into society at two years old; that they return as grilse the same autumn; and in the following spring or summer (as the case may be) come to pay us a visit and leave their cards as Mr. Salmon. There; we have put our foot into it with a witness, and shall possibly receive a rap over the knuckles for *having* an opinion. If we must, we must; but believe me, gentlemen, you will have all the switching to yourselves. I shall bear with patience, and suffer without retaliation. Let us return to the starting point once more for a moment. If the Spey produces as great a weight of salmon as some of the smaller counties do of mutton, what would the whole county in which the Spey wanders produce, if all its rivers and lakes rendered their due proportion? Why, a great deal more. But

---

* Since the above was written, there is every reason to believe that this argument, however specious, is incorrect. In fact experiment, so much more potent than hypothesis, has proved the "half-and-half" theory to be true; still as the doctrine is not yet generally accepted, the text (though in our opinion erroneous) has been allowed to stand.

is it certain that even the water in question can give no more? If to this be added the consideration that salmon constitutes only *one* crop, and that these water farms are capable of producing two crops at the same time, may we not say of our thesis, Q.E.D.? The question of the age of the smolt, and the time of the return of the grilse, are matters in no way affecting the success of the fish farmer. The one *will* go down, and the other *will* come up, in his season; yet that the adolescent salmon returns to the rivers after an uncertain period, ranging from five or six weeks to three months is, I believe, indisputable.

In "mine own" especial water, about the last week in May, small grilselets (from one pound to twice that weight) appear. These gradually grow larger, till about the 10th or 12th of June they begin to be stopped by "the breast" of the cutts. Previously they were able to slip through the opposing bars. Does not this seem to favour the idea of a rapid but continuous growth? The average weight of grilse may be taken at from $5\frac{1}{2}$lb. to 6lb.; had they been roaming the seas for fifteen months, would it not be reasonable to suppose they would have attained a more uniform size—in fact, have reached their majority? We certainly see some men of six feet, whilst others are only five feet seven inches: but, taken as a whole, men are pretty uniform in height, and all the inferior animals—race, food and temperature, being taken into account—are likewise uniform; but why one young gentleman salmon should be five or six times as big as another of the *same age*, I cannot understand. The difference may be accounted for if we suppose growth to be at the rate, let us say, of one pound per week, and the difference of time between the capture in the same ratio—but hardly if we accept the "two years theory."

This paper is so thin that anything heavy would make a hole in it. Philosophy must be written not on straw, but extra fool. Should any reader, however, desire wisdom, let him read the second chapter of Mr. Russell's admirable book, where he will find wit and wisdom, kindness and good temper happily blended into a very pleasant mixture. If there is a dash of the lemon, there is plenty of sugar·

and as the spirit comes from his private still, we may be sure the author of "The Salmon" has provided "the material" in full quantity and quality to wash down his fish.

If there be one thing I hate more than another, it is argument. It may make enemies, but never yet cemented friendship; and as for conviction, who ever was convinced by it? The rule is, argue with a doubter, and you make him an infidel; bother a man who has no opinions, and you make him as obstinate as a mule. Oh, I hate arguing! and if anyone said, "Pray allow me to convince you that the moon is composed of green cheese," I believe I should make him a bow, with "Sir, I am entirely of your opinion."

With a sigh of relief the pen was here laid aside. I was on the point of meditating a pipe, so of course felt better. Through the window came a pleasant air, rustling the white dimity curtains. Outside the door, too, there was a whispering, but not of the summer air. With a light knock, Willie entered. "There's a nice breeze a-just springing up," he said, "and a light bar of clouds to the windward; maybe, master, it would do you good to see them, and Michael has a prime basket of drakes." Fully calculating that the invalid was *hors de combat*, he had doubtless intended to enjoy the day in a private piscatorial manner; but the unexpected rising of the wind and clouds brought the faithful fellow back to see if his master could be tempted.

Vexation on the score of Dereveragh was nearly over—so was the argument—so was the headache; and by the time we reached the shore the vapours grew lighter and lighter, and so faded away out of sight.

Till after midday the lake had been impracticable, and now this marked and unlooked-for change evidently made the fish in a most obliging frame of mind. They received, as it were, an unexpected windfall, and seemed disposed to make the most of it. Near our end of the lake three boats were drifting, into two of which trout were lifted as we approached, whilst the third appeared more heavily engaged with the enemy. We had been watching this one perhaps for twenty minutes, and ten more elapsed before we came within hail; "Pray keep farther off, sir; I have got a splendid trout, and would not lose him for the world." We lay on our oars, and shortly after saw a very nice fish secured. "I have to beg your pardon," said my new acquaintance, whose neat dress and neater appointments savoured strongly of dear old London, "for calling to you just now: pray excuse me; in the excitement of the moment, I may have been a little delirious. But do just look here; did you ever see such a beauty?" It was certainly a capital specimen of a Belviderian, weighing from $4\frac{1}{2}$lb. to 5lb. Never but once before had I seen mortal creature so happy. He trembled all over with pleasurable excitement, and his voice shook whilst inviting me to admire the goddess of his idolatry. Had I at that moment announced him heir to 1000*l.* a-year, I do not believe he would have cared one farthing for the intelligence—he was so full of joy, there was no room for more. I was reminded of my first salmon, which, speaking correctly, was but a miserable grilse of 4lb., yet the world never held such a glorious creature. I dared not touch my prize, lest I should defile it. Shape, colour, all came back to me now, with the happy exaggeration of that hour. The pocket handkerchief was again wetted, and the immortal one carefully swathed therein. No young mother ever carried her firstborn so tenderly as I bore that wretched little brown fish home. Placed in the largest dish the house contained, I worshipped him. Had a painter been near 10*l.* would have been cheap for his likeness. I wanted to have him embalmed. I longed passionately to take him to bed. Ah me! I shall never again meet such another. The redskins in their happy hunting grounds enjoy for ever and ever the zest of the first chase, and now here, in this work-day world, stood a man feeling what I once felt. How I envied him; yet had his story been known to me then, perhaps my envy had been less.

That night, over a quiet cigar, he told me that ten years had elapsed since he had touched a rod. "I was in Cumberland then," he said, "with my brother; over-fatigue brought on fever, which ended fatally, and then I lost the dearest friend I ever had, or ever shall have. Till to-day I never dared to look at it, and now"—with a smile on his lip and a tear in his eye—"I am half ashamed of being so happy. Poor Ned, had *he* only been here!"

As to numbers, this proved our best day on the lake; for three hours "the rise" was incessant; twenty-three fish came to our lot, the odd one falling to the share of the professor, who noticed the fact with a solemn countenance and an ill-concealed triumph.

CHAPTER XVIII.

We go to Castle Pollard—Fish Dereveragh for two days—Return to Mullingar and Belvidere—Visit our old acquaintance Lough Owel—And set out for Boyle.

May 29, 6 A.M.

THIS morning our little household is in a high state of activity. *Madame et sa femme de chambre*, in full travelling costume, are hard at work, cramming into a carpet-bag articles which by no possibility can be required. Such an opinion being expressed, the cry, "Turn him out, turn him out!" is too unanimous to be resisted—objector instantly silenced. Willie, too, is there, locking the basket which holds all our manufacturing treasures. "You are surely not going to drag *that* to Castle Pollard, when all we *can* want will be a few small hooks and some light gut!"

"Sure and I am, though," said he, deliberately placing the strap over his shoulder. "How much would we expect to see else when we cum back? May be, if an honest gintleman looked thim things over, we might find the kiver, or even the bottom; sorra a thing else."

No larks in the world are so light-hearted and vocal as those in the dear island; the whole summer business of their happy lives seems to be singing from morning till night, and now, having breakfasted, they were up in the blue sky carolling *gloria in excelsis*. I rather envied those birds. No morning meal for me, nor any immediate prospect of such a thing; the car is safe not to be at that wretched roadside station to which we are bound; should it by any extraordinary luck be waiting, a trace may break; then the driver must stop at least four times to light his pipe; whilst the landlord will not suppose we want anything at such an hour; then perhaps, I shall remember being coughed down, and growl at being twitted with *always* wanting food at inconvenient times. Now, this is one way in which good people get into a pet before there is any occasion; for the car did meet us, breakfast was ready, and the account of the fishing highly favourable. Yesterday several six and seven pounders were bagged, and one rod was *reported* to have killed sixteen fish. For the next hour it will be useless to embark, so we may employ the time in taking a more extended view of the lakes in Westmeath, Sligo, and Roscommon than we have hitherto done.

Hitherto they have only been considered with reference to the drake, which in general is supposed to be the Alpha and Omega; but, like many other articles of popular faith, this is an error. Nor am I quite prepared to admit that the May-fly fishing offers the best sport these waters can show; for it must be remembered that, with very few exceptions, they hold pike and perch, as well as trout, and that the *Percidæ* here run large, three and four pounders being nothing remarkable. It is not difficult, therefore, to imagine how excellent the trolling must be, either before or after the reign of Prince Draco. With the fly, trout are of course only to be taken, but in spinning, the angler goes in for all; far heavier bags are to be made, and, besides, there is the charm of variety. You get hold of something heavy, and for ten or twelve minutes are in a delicious state of uncertainty as to what you *have* got. I have heard several gentlemen, whose property lay in the district, and whose opinions might well be considered conclusive, say they preferred April, July, August, September, and October, to May. Of course the blow-line will always have warm advocates; its delicacy, deadliness, and the skill required in using it successfully, deserve all that can be said in its praise; yet still, you may take my word for it, the early and late fishing on these glorious lakes is not to be despised.

If poor Mac's politeness, not to say his reason, is to be preserved, we must hurry to the shore, and Willie must be informed that he has no right whatever to improve another gentleman's property against his consent. 'Twould make any Irish saint swear to see him. He has positively turned Mr. M'Cutcheon's yacht bottom upwards; probably, too, has called her "an old basket," and, with a stone for a mallet, and an old knife instead of a caulking-iron, is actually hammering "lint" into the seams. That fellow's impudence "beats all."

Castle Pollard is situated about the same distance from Dereveragh as Boyle and Mullingar are from their respective lakes— that is to say, about three miles. With such charming sites at command, it seems strange that neither of these towns should have availed themselves of the advantage. In the good old times, when every man brewed for himself, water, perhaps, was considered a dangerous element. If this be not deemed a good reason why the towns above mentioned were placed as far as possible out of its reach, I regret being unable to offer a better. Dereveragh, seven miles long by three broad, though not possessing beauty of a striking character, is yet well worth a visit for its quiet loveliness; so, at least, I thought, as we ran our boat over the pebbles into its clear waters, smiling and dimpling in the summer sun.

With a long drift before us, my *fidus Achates* seated himself on the bottom boards, and commenced a fly for the Erne. "I've got him!" The artist merely glances at the eddy caused by the descending fish, and then, for more correct information, at the curve of the rod. "He won't be ready these ten minutes." Nevertheless, the handle of the net is brought across his knees, and the golden hackle wound with admirable precision at the front of each roll of tinsel. Then he looks about him once more, and selects four toppings of the exact length required, and sets them carefully on. Shall he produce any further? He is doubtful as to the propriety of opening a paper containing sprigs of bustard, mallard, ruff, and the like. This should be done carefully, especially in the wind; so, placing the half-finished parson between his lips, he gets up just at the right time, and does his work with the usual neatness. "Nigher six than five and a half," he observes, when calmly crimping the unfortunate, "and the mistress shall have him roasted for lunch." The sport soon grew admirable—no quarter of an hour passed without some event. Three were lost in succession by the mouth giving way; next five were secured without accident, of 2lb., 3lb., 3½lb., 5lb., and 5½lb., and then the best fish of the day was hooked. How he laughed at the gossamer thread which held him; it seemed mere pastime to dart off with fifty yards, and throw a somersault that would have made Blondin sick with envy; but we must all die, even as this strong and beautiful creature, who was put out of pain so suddenly by a judicious rap on the *occiput* as not to hear the executioner remark, "'Deed now, master, but he draws eight and a half." About midday the breeze fell off, and the trout, after "tiffin," lay down for a siesta under "the glassy, cool, transparent wave," as Milton sings. The *chef* had not forgotten his gracious promise, and proposed landing and lunch, an offer the entire ship's crew hailed with three cheers. Did you never see fish roasted *sub Jove*? Well, I hope you soon will, of your own catching too; meanwhile, allow me to tell you how an experienced cook did it: From yonder cabin some live coals, supported on an armful of peats, are brought—there are plenty of stones on the beach for our fireplace—the glowing cinders are piled in the centre, the turf arranged on end in contact with them, and some bits broken to fill up the crater. The mess consists of five, and the caterer serves out a six-pounder and a four. The fish is ready as soon as the fire, cut in slices, with a peeled osier inserted into each. These are placed upright before the fire (supported by a long sod cut for the purpose), and dexterously turned by the forefinger and thumb of the accomplished *chef*. If this meat be eaten, as good old Izaak says, with a thankful heart and good appetite, in my opinion it won't disagree with you.

The boa, after sucking down a sheep, requires forty-eight hours' repose before again feeling comfortable. Some of the crew felt exceedingly like boas after dinner. But the breeze was once more playing a game of romps with the lake before going to rest, and two heavily-gorged animals had to be roused into what was unquestionably a painful state of activity. Again the sport brightened up as before, but in a couple of hours the wind sank for the night, and we pulled for the shore over a long stretch of water, whose surface was smooth as polished glass. Ten fish lay on the grass, two more were chiefly carried by parties whose names are sacred; one dozen in all. Well done, Dereveragh!

If required to name the day on which the May-fly makes its first annual visit to this lake, I should fix on the 18th of May. Of course a long and cold spring retards the development of the caddis, in the same degree that warmth and sunshine contribute to its more early maturity. No season could be more genial than the present, and as a consequence the drake "was up" some days prior to the date above mentioned. Indeed, these beautiful insects had fluttered away half their bright brief lives when we arrived; but the sport had reached its climax, for the trout, fully alive to the dainty, were not as yet surfeited with it.

A twice-told tale grows wearisome, however well narrated, and must especially be avoided in a work so unpretending as this. Suffice it, then, to say our second day proved less productive than the preceding, both as to number and size, for out of eight fish brought to bag, one only reached $5\frac{1}{2}$lb. And now standing, perhaps for the last time, on the shores of Dereveragh, I could not but turn to take one long lingering look at the place where two such happy days had been passed. In this uncertain and anxious life who would not feel grateful to a spot where he had found such wealth? Then the thought so common to man rose within me, "Shall I ever visit it again, and will there be no one of the dear faces now round me absent for ever?" Instinctively I drew closer to them, as if (idle dream!) proximity gave security. In sober mood I drove back to Connel, paid our moderate bill, and set off for Mullingar as the shades of evening began to gather round us.

The reader may like to know that he can be boarded at the Pollard Arms for 2*l*. 14*s*. per week, which includes car-hire to and from the lake each morning and evening. When it is considered that for this sum he has first-rate fishing, bed and sitting rooms, three meals a day, and twelve drives, I think no reasonable man would object to the charge.

Beautiful Belvidere lay sleeping lazily in the sun, as fresh and fair as when I left her, and as she will do a hundred years hence when some stranger comes to say farewell, as I do now. We have an affection for this water, for it was the first on which our blow-line ever sailed. Often, when hundreds and hundreds of miles away she has visited me, smiling as she now smiles, and that dear familiar face has comforted me in anxiety and soothed me in sorrow. What could a friend do more? True, like many other early companions, she has not proved "all my fancy painted," for I have since found many more trustworthy. But pray, have not you, sir, some early acquaintance of whom you feel rather ashamed, and long since acknowledged undeserving your regard, to whom you cling, nevertheless, merely for the sake of old times? Such weakness is doubtless unworthy a philosopher; but then I make no pretensions to so high a caste, and without shame say, the memory of "young love" is very sweet. After Dereveragh, my quiet friend seemed tame and dull, and at three p.m. I bade her adieu, leaving the men to take the boat to Lough Owel, and bring back "the game"—eleven head, no one of which weighed 3lb.

Lough Owel bears little resemblance to her sisters, being surrounded by shores far more bold, broken, and bare. Lying in a vast rocky basin, composed probably of limestone, its clearness and purity are remarkable. Over its entire surface myriads of bubbles rise from unknown springs, and, in fact, the lake is one vast fountain of delicious water. This, combined probably with the clean bottom, gives the trout the peculiarly silvery character that distinguishes them from all others with which I am acquainted. We found our boat drawn up on the south-east corner, near a circular fairylike island, planted with larch and flowering shrubs, and, launching, pulled for the western side, in order to make our first drift towards a high headland on the opposite side. Lough Owel was a special favourite with Willie, being, as he said, "a place where a fish in earnest might be killed," so I gave him a day; nor was it long before his line was sailing gracefully, far in advance of our humble bark. Here and there, at long intervals, the small circling eddy of some rising fish was seen as we glided on; but nothing came in our way till within two or three hundred yards of the rocky shore, when a trout sailed up, dexterously sucked off my fly, and disappeared. There was a momentary glimpse of a very broad tail. "Out with the paddles, and over him again!" but before the words were uttered, the folly of the order became apparent. The first dip of the oar would have driven the fish from his ground, so the boat was allowed to float silently on; accurate marks were taken, and on reaching the cliff, we pulled cautiously along its base before again taking our station far above the spot where the charming vision faded from our eyes. Every moment made me feel more and more certain of being in the exact line. Now the fly must be within five yards of the place—now within two—now within one. Can we have passed him? There is the smallest conceivable rise—a backward motion of the rod, and such a swirl! "He's got what he won't get rid of easily. That's fine! Och, but that's beautiful! Ah, master! sure there's nothing like this in ould Ireland, any way at all."

Thus spoke my faithful servant, instinctively charging his pipe, whilst a faint smile stole over his honest and sober face. Now rooting at the bottom, now rolling over the surface, again and again flying as if life depended on his speed, what a gallant fish it was! Little by little his efforts grew more laborious and less effective. Presently the broad tail which led to his destruction, scarcely possessed the power to keep that small head under water. More faintly still he fluttered from the fatal net, now it is over; nature can do no more, and like a log he is drawn slowly and steadily towards the boat; another foot and he is safe and on board. I would have walked all the way from Dublin for that one fish. "Ten pounds and a quarter! No, not quite a quarter (our clerk of weights and measures was very precise) call him ten pounds lucky. That's something like a trout." Over and over again the same course was tried, in the hope of meeting another of the same class, but in vain. At length we resigned it reluctantly, and commenced a fresh drift over the broadest part of the lake in a line with Church Island. Half way down the shore of that low rocky reef a good fish rose right ahead. Slowly the fly sailed straight towards him. "What's that?" My first thought was that Willie, who just before was sitting on the gunwale, had tumbled head-over-heels into the water. But no; there he sat, composed as ever. "He's an awful monster, master; as big as a salmon." To jerk the line out, reel sharply up, so as to ensure my companion fair play, was but the work of an instant. Had it not been for that startling plunge he might have been fast in a rock for anything I could see to the contrary. Fish have temperaments various as their captors; they are shy, bold, cowardly, volatile, sulky, or determined, and the one now under treatment combined the latter qualities in about equal proportions. For a full hour we saw nothing of him, and all this time had been drifting deeper into the rocky and shallow bay beyond the island. "Pull, pull, I'm fast! He's sat down. Oh dear, oh dear! what will I do? Pull, pull for your lives!" A few dashing strokes brought the boat over the exhausted monster; the line was free, and the battle over. There he lay on the bottom, with his great side leaning against the rock that refused him shelter. The water was barely 5ft. deep; off went the net, on went the gaff, and then we found leisure to admire our prize. Perfect in make, exquisite in harmony of colour, in weight 13lb.—truly he was a picture; glorious in life, beautiful in death, it may be long before his fellow is hung with such a thread. As may be imagined, all that occurred subsequently was tame. Two more, however, of 3lb. and 5lb., wound up the best day I ever saw with the blow line.

We lived on the lake for the remainder of the week, meeting with fair sport, and on Monday set out for Boyle, where, from intelligence received that morning from Sergeant Nameless, of the Greens, great things seemed to await us.

CHAPTER XIX.

Irish Ruins—Church Islands—Things in General—Boyle—Lough Gara—Lough Key—Lough Arrow—Prophetic of Good—We go to the Erne.

Boyle, June 8.

IRELAND has been called "the land of ruins." Poets have employed the theme to make us sad—orators to make us savage. The former asked only a sentimental tear, but the latter, by party legislation, senseless clamour, abuse, and bigotry, for many and many a year raised men's blood to the boiling point, and scalded poor common sense and charity nearly to death. No one need deny Ireland to be a land of ruins, but this is a far different thing from a ruined land; and that she does not present this mournful spectacle is certainly not the fault of the oratorical quacks, who not so long since undertook to cure all her earthly ills. She is pre-eminently' a land of ruins, and possesses monuments as old, if not older, than any other country in Europe, which, could they be deciphered, would afford marvellous ethnological interest, and throw a light on peoples and races whose origin, civilisation and habits are now lost. Pictorial blocks, inscribed stones, Cyclopean forts, graceful towers, tumuli, earthworks by lonely strands and stormy headlands, ecclesiastical ruins, military ruins, and, worse than all, clusters of roofless cottages in deserted districts, swept bare by emigration, famine, and fever, all justify her claim to the mournful title. These deserted dwellings fill the stranger with horror, for they force on his consideration fearful pictures of want, sorrow, and suffering, endured before the last miserable creature passed from the spot where so much wretchedness must have been undergone.

Whilst we renovate and investigate ancient ruins, may Heaven avert new ones from the land! There is one order, however, which more constantly comes under the angler's notice than under that of other men—remains of ecclesiastical edifices on the lakes. Few of these waters are without a Church Island, where roofless cells, solitary and crumbling, set us thinking of the dark days which made such situations necessary. These lonely spots are singularly interesting and suggestive, and without wandering into dreamland—the stranger will be apt to draw two conclusions: from their number—that prodigious efforts must have been made to introduce the only true civiliser; from their situation—that the state of society was considerably worse than that which existed in New Zealand forty years ago, where the amiable natives did nothing worse than cook a curate occasionally. I do not say that these deductions will be accepted, nor have I any authority for asserting that they are correct; but if a man locks and bolts his door, puts up iron shutters, fills the moat, and hauls up the drawbridge, it looks as if he rather mistrusted the character of his neighbours, and leads to the belief, that his exhortations to "do as he would be done by" fell on the wayside. The lot of these poor preachers of peace and goodwill seems to have been cast in evil times; doubtless, they sowed diligently and reaped a scanty harvest—attempted much, but effected little, save to themselves.

A writer whose wisdom has stood the test of centuries, and will last whilst the world endures, says: "There is nothing new under the sun." Our application of electricity to a few lines of wire—is that new? 'Tis as old as the hills, ay, and a good deal older than any hills with which we are acquainted. Why, the day when the blessed sun first shone on Eden he managed more miles of telegraphic communication than man ever made or will make. Each morning he sent a message to Adam and Eve to rise and be thankful; every moment he forwarded orders beyond the most advanced pupil teacher's power of numeration, to flower and tree to put forth bud, blossom, and fruit. Well, perhaps, there is nothing new, and we lead a sort of horse-in-the-mill life; but these animals, being popularly supposed blind, fancy perhaps that they are always going straight on. Some of us, too, may be blind and fall into a similar error. We have quitted Mullingar, and are now in Boyle. We have left one set of lakes where we sat all day in the sun and wind, reddening our noses and otherwise injuring the complexion, and are come to another set of lakes where we intend doing the same. There does not seem to be much novelty in this, but for the life of me I cannot get my rebellious members to agree with the dictum. The feet will speed lightly towards Lough Gara, the hand will grasp the rod more eagerly, and the eyes will grow brighter. Bah! Family quarrels are intolerable. *Peccavi! peccavi!* There, rebels, will that content you? and if the plain truth must be spoken: "Gentlemen of the opposition, I most heartily agree with you."

How joyously we stepped out of Boyle side by side with the strapping sergeant. Names are not things to be lightly mentioned. He might have been sergeant of militia, sergeant of marines, sergeant-at-arms, or our honourable friend Serjeant Buzfuz; at any rate, he was Captain of the Guides, and ought to have been Marshal of the Lakes. As we have recently seen a good deal of fishing with the green drake, it will be more advisable in this chapter to take a general survey of the waters of the district, and say as little as may be on the more pleasant subject of practice, remembering the proverb that "Too much, even of a good thing, is good for nothing."

Roscommon is bounded on the north-east by Leitrim, and on the east by King's County and Westmeath, from all which it is separated by the river Shannon. The area is estimated at 609,405 English acres, of which 131,063 are unimproved mountain and bog, and 24,787 lakes. The interest of the sportsman may therefore be considered as fairly represented by these freeholds of nature. The general surface of Roscommon is either flat or gently undulating; there are, however, some mountains, the principal groups of which are the Braulieve and Slievh Curkagh. The county belongs to the basin of the Shannon, except a very small portion at the western extremity, which is drained by the Moy. The Shannon, about five miles from its source, enters Lough Allen, flows through it, and forms the north-eastern boundary of the county; breaking from this lake, it runs along the edge of Roscommon to Carrick, where it receives a stream from Lough Key; from Carrick the great river pursues its course along the border, passing through Lough Corry, Lough Bodarg, Lough Boffin, and Lough Forbes, to Lanesborough, below which it enters Lough Ree. The extent of some of the principal lakes is as follows: Lough Allen, seven miles long by three broad; Lough Bodarg and Lough Boffin, forming one continuous sheet of water five miles by seven; Lough Forbes and Lough Ree, seventeen miles long and seven broad; Lough Gara, five miles by three; Lough Key (otherwise called Rockingham), about three and a half miles; and Lough Oakport, smaller, which communicate with the Shannon by a stream called Boyle Water. Seven or eight others might be mentioned, but enough, in all conscience, have been enumerated. Here, indeed, is *l'embarras de richesses*, for all hold fine red trout; and, as no one mortal man can fish them all in the month which divides the salmon from the grilse season, it behoves him to take counsel and select the best. It has been shown how we have spent the interval, and the line of march we have taken. Others, holding some of the waters above mentioned in great favour, will, perhaps, maintain we might have chosen more wisely. Very possibly; but if they are pleased, I am content. Having skimmed like a swallow lightly over the waters of the district, we will perch on the church tower of Boyle and look nearer home. This town lies on the high road to Sligo, on the "Boyle Water," which flows from Lough Gara into Lough Key, and, in the reign of John, a Bernardine abbey of great wealth and importance took the place under its wing. If it continued to grow from that time to the present, it must, in the days of the good friars, have been much too small to go alone. The older portion of the town stands on the northern bank of the river; the more improved part on the southern; but, notwithstanding the improvements, a very matter-of-fact writer observes, "out of about five hundred houses three-fifths are miserable thatched cabins, and half the remainder are little better." The stranger, however, need not be alarmed on the score of his comforts, as he can either stay at an "hotel" sufficiently comfortable, or procure lodgings where, if not too luxurious, he may feel at home.

I fear my friend the sergeant will be wroth, for he has been kept waiting an unconscionable time at the outskirts of the town, whilst I have been flying over the country and twittering on the parish church.

My friend thinks we shall find matters rather dull on Gara, as it is the earliest lake in the neighbourhood. Nor do I doubt the correctness of his opinion, for the fly rises on this extensive sheet of water about the 8th or 10th of May, so that by this time the fish are sure to be suffering from indigestion, the product of over-indulgence. Nor, indeed, is Gara, under even the most favourable circumstances, comparable either to Lough Key or Arrow, as its trout are comparatively small, and suffer much both from nets and cross-lines. Still I was anxious to spend one day on its broad bosom, visit the islands, and make its beauty mine for ever. A pleasant walk of forty minutes brought us to the lake, where we launched, and paddled off to the best fishing-ground, some two miles lower down. There is to me a peculiar charm in all islands, for they seem to possess peace without dullness—solitude without desolation—not to be found elsewhere. Derrybeg, Annough, Mackmoragh, Inchmore, and many others all tempted us, when sport failed, to land; but the sergeant was of a temperament so hopeful as always to be convinced there was a flaw of wind somewhere else, the consequence of which was, that no sooner had I begun to get cool and comfortable than I was hurried off in doubtful chase after some fugitive breeze. All that men could do, we did; and whilst a chance existed, persevered; and when compelled to desist could only count between us seven fish, not one of which exceeded 3lb.

It has been already observed that the drake does not appear simultaneously on all the Mullingar lakes, but, obeying some invariable natural law, rises first on one and then on another, which, by the way, is an excellent arrangement for the angler. Here also the same mysterious order is observed, the insect coming into "mid air" first on Gara, next on Lough Key, and lastly on the Arrow, where it remains nearly to the middle of June. To attend the funeral obsequies of fair May-fly is impossible, as we have made arrangements to be at Ballyshannon by the 7th or 8th of the month.

The short time left at our disposal, therefore, must be divided between Key and Arrow, probably the two best waters in Ireland for blowline fishing. Whilst strolling over the pleasant mile and a half which separates Boyle from the former water, I re-read a note received on the morning of our leaving Mullingar, which, being pre-eminently practical, is here presented to my friends :

Boyle, May 25, 1865.

My dear Sir,—You ask me to send you an account of my proceedings on Lough Key. I do so with pleasure, but pray come and see for yourself. Let me, however, first say a few words about one day's angling there in the season of 1864. My attendant was William Ross, an exceedingly intelligent and able man, and with his help we killed (on the occasion referred to) five-and-twenty trout, eight of which were above 7lb. each, and twelve others over 4lb. each. This was, Ross said, one of the best bags almost ever made.

"Never mind the rest of the note—" crushing it into my pocket. "A great achievement has been wrought; what was done once, may be done again; and who knows, eh Willie! but that we may be the fortunate individuals?" With a longer stride I hastened on; there stood the field of battle, and we resolved, if possible, to go in and win. Unlike Lough Gara, the water on whose margin we stood is private property, and, as neither cross-lines nor nets are allowed, it is indeed an angling paradise, where no evil thing comes. The drakes had been "up" about ten days, and were now sitting on almost every leaf, or sunning themselves on nearly every stone. The excessive heat which cheered them chilled our hopes; to-day would not see the crowning victory. Well, life may not be one long triumph, and the best soldier can but do his duty. Over the blue waters we drifted with a lazy motion, passing many a lovely island whose name should not be unrecorded here; Church, Orchard, Sally, Stag, and Crane, and many others, were *noticed* (I like to be accurate), for we did not land on any : who would, with such a letter in his pocket? But we must not linger on description. Considering the weather, we did wonders, two rods taking twelve good fish, the three best being a trifle under 19lb. Two more happy days were spent on Lough Key, during which the sun forgot himself, and behaved as he ought to have done in the tropics. Of course we fished under unfavourable circumstances; but the blow-line when properly managed rises above most of the difficulties created by weather. With tackle of any other description sport would have been almost an impossibility; but with this, should there be only the lightest conceivable air, a man will seldom return disappointed. More favourable atmospheric conditions will of course largely contribute to the chances of success; but the day in which an angler writes in his diary the ominous word "blank" must be bad indeed.

During the past season four or five salmon were taken on this lake, and one or two during the present; but as yet the numbers are too inconsiderable to make this fish of any importance.

Within the next few years, perhaps, some future chronicler for *The Field* may have to record, "splendid grilse fishing on Lough Key;" everywhere our wise law is producing fruit; good streams are becoming better; bad ones becoming good; and rivers, now exhausted, or by natural obstacles out of the reach of the most adventurous salmon, here and there begin to show the first promise of the coming harvest. Not only will that Act increase the number of waters for sporting purposes, but it will do far more, it will *decrease* the heavy rents hitherto demanded from the angler; not that I would be understood to imply that such charges were or are exorbitant; far from it; the goods were exposed in a fair and open market, and the prices asked cheerfully paid. Local reputation will in many cases keep up for a time former terms; but as in general society the poor far outnumber the rich, so amongst the brotherhood of the rod those who with difficulty make both ends meet greatly exceed those who can bring the ends together, and moreover find a good piece to lap over; thus men who are unable to pay large sums for their recreation will gradually hunt up new quarters, meet more fortunate friends and proclaim *their* success, when it will be found that many an impoverished lake and river has suddenly grown wealthy, and is entitled to take rank with the best. The consequence of these changes is sufficiently obvious; there will be more goods in the market, and the value of the stock must diminish in the ratio of its quantity.

I linger over the sheet as loath to leave the subject; but the best friends must part, and we have come to that inevitable hour, on the shores of Arrow, the last of our green drake lakes. This sheet of water, without presenting any striking beauties, yet has charms of a pleasing kind; " there are sloping, green, and cultivated. banks, finely wooded promontories, low, but stretching far into its bosom," with many an emerald isle sleeping on its blue surface. This morning, when we left Boyle, we quitted it for the season, and looked our last on Lough Key—the splendid surrounding woods of Lord ———, and the venerable ruins of the Abbey—one of the most beautiful in Ireland. Nor did we pass the comfortable but unpretending inn without a sigh, hoping devoutly that during the remainder of our journey we might always find one as good.

It is needless to record our sayings and doings on the silver Arrow; they have been already told at Belvidere, Dereveragh, and Lake Owel. Suffice it to say the sport was excellent, and that in four consecutive days thirty-one trout fell to my rod. In point of size they were very fair, the largest weighing rather over eight pounds and a half. . . . . . .

The day is over, and we stand on the hot and dusty road looking up the long slope which leads to Boyle.

"Here they come, sir!" At that moment I did not feel as a model family man ought to have felt. The occupants of the rapidly approaching car seemed not so much friends, as savages about to tear me from what I held so dear. Whilst we drove away I watched the lake as if it wore the form of some departing friend. I was very dolorous, and looked so.

"Come, cheer up! What would you have?"

"I would have the lakes."

"What! and give up the Erne?"

"No."

"But you cannot have both. You must renounce one."

"I cannot!"

"What is to be done? Don't threaten to shoot yourself like Scythrop Glowry. There, light your pipe: already you have 'One auspicious and one drooping eye.' You will forget your lost love to-morrow, when you stand once more on the dear old bridge of Ballyshannon."

CHAPTER XX.

The Erne—Early morning—The Bridge—A "great" misfortune—Subsequent success—The Colonel discourses—Draughting under the Falls.

June 12.

THE church clock struck three as I lay broad awake in my comfortable chamber in the Mall, waiting the expected signal announcing that Pat and my *fidus Achates* were at their post; yes, wide awake, for who could sleep on such a morning? Through the open window comes the balmy breath of the sweet summer, and the minstrel thrush is humming over the song he will sing so soon to a drowsy world. Beautiful Erne, I cannot see you; yet I feel your bright face will smile a welcome to an old *adorateur*. Queen of streams! thou art peerless amongst the waters. A very Phœnix of rivers, you burst in your might from the parent lake, and after a too brief race of four miles, die in your prime, and drop into the eternity of Ocean. No dull stagnant life is yours, but onward, ever onward, in beautiful variety—splendid in your streams, deep and wide in your pools, grand in your falls. Many a happy day have I whiled away on your banks, sweet Erne!

Time did not, however,
Keep pace with my expectancy and fly.

Four was the hour agreed on, but it wanted sixty minutes to the time, and who would voluntarily submit to half or three quarters of an hour's misery if he could help it.

To spring out of bed and gain the window was the work of a moment. There, on the opposite doorstep, sat Messrs Willie and

Pat, talking as calmly as if it were midday, instead of only three hours after midnight.

"Holloa, Willie, why didn't you call me?"

"Your honour appointed four," observed Pat. "All's quiet in the town. Not a ghost of a soul's stirrin'; we come early for fear of being late. Niver a doubt but I'd have gravelled the winder had there been any need; but things ain't as they used to be."

We had been so fortunate as to obtain our old quarters in the Mall, a site indeed quite to my taste, for it was within a hundred and forty yards of the bridge; and what did that imply? Why, simply this—that I was hardly a minute's walk from *the best* cast in the kingdom. The water thence to the falls is reserved, but my kind friend the lessee had placed it at my disposal, and I longed to be there.

The dear old bridge, scene of many former pains and pleasures; of defiance to foes and plots against friends, shone bright as ever in the morning sun. Each stone on the parapet was graven on my memory, for had I not seen it every hour in the twenty-four—shivered there at ten, eleven—

> In the dead waste and middle of the night!—

and as for two, three, and four—they were parts of our daily life.

"Well, Pat, who have you got here this season?" I asked, as the line was being passed through rings.

"Some of your honour's friends; and the Colonel—you'll be glad to hear he's come."

This was good news, indeed. The stout soldier was so old a friend that I knew him before my lips could well pronounce his name. We had not met for three years, I having during that time rented a river farther north. Bright, genial, and courteous, his society was a privilege; he was better than a book; had haunted the Erne with men whose active lives were over; remembered bygone scenes and ancient comrades, and spoke of them with a gusto and vivacity rarely met with.

"Will we try the parson first?"

"Oh, by all means, Willie. Is the thread good?"

"Never a better was wetted," he said, giving me the butt.

Anyone possessed of hands could float a line down a stream, but *that* would not have been fishing our bridge. First, it must be tried close to the arches, and this can only be effected by keeping the point near the water, and the rod parallel to the masonry; then a little more line may be paid out, and the glittering fly made to dart *across* the rapid, play in the eddy, and so skim back again into the current; and, lastly, more and more length is given by slow degrees, till that portion of the water has been fairly tried. Now there are many arches (some far better than others), so it may be easily imagined we have sufficient work on our hands, till a breathless messenger announces, at half-past eight, "Breakfast is ready." The third and fourth streams from the north side were especial favourites, but each was worked in vain, with two or three changes. This was the more vexatious, as the wide sheet of water between us and the falls was alive with fish, springing high in air or casting themselves horizontally over the surface, often showing their broad and silvery sides distinctly for many a yard as they dived below. It needed not the magic ointment of the dervish to see that a treasure lay there; but now to win it was the question.

It is hardly possible to have too much line for this throw, as the angler is well-nigh chained to his post. On the south side there is no possibility of following a fish, and on the north the propriety of such a step is very questionable, for it can only be done by dropping the rod to your attendant as he stands below. Supposing such a transfer safely effected, you cannot follow more than fifty or sixty yards, when the depth of the water forbids all further advance. But it is not often a fresh salmon takes this steady downward course. Desperate runs in the direction of the falls are inevitable; but in nineteen cases out of twenty, while strength remains, he will again head up stream, and eventually come within reach of the gaff.

"What! never a fish?" said an ancient professional, who, too old to follow the river, yet haunted the bridge. "Will your honour let me look at your book?"

I assured him everything it contained had been tried, and found wanting.

"Your honour has not wet this the morn," he observed, slowly drawing a gaudy article from one of the pockets. I had frequently tried it, for I was proud of the handiwork, but had at last thrown it aside as worthless. "It *might* do," he said, running critically over the composition. "Gold tag, topping, kingfisher, and a turn of ostrich; that's a good tail, any way. Puce silk body, bright claret hackle, fiery brown pig's-wool, and jay at the shoulder." "Is there four or five jungle cock in the wing?" "Well, it *may* do." "Try it your honour, any way." Scarcely had the fly touched the water, when a monstrous salmon made a charge at it. I knew he was well hooked. "Mona mon diaoul," exclaimed the veteran, "but he's the best fish that's been stuck this season." "He's forty pounds if he's an ounce." His activity and strength exceeded anything I had ever conceived. Again and again, at a single dash, he tore the whole line (140 yards) from the wheel, but by great luck always turned at the critical moment. I felt from the first a terrible misgiving that the business on hand was more than I could manage, and looked anxiously for Pat, who had gone home in the hope of producing an article more captivating than those hitherto employed. "Whish— he's off again," now leaving me scarce an inch on the reel, now encumbered with a hundred yards of slack; now dashing to the right and then to the left, with such startling speed and determined perseverance as kept me in constant difficulties. "Ah! there's Pat at full speed." "More power to yer elbow, yer honor; I heard the music up by the church, and that's a quarter of a mile. Tare-an'-ouns, but he's a tatterer."

Verily I had caught a tartar; the strength of the fish, the necessity of holding the rod up, and the weight on the line, had "kilt me entirely." I was dead beat. My arm refused its office, and if life had depended upon it, I could not have worked at the wheel a minute longer. Gladly I handed the rod to Pat. The change was scarcely effected, when the monster once more dashed down the water at headlong speed. Pat saw the crisis was at hand; he looked pale, agitated, but determined. By the time the last inch of line was off the wheel the butt was pointed in the direction of the fish, and the top well over his shoulder, to break, if possible, the force of the rush, by the elasticity of the rod. This *might* have succeeded with a smaller fish, but would, I felt, be useless here. It required his whole force to keep the rod in the proper position. Twice the gallant salmon made desperate charges, yet the good tackle stood; a third succeeded. By sheer force the rod was drawn into an horizontal direction, and the line, an instant before tight as a harp string, flew loosely upwards. The poor fellow turned an appealing look at the great master. "All the sons of men could not have helped it," he said, soothingly; "man could not have played him better." Here was, indeed, a downfall to my expectations. It was the only chance that ever fell to my lot of achieving real greatness. I said not a word. What my feelings were it is needless to say; they may be more easily imagined than described. It was no use grieving over a broken thread. The casting line, composed of stout treble gut (with the exception of a capital single thread on which the fly was tied), had luckily parted in the middle, so the loss of tackle was nothing. Damages were soon repaired, and the "parson" was in a few minutes swimming seducingly across the streams of the fourth and fifth arches. "Hooroo! that's something like. Murther! but he's missed it." Scarcely had he spoken before the same fish turned at the brilliant insect and took it. A furious run of eight or ten feet ended my hopes; the mouth had given way. Willie was in despair, Pat more than ever convinced he had met "an evil eye," and that no luck could fall to our share. His mind was disquieted; thrice he enumerated every ill-favoured old lady of his acquaintance, and still was unsatisfied; he could fix with certainty on no one. Memory was treacherous. Might he not have omitted an item in the reckoning? Possibly. And a fourth time the summing-up was recommenced in hopes of a different result.

"Molly M'Gowan—bad luck to her. But sure it wasn't her; didn't I bestow her a stone of praties not a month ago? She wasn't the witch. Biddy O'Brien," continued the persevering calculator, scoring her off on the first finger of his left hand—"Biddy O'Brien!" the groaning of the wheel cut short further investigation, and the spell was broken by our landing, about half an hour afterwards, a beautiful fish of 18lb. But fortune had not yet done with us, for within the next forty minutes another salmon of 16lb. lay cooling in the shallow edge of the stream; whilst a third, larger than either, was giving me full occupation in a series of runs, so desperate that nothing but a first-class wheel could have stood the work. In the midst of one of these, a light hand was laid on my shoulder and a well-remembered voice said—

"Well done, Walter! This is like the good old times. Polish your man off; I can wait."

Short greeting was given to the Colonel then; but, when Willie had gaffed the fish (he was nearly 21lb.), I found leisure to say, how happy it made me to see my old friend once more.

"Ay," he said, "I heard you were here, and came to rob you of an arch or two. Privilege of seniority, you know, Walter—one of the few good things one gets in exchange for time."

Wiping my forehead, I murmured something about having done enough for one morning—Heaven forgive the deceit!—I could have worked for the next forty-eight hours without food or rest, and, reeling up, stood by the Colonel's side, watching the wonderful skill with which he fished the water. Playing his fly with unceasing activity—now close to the masonry, now in the current, then with a graceful curve into the eddy, and so back into the stream again—he ran on in a full flow of pleasant chat.

"What a place this is to me!—it is full of memories; *here* old times, lost friends, merry plots, and innocent counterplots, all come back as fresh as May. What fun I have had! You don't remember old Tom? Many years before you became one of us, Captain —— 'outdid his former great outdoings,' killing upwards of a hundred heavy fish in the short space of six weeks. Various attempts were made from time to time to despoil him of the property here, but without success. Four, half-past three, three, and even half-past two had been tried in vain. Come when the invaders would, the Captain was on guard. Poor old Tom Lightly (he's dead and gone now) was, at the time I speak of, my attendant, and in an evil hour persuaded me to try my fortune. I consented; ordered him to watch the Captain's retirement that evening, occupy the post with my rod and gaff, keep watch all night; and call me by peep of day. Before turning in I took a look at Tom, and found him with a roaring turf fire in one of the niches, his pipe going merrily, and the bottle of whisky I sent to help out his watch, half finished. All was right, and I went to bed with a mind at ease. About half-past two John and his master rounded the corner, not a little alarmed at the signs of occupation evinced by the blazing fire. All was still. They took a closer look. Could they believe their eyes? Yes; there stood the bridge, solitary and unoccupied; once more they were in possession. The mystery was soon solved. Sheltered from a sweeping northerly wind in a friendly doorway, lay old Tom, fast as a watchman, his master's rod across his knees, his pipe smothered in its own ashes, and the bottle empty. Whether the wind had half frozen the old fellow's blood, whether he had walked in his sleep, or whether Tom became rather blind and lost his way, no one ever knew. Merely to hint at the subject was a broken head. John was in an ecstacy of delight—to think of two Christians, comforted with a reasonable night's rest, outwitting those who had 'outwatched the stars.' It was better than a month's wages. There was a further triumph which suggested itself to the malicious John, could old Tom but be roused to a sense of his miserable condition by 'a grand instrumental crash.' To wake and find the bridge occupied would be something; but for Tom to start up and find the Captain 'stuck' in a twenty-pounder, would be Elysian. Hardly was the wish formed before the music of the wheel announced its fulfilment. Hitherto John had with difficulty restrained his exultation; but *now* the measure of his joy overflowed; this crowning triumph was more than mortal could bear in silence. He could contain himself no longer, but gave vent to a yell that would have done credit to a whole tribe of redskins. Such an assemblage of terrified heads as it drew to the windows of the 'Purt' had never been seen at three a.m. in the memory of man. The general opinion was that the cholera had 'tuk the pegs.' It startled the Captain; what wonder that it woke old Tom? He saw the state of affairs at once; dared not encounter the jokes of the delighted John; modestly observed, if St. Patrick was to order it, he'd not watch the bridge again if that born devil, the Captain, was within twenty miles of it; turned tail, and fairly bolted. Next morning Tom was reported absent. For a whole week my servant returned the old fellow *non est*. I was growing seriously anxious on his account when, late on the ninth evening, he made his appearance in the coffee-room. I hardly knew him, so pale and gaunt had he become. By degrees I learned that, knowing the merciless quizzing he must endure, he dared not return, but had been wandering in the Leitrim mountains from one cottage to another, till the present moment, when he hoped the affair had blown over and been forgotten. I ordered him to call me early. 'I'll do it, your honour; but och, Colonel dear, niver breathe the laste taste in life about the bridge.' Welladay! Many a pleasant hour have I passed on this spot with friends I shall never see more." Here the soldier brushed half an inch of white ash from his cigar—a silent comment, perhaps, on the perishing nature of sublunary things, and continued: " Tom had a tenacious memory; he owed the Captain 'one,' and was not likely to forget it. He was biding his time. Now, the commander and myself were next-door neighbours. One stormy night, about eleven, Tom placed himself under the Captain's window, hemmed, coughed, whistled snatches of a song, and, pausing between whiles, listened intently. If the Captain slept like a lynx, he was wary as a hawk, and Mr. Lightly was afraid of over-acting. The bait took; he heard his victim bounce out of bed and cautiously approach the window to hear what was going on. 'Hist, hist, your honour,' said Tom, addressing his sleeping master, but so softly that, though perfectly audible to the ambushed commander, it would hardly have waked a watch dog. 'Hist, hist, your honour, if ye arn't down in five minutes, bedad but we'll lose it,' adding, in a yet lower tone,

'The Captain's awake.' This was enough. Tom knew his man would risk life rather than lose his favourite throw. In less than a minute the door flew open; out rushed the deluded angler half dressed, ignorant of the hour, in a drizzling rain and westerly gale, to bide, as best he might, their pitiless buffeting through the long, long night. Tom was revenged. He had paid his debt and a little over. The whole was a ruse, for I never dreamed of again entering the lists against the invincible commander; and the hit consisted in giving him a Roland for an Oliver in the shape of an unnecessary airing of five or six hours on a squally night on one of the most exposed spots in the barony."

Anxious to give my companion full possession, I soon wished him good sport, and strolled up the Mall. Having a few minutes to spare, I determined to walk a couple of hundred yards farther, and see what was going on under the falls. Throwing myself on the grassy knoll which overhangs the fishhouse and the leap, I watched as delightedly as ever the operation of draughting. A stout, well-manned boat had just pushed from the shore, and was pulling at great speed towards the foot of the cascade, the captain in the stern delivering the heavy seine net as the crew dashed on. Now they are within a foot of the mighty sheet of falling water, and, turning close under a smooth rock on the southern bank, head back to the starting point. The corks now show the circle is complete. All hands to the ropes. Narrower and narrower grows the prison, more desperate the struggles of the captives, more keen the interest of the spectators. One heave all together, boys, and a hundred splendid fish, such as no other river can show, unless, perhaps, it be the Spey, are bounding on the floor of the boat. No time is lost between death and interment. A few moments only elapse ere the salmon are weighed, iced, and screwed down in the coffin-like boxes in which they are conveyed to Liverpool, London, and perhaps Paris. I have said they were such as probably no other river can show—admire their exquisite beauty of form and colour—look for a moment at their size! There are a few of twelve, more of eighteen, numbers from twenty to twenty-five, and perhaps two or three between forty and fifty pounds each. This draughting had been going on for hours, yet so great is "the run" that the last haul seemed to equal the first, and already numbers of new comers are even now leaping at the falls.

"Ah! breakfast is ready is it, Willie?" 'Twill be an idle ceremony, for this sight always spoils my appetite for beef and buttered toast.

CHAPTER XXI.

A Piscatorial Republic—"The Bank of Ireland"—Moss Row—The Captain's Throw—The Lost Gaff—"Luck's All."

June 17.

THE Erne flows through the town of Ballyshannon, dividing it into two unequal parts, the principal of which is on the north bank, where the ground rises rather abruptly, showing to great advantage its sunny gardens and pleasant dwellings, whilst a fine old church crowns the summit of the hill. From the east comes the rushing river, whilst to the west stretches a long range of sandhills, guarding the lough from the wild fury of the Atlantic. A solid mass of rock crosses the bed of the stream, which, thundering over the obstacle, drops in an unbroken sheet into the estuary, and is soon lost in the wide waters of Donegal Bay. A finer entrance can hardly be imagined, yet the Erne is not a spring river. Some early fish are taken, but the true run commences about the 1st of June, and consists exclusively of salmon, which are followed by the grilse three or four weeks later. Happy is the man who welcomes *these*, but thrice happy is he who meets the glorious creatures which throng hither in the first days of summer.

Every river has some peculiar characteristics, one of the distinguishing features of the Erne being a decided tendency to remain constantly in good angling trim, in which amiable eccentricity it differs from most of the other streams in the kingdom. In one, during the hot months, sport becomes impracticable from want of water; in another, wind is a *sine quâ non;* in a third, not a fish will move unless the day be dull, dark, and breezy; whilst a fourth may have an obstinate predilection for becoming flooded on the smallest provocation. But here, whether the season be dry or wet, about an equal number of "throws" are always in order. Summer floods (in the usual acceptation of the word) are unknown; sun, wind, and clouds are things of comparatively little moment, and every morning ushers in a fishing day. In fact, Lough Erne has its summer and winter level, from which it rarely varies, rising periodically during the latter season, in the ratio of the rains. This, of course, regulates the height of the river; but the lake is so enormous, and the tract of country whose drainage it receives so extensive, that in the driest summers the volume of water discharged is always great. "Our pet" possesses another virtue, that of being seldom discoloured, as all the large tributaries lay near the head of this inland sea, in which the rude mountain torrents grow quite genteel and refined, long ere their waters reach Beleek. Desperate and long continued storms may occasionally shade the Erne, but even then a fish may be killed; and at the worst a few hours will restore it to its pristine brightness.

A society so respectable as the Piscatorial Republic on the banks of the Erne could not, of course, exist without a code for its own special government. All questions of right or etiquette that arise are settled by reference to a *lex non scripta*, in which our sporting attendants are well versed. Unlike other jurisconsults, their decisions are uniformly governed by sense and justice; and as the laws are seldom strained to suit private purposes, appeal to higher authority is rarely necessary; peace and harmony prevail, and we form, in fact, a model state. By one of these traditional rules any angler who first occupies a lodge may retain it *à discrétion*, and as the casts are well defined, each subsequent comer passes on to the next he may find vacant. . . . . . .

The heat is awful; to be out in such a day would almost justify a man's friends procuring him furnished lodgings in Bedlam. In the full blaze of the sun a Bengal tiger might feel at home. The windows are open, the blinds down, yet the wax is melting on the paper where I am fabricating a pair of flies for your benefit, my dear sir. The mysteries of Eleusis, which stood on the Lake Copais, were not more carefully guarded than the secret of a killing fly by a zealous artist ; but you are one of us, so enter the Penetralia and behold. An O'Shaughnessy, suited to the weather and state of the water, is strapped to a thread of single gut. Gold tip, a turn of bright blue silk, another of crimson ; topping, kingfisher's feather, and a roll of black ostrich, form the tag. The body is made of rich yellow floss, gold tinsel, and hackle of the same hue. The wings consist of four or five toppings, six or eight orange feathers from the toucan, a few strands from the cock of the rock, four fibres from the tail of the golden pheasant, and two long crimson horns. A black head completes the elaborate production. This is the favourite lure, and is considered by the learned as the best that can be "put over a fish ;" and now, having finished the fly, the next thing is to try it.

Our plan for to-day is to reach "the Bank of Ireland," if possible before the doors open for the admission of the public ; to work there for two or three hours, and then take each cast in order back to the town, following the *south side* of the river. Over the bridge we hurry, up the hot and dusty road for a short distance, then across a field or two, and so reach Kathleen's Fall. From thence to Stonewell is an unbroken succession of lodges, but there is no time to try them. Straight on we go ; over the green swell above—" the grassyard,"— over walls and rough pastures, till we reach the ornamental grounds behind the "Captain's Throw." Still onward ; through plantations, over more walls, past a considerable stretch of coppice, when we plunge downwards and find "The Bank" without a customer. This throw is indeed perfection—long, deep, and broad, with a splendid stream, running with decreasing force to the end, but which requires some neatness of execution, as a high wooded slope rises abruptly from the edge of the river, and forbids casting in the ordinary manner. Of course the newest fly was slipped on the line. How my hands trembled; for each moment I expected a rise. Over the left shoulder flew the line, which, guided by a light touch of the right hand, shot straight as an arrow far across the water. A dull ruffle, an upward motion of the rod, and a good O'Shaughnessy sinks deep in the jaw of a fifteen-pounder at the least. Speaking of one of the smaller rivers, a friend once observed, "Do you call *that* sport? Why the poor beasts cannot turn round in such a ditch." But here no one could complain of wanting space. How these fish fight! Weight and water are all in their favour, and our antagonist made such good use of his personal and natural advantages, that half an hour elapsed before my man got a chance with the gaff, and was able to land as handsome a sixteen-pounder as anyone need desire to see. This agreeable commencement put us all in high spirits. A dark fly succeeded "the parson;" an olive officiated as clerk to his reverence, and was in turn followed by an "orange grouse." Now to go carefully over "the bank" four times, implies a considerable amount of exercise, so we sat to consider what was next to be done. For the last hour Pat had been busily engaged in dressing "an infant phenomenon," which he was, of course anxious to trot out. This, too, failed; and as nothing more could be done, we tied our prize "head and tail," and moved on to the stream below. Hitherto we had been favoured with only a single chance, nor did it seem an easy matter to obtain a second. Under the waving woods adjoining my friend ———'s pretty villa, lay some likely spots, each of which was carefully but vainly tried; and now, here is "Moss Row," as good a "rising throw" as any between the bridge and Beleek. By keeping pretty constant possession, and by dint of hard work, I managed this season to obtain a sort of prescriptive right to the row, and considered myself in some sort as proprietor of the property; but like other potentates, I too had my cares of state.

<blockquote>Uneasy lies the head that wears a crown.</blockquote>

I proved no exception to the rule, for it required the utmost vigilance to maintain and defend my sovereignty. If excitement be a charm in angling. the sport here must be enjoyed in its highest perfection, for friendly rivalry, plots, plans to be formed, and designs to be traversed, keep us constantly on the *qui vive*. Did I relax my watchfulness for a day, another hand was sure to snatch at the reins. Did I fail to take a fish, I was mercifully left in undisturbed possession; but if success attended me, fresh efforts were regularly made to dethrone me on the morrow.

As a general rule, all the casts on the south correspond with those on the opposite side. There are, however, two exceptions—Laputa and the point of the Mullens, both of which belong exclusively to the north shore. Each is excellent, but the latter has a high reputation for holding fish of extraordinary size. That this character is deserved cannot be doubted, and once (I say it with shame) I endured an hour's unutterable anguish whilst watching Capt. M—— kill there a salmon, which weighed between 36lb. and 37lb. In this noble river nothing can be done without constant and deep wading, two or three pools only being fishable from the land, but our professionals are amphibious, and as much at home in the pure element as so many ducks.

Whilst drawing on my boots and getting ready for a turn in "the Row," Willie seats himself under the shade of a friendly thorn, opens the basket, and prepares for half an hour's work. With Pat close at my back, to aid and direct my course, we gain the point whence the stream can be most advantageously commanded. At the third cast a glorious fellow rose and refused the fly, which was allowed to float quietly on, when the line was gathered in by hand, to insure its coming over him again under conditions exactly similar.

"Worn't he a large one?" asked the artist, who, guessing instinctively what had happened, hastily shut his shop, and was now paddling close behind me with "a change." "Shure he *wor* a big one, for I seen his wave roll *up agen* the current. Will we try him with this?" producing his favourite light donkey fur with jungle cockwing. A couple of short casts brought the tackle to its full stretch, and the third sent it light and true to a point from whence the glittering insect must pass over our friend's head on the *turn.*

"Sweet father! but that's nate," remarked Pat, his head admiringly on one side, as the salmon, feeling the point, plunged savagely on the surface for a moment. "Musha, but the crayther's eight-an'-twinty-pounds." He seemed possessed of all the divine fury of an ancient sea-king—now in the air, coming down again with a crash plainly audible above the rush of the river—now rattling along at railroad speed. What an absurd sight we must have presented to any calm philosophical looker-on, reeling, tottering, slipping, splashing, struggling, gesticulating, and all because a poor fish (having taken service with a hard master, by mistake) was now trying to run away. Ten minutes—twenty, thirty—passed, and still the contest raged fiercely as ever.

"Mind him, for yer sowl mind him! Och, the devil mend him; bad luck to that same for a salmon!" screamed Pat, in the wildest state of excitement, as the captive, after a furious race, took an awful perpendicular leap. "He's off; no, he's on!" sprang involuntarily from my lips. I *felt* that for an instant he *was* free. Had there been time I would have staked my last farthing on the truth of that belief. Yet, there he was, firm on the hook, tugging laboriously at the line, seventy or eighty yards above me. But the fight was over. That last rush had broken his heart, and, yielding to the pressure of the rod, he came weltering down the stream. Cautiously avoiding the tackle, Willie placed himself in line, and with his usual quiet skill gaffed as gallant a fish as ever died a death of fame. "I'd have sworn," he said, thrusting his hands into the gills, "that the baste was hooked fair; such a pig, too, and him wid the steel in his side."

After so much excitement, pipes all round were inevitable. As the smoke curled up amongst the green leaves I heard, "Blest if it ain't queer; look at his mouth, Pat." There, over the inferior jaw, was a long rent. Under the great strain the sharp weapon must have cut its way out, but how it had taken a fresh hold was past my wit to explain. I accepted the fact and was satisfied. Whilst meditating on these things, a light step sounded over the shingles, and my friend L—— stood before me. "Look here," he said, pointing in great glee to a particularly handsome gaff in all the splendour of unsullied brass and steel; "I shall not want your unwilling charity again, you niggardly Walter. Here, what do you think of this?"

I could not but admire the implement.

"'Pon my life, though, I wish it was safe back again in Beleek. Rowley was very unwilling to lend, and gave no end of directions about care, and all that sort of thing."

"Why don't you give it to my man, he'll keep it safe. We shall be all together for the rest of the day?"

"What are you going to do next? Is there any one at the 'Captain's Throw?'"

The latter question I could not answer, and, with respect to the former, "I intended to try 'the Row' again, and afterwards follow the stream down towards the town."

"I shall go on, then," he said, "and wait for you at Alt More."

After giving the water sufficient rest, we tried it again and again. But the lodge had been thoroughly upset, and nothing more could be done, so our guide considered it high time to move on and inquire after the fate and fortunes of my friend, more especially as he thought that once or twice suspicious sounds had floated up from his neighbourhood. As we advanced, Mr. Pat was in the act of remarking, "that the captin must be doing something, or never a bit of him would have stayed quiet so long," when a terrific howl cut him short. The start would have done credit to the Great Liverpool. Off we went at score; neck and neck: took a rasping fence at the same moment, floundered through some soft ground, and entered the thicket. Here the guide, who knew the paths, shot ahead, and we paused to catch the direction he had taken.

"Stones, Pat, stones—those ain't big enough—where the deuce is the master? I've been shouting this hour. There's not a bit of skin left on my throat." Guided by the voice, which resembled that of a trumpet labouring under severe catarrh, we soon came up

"Now, now, he's under the rock. Och! murther, Captin, dear, mind the line." Splash, splash, splash, went stones. "He's in; he's out; confound you, throw. No, no; hold hard," were some of the contradictory orders that greeted our arrival at the scene of action; and what a subject for a painter! L——, pale and nervous; Pat, fiery red, from his frantic exertions in turning up morsels of rock. Our position, far above the water, enabled us to see at a glance that my friend had, indeed, found a prize. There he lay, heading the stream, but dead beat; nor was the victor in much better condition, for his white lips and trembling hands marked the extremity of his agitation. Now was the moment, as the fish neared the surface, and, yielding to the steady pressure, edged towards the shore. To seize the gaff and slide down the face of the rock, was to Pat scarcely the work of a moment; a single foot nearer, and he has him. With extended jaws the helpless monster is drawn, inch by inch, closer and closer. Now!—the descending weapon fell short, and scared the quarry, which, with a last laborious effort, paddled a few yards farther from the rock, rolled heavily over, and floated down the stream. Yes, down! for the hook had slipped. I dared not look at the bereaved man, but gazed wistfully at the exhausted salmon as he glided over the smooth yet rapid water, and disappeared in the torrent below. With desperate calmness my unhappy companion reeled up the line, looked at the fly, pronounced all right, handed the rod to Pat, renounced its use for ever, apologised in good set terms for the trouble he had caused us, and professed perfect readiness to return home when it suited me. His misfortune was beyond the reach of sympathy. But Willie had yet his own source of consolation to offer. He held out his pipe—"Take a blast of that, Captain, and may be 'twill settle you."

A silent walk of half an hour is a wonderful restorer of the temper, and by the time we reached Allingham's Point the disconsolate had forgotten his vow, and was again eager as ever once more to try his fortune. Interested in his success, we sat on the bank to watch the result. True flew the line, light fell the fly. About the middle of the cast a fish met it, and after something less than half an hour's very pretty sport I broke the spell by landing a silvery sixteen-pounder. Leaving my friend wonderfully restored and tranquillised, to finish the throw at his leisure, I hastened on to "the Sod Ditch," and close to a sunken rock, was once more successful. The heavy stream and level margin were great odds in my favour, and Mr. S. was soon well under command with the dark line of his back above the water. "Keep off you, sir," to poor Willie, who was calmly waiting his opportunity, "I'm going to land this one," and suiting the action to the word L—— dashed at once into the stream and made towards the fish, which slowly retreated as the enemy advanced. On he marched, up to the knees—over the knees —to mid thigh; now the hips are covered, but at length he stands face to face with the foe. I saw the gaff poised, and "felt" the dull sound of the stab. With a heavy lunge the wounded animal wrenched the smooth and polished handle from his hand. For an instant fly, casting-line, the luckless weapon, the living and the dying, were all "in wild confusion blent." For twenty or thirty yards we watched the polished lignum vitæ shaft whirled round and round, and then vanish. The discomfited hero's look of real distress and comical dismay were irresistible. "Oh, dear! what will Rowley say? Why don't you swear at me? I know you're in a towering rage, and 'twill do you good. You'll feel easier afterwards; why *don't* you swear at me?" Four days after a fine salmon was found dead on the shallows near the town. His size and the great rent through the back assured us that we looked on the immediate cause of the Major's grief and L——'s chagrin.

The afternoon—fulfilling its earlier promise—was throughout intensely hot. Experience, however, had long shown that downright hard work will effect more on the Erne than on any other of the Irish waters. Indeed, the river is a perfect paradox, a sporting contradiction; and it has often been found that days seemingly the most favourable too frequently turn out blanks, and that weather, apparently impracticable, constantly affords first-rate angling. In short, the professionals seldom like to stake their reputation on a promise of success, and the eager and confident, "Well, Pat, this looks something like, generally meets with the damper, "May be it is; your Honour should know best; *but luck's all.*"

CHAPTER XXII.

Ballyshannon—Salmon Leap—White Trout—Evening—The Grass Yard—How Pat was brought to Life—The Colonel Tries on his Boots, and John doth a Tale unfold.

June 23.

The real run of fish in these water, though enormous, is very limited in point of time. Taking the average of different seasons, it may be said to extend from the 1st of June to the end of July: a few hundred stragglers are, however, caught during the next twenty days, and some earlier salmon are secured in May, together with a few in April.

An idea may be formed of the numbers which enter the river from the fact that during the height of the season it is not uncommon to secure six or seven tons a day, the greater part of which are taken in the pool below the falls by draughting. The high grassy banks, which there rise from the water's edge, form a favourite resort of strangers as well as residents, who appear year after year to watch the operation with undiminished interest. Eas-Aodh-Ruaidh, or Red Hugh's Fall, called with more brevity and less dignity "the leap," extends across the entire bed of the river, and at low water has a perpendicular height of 12ft. All fish that pass are safe, for no net ever robs the Erne of its treasures. Thanks to the falls there is always a noble stock to benefit the property and rejoice the sportsman; a stock ever increasing through the season, and only diminished by the angle. In most of the other Irish fisheries the upper waters depend on rain for their supply; but here fresh salmon are continually entering the river, and at spring tides hundreds pass every twenty-four hours. At such times it is highly interesting to watch the desperate efforts of the silvery creatures to leap the barrier as the tide rises. For a few seconds all is still; then, perhaps, a monster bounds from the water and is seen for an instant quivering in the air ere he lights on the very edge of the falls; for a single moment he struggles with the descending torrent, shoots through it like a stream of light, and disappears in the calm deep sheet beyond. As if encouraged by this success forty or fifty, perhaps, dash simultaneously at the cataract. Some succeed, but more fail, to renew their attempts again and again till finally triumphant.

Between this point and the Abbey of Asheroe, where a small stream enters the estuary, there is in August and September very good white trout-fishing, which, however, requires the use of a boat. In May and June large numbers of brown trout, returning from the sea, loiter for a time in the brackish water and afterwards ascend the river. Every day in summer, diminutive boys may be seen seated on the rocks angling for these fish (which run from two to five pounds) with a skill beyond their tender years. They seem to take to it quite naturally; perhaps the art has been transmitted to these urchins from a long series of ancestors famous in all the mysteries of the gentle art. The *regulars* of the Erne, in casting, fly-tying, wading, and patience, are, in my opinion, unrivalled; if to this be added that, as a class, they are a most respectable set of men; I think they may fairly be said to stand at the head of the profession. During the present season the river from Ballyshannon to Beleek is let to nine rods, but I have no warrant for asserting that a similar arrangement will prevail in 1866. The bridge and the pool below, are reserved. . . . . . Dinner is over, and the evening feels less sultry than usual, for a pleasant northerly air curls the stream and whispers hope. As a general rule salmon rise best from 10 a.m. to 4 p.m.; and this remark, which is true of most rivers, is particularly applicable to the Erne. Still many a fish is killed here both earlier and later by the persevering angler, though it may be questioned whether the gain repays the toil.

The broken water above Kathleen's Fall will give us nothing—

Log-a-Thrummain turns a deaf ear to our entreaties—the Angler's Throw sees us wade in vain—in the Sod Ditch two or three heavy fish are rising to please themselves, but refuse to gratify us—Allingham's Point is as quiet as if it had never held a salmon. We are weary, the river is dull, and everything seems flat and unprofitable. Shall we return and join the Colonel, who is thrashing away below, or first try the Grass Yard? Pat thinks our friends have shut up for the evening, Willie rather inclines to the same belief. In my heart I feel they are right; but, being by nature obstinate, cannot confess it. Regularly done, we scrambled along the rough and rocky way, crawled up the bank, and so gained the yard. For once in his life my poor companion took the rod reluctantly, and waded, I fear unwillingly, into the strong stream, to a point that gave him full command of this splendid lodge. Never had he operated so execrably. I should have been sorry to swear he was not fishing in his sleep. "There, that will do; come along. It is no use." Thirty or forty yards higher up the evening breeze faintly ruffled the flat, near a low ledge (fantastically carved by the winter floods) where occasionally we had succeeded. "Give me the rod, I'll take a throw there before we go." My tired comrade listlessly went through the ceremony of presentation, and I delivered the kind of cast a man is apt to make, when faint and hopeless. From sheer laziness the fly was played close to the rock, where a spanking salmon sailed quietly up and took it. I saw the fair deceiver disappear within his jaws, opened like two white arms to receive her, and, completely surprised, forgot courtesy—my great obligations—all the proprieties in short—and struck him rudely and furiously. A loud crack announced that the full penalty of violated laws had overtaken me, for the ill-used rod had snapped short off about six feet from the point. It fell, however, into hands which could be relied on in any emergency. The butt and wheel came necessarily into my department, and by keeping the broken parts as nearly as possible in one line we managed "the runs" very satisfactorily. Once before, a similar accident befel us, on which occasion we passed through the trying ordeal with credit. The water was still and deep, the ground favourable, and each moment our hopes rose higher and higher. Had Pat been at his post, once already he might have been secured. "Pat, Pat, where are you? Pat, Pat, hullo-o-o." It was like calling "spirits from the vasty deep;" my tricksy familiar heeded not. 'Twas too bad. "Here's another chance." In the midst of a furious tirade against poor Patsy, by good luck I stumbled over the gaff, kicked it to the delighted Willie, who, in a second afterwards, with an indescribable grin (his nearest approach to any outward manifestation of pleasure), landed a fish of $21\frac{1}{2}$ lbs.; and in another minute we stood over the deserter, stretched at full length on the shingles fast asleep, in happy unconsciousness. Anathemas had not disturbed him, vows of vengeance had not broken his rest, which would probably have lasted till morning had not some malicious person recalled him to a sense of his degraded situation by tickling his nostrils with the tail of "a cold, moist, unpleasant body." On our return we found the Colonel near Kathleen's Fall, winding up for the night.

"Well, Walter, you really work like a horse, and ought sometimes to get your corn. Come and rest. 'Tis a cool, delicious evening. I say, Pat, let me look at those boots." Taking a pair of Cording's stockings in his hand, he continued, "Light and admirably efficient; there were no such things when I commenced my career here five and thirty years ago. Heavy leather inconveniences were the thing then; take a cigar, and hear what once happened to me just at this place, on such an evening as this, in the far off days when, tough and active as a gorilla, I hooked a 17lb. salmon. After two or three heavy runs he flew down the stream, when it became instantly necessary to head, and close with him before the torrent twisted the slack amongst the rocks. In floundering to the bank I was soon up to my waist, and as may easily be conceived, six or seven pounds of water on each leg were heavy odds against winning the race. Still it *was* won, and in fifteen minutes my antagonist was dead beat and safely landed by Mike—he's dead and gone now— who was at that time my attendant and backer; and to do him justice a better fellow never handled a gaff. After an exulting whoop I lit a cigar with infinite satisfaction, pulled off my boots, poured out the water, and hung myself out to dry, here above Kathleen's Fall. Carelessly casting the line as I sat dangling my legs over the water, the fly was instantly taken by a regular rasper. I was up in a second. Mike was utterly bothered by such an unusual combination of circumstances; a lodge, where our salmon was safe not to remain five minutes, bare feet, and two hundred yards of the sharpest and most broken rocks in all Ireland on the very course he was sure to take, and that, too, at a pace requiring the utmost exertions of an active man to keep up with. 'Holy Mary,' he exclaimed, in an agony of despair, 'oh, Holy Mary,' what a murthering sin, and him, too, so big! the ould rogue, bad luck to him, we'll be bate entirely.' 'The boots Mike, the boots!' I roared, with an energy corresponding to the excitement of mind and anguish of body. Had I gone barefoot on a pilgrimage to Loretto, I could not have suffered half so much. Poor Mike pulled manfully at the reeking leather in the almost hopeless endeavour to get it on, whilst I kicked like a madman to help him. 'Hould him, hould him, your honour!' and faith it was time, for the fish was within six inches of the edge of the torrent. By great good luck he turned and shot up the water like an arrow; we breathed again, and for a moment felt secure. By desperate struggling and pulling we contrived at length to get one boot on and the other partly so; but a rebellious fold still held out in spite of our superhuman endeavours; whish, whish, wh-i-s-h, groaned the wheel: 'he's over,' and away we went, tumbling, scrambling, jumping, slipping, and recovering, bruised and breathless. The gallant foe made one vain effort to head the stream. Those few seconds enabled me to come up and bring him under the rod. It was now ten to one on the fly, and in a few minutes after Mike landed a splendid fellow of three-and-twenty pounds."

Many a star was shining in the deep blue sky, and the moon had risen over Stonewall, yet the commander showed no intention of breaking up his bivouac.

"Is that Causan-a-Mhanaigh where the moonlight rests, John?" —to his squire.

"Faith, then, it is the Monk's Path; and the best o' raisons why it should be called the same." Here John seated himself on an opposite fragment of rock, with an air half solemn, half mysterious. I saw he was in the legendary vein; so, charging the meerschaum, I resigned myself to the infliction.

"In ould ancient times in the mountains beyant, there lived a raal gintleman, Ruaidh O'Rooke. Now, Ruaidh, your honour, was a wild slip of a boy who spent his time between gamin', dancin', huntin', drinkin', fightin', and the girls; and it chanced somehow, quare enough, that he spint all his money too. Now, Sir Phalim, the master's elder brother, was not sich a gentleman as Ruaidh at all, at all. Not a pin cared he for the ladies—seeing he was married; so for that matther was the master—and as to dogs, not a sowl of 'em dared wag a tail in his company but one ould wolf-hound, a great favourite, d'ye see. His only divarsions were readin' in a big book, as dull and silent as himself, or stalkin' over the hills with Dhugh (for that was the baste's name) at his back. Now, seein' the master spint all and Sir Phalim not a copper, small blame to him for borrowing what what was no use in life to his brother. But when the scholar came to know it, och, blood and turf, but he gets into a tunderin' passion, bade him begone, and make a fortin as good as he'd marred. Yer honour may take your book oath the master didn't lave his blessin' behind him. Mary stand atween us and evil—wasn't there a too-roo that night at the castle! Such murtherin', screechin', and yellin', rampin' and tearin', howlin' and moanin'—the Lord be good to us! Not a mother's son closed an eye, and when mornin' came there was the big book, but devil a sign of Sir Phalim or his dog. All this was mighty strange. At last the praist, with the tooth of St. Bridget, knocks at his door; and who but the raal clargy dare venter? All was still, and his riverence lifts the latch, and sure he'd been kilt entirely savin' the relic; for there lay Sir Phalim with a black mark round his neck, stiff and cold, and the dumb baste by his side cryin' like any other Christian. In course of time the master was found, and mighty pale he turned with grief, and mighty fond he got of his brother's wee daughter, and a beautiful crathur she grew, and all the world knew that she was to have her uncle's eldest son, for the great fortin, says he, came by her and should go to her. But the lady lived in the heart of the youngest, and loved a fond glance of his eye more nor all the lands of the other; which, as yer honour knows, was very parvarse. When the master came to know it he wasn't mighty well pleased you may be sure; so he founded that abbey yonder for the glory of God, and piously made his younger son prior of the same, and there stands the old walls this blessed minute. But the lovely lady, as bright as the moonlight, took sick and was like to die, till, night after night, unknown to a sowl, the prior crossed this spot to comfort the sick, and before the eye of the mornin' was opened, stole back to his convent to hide his Christian charity. The lady recovered, and for love of holy Church came evermore to this place with his riverence to receive his blessin'. One morn she niver returned, for the monk was found drowned in the ford, and the maiden cold and dead where the Colonel is sittin'. Thus your honour sees how, all along of Sir Phalim not livin' as a gintleman ought, nor lendin' his money, the devil flew away wid him; a swate young crathur broke her heart, a holy saint was drowned, and how evermore this strame was called Causan-a-Mhanaigh, or the Monk's Path."

I looked wistfully at the deep and dark river; the time, the place, the faith of the narrator, and the simple tale of love and murder, produced their full effect; and I am ashamed to own how often that night I thought of the ill-starred monk and hapless maid.

CHAPTER XXIII.

The Colonel takes Command of an Expedition—Through many Dangers we arrive safely at Beleek, and troll on the Lake for anything we can catch—After Mess the Crew cut their Sticks, but subsequently return to Duty—A desperate Character—Westward Ho!

June 27.

My stout old friend the Colonel, though fast verging towards the fatal "three score years and ten," is yet hale and hearty; place him in a boat, and he will work as well as the youngest; but he finds the world rougher than it used to be, and detests all unnecessary pedal locomotion. Without

Larding the lean earth as he walks along,

the commander yet agrees with honest old Jack, that "eight yards of uneven ground is three score and ten miles a foot with me," and in this mood proposed, as we strolled towards the town, that we should visit Lough Erne. To me his wish is law. So it was settled then and there, under the quiet stars, that we should start early on the following morning for Beleek, and declare war against the trout and pike.

We had been busily engaged in preparing tackle for the expedition; had finished the morning meal; packed up a basket of provender; and yet it was not eight o'clock, at which hour the Colonel had covenanted to be at my door with chariot and horse. With him "promise" and "perform" were synonymous, and, as I conjectured, on the last stroke of the hour he drove up. What a conscience that man must have, to expect one wretched animal to drag a lady, five stout men, three baskets, and two heavy hampers all the way to Beleek! But so it was to be. With the exception of the Colonel, we walked up the steep street, and then rolled heavily along the old road, past the pretty villa of Laputa—by heath and moorland—by rock and coppice; came to a stand from a fractured trace, near the hospitable Mullens; repaired damages, and, passing "the point," wound our slow way up the opposite hill, and there fairly broke down. Brought thus to a stand, we paused to look about us. Around lay an extensive planting of Scotch and larch firs, filling the morning air with their sweetness. Our position enabled us to trace the road we had hitherto followed; to see many a comfortable cottage with slated roof and well-glazed windows, each one a panegyric on the owner of the property; whilst far below, the river, rushing through wooded and overhanging banks, toiled and raved with unceasing din, foaming on in beautiful variety, till it swept round the Mullens and was lost to our gaze. Under a heavy press of rods, baskets, cloaks, and hampers, we staggered into the little hamlet of Beleek, once famous as a military station, commanding the passage between Fermanagh and Donegal, and now illustrious as possessing an admirable fisherman's rest, where some of "ours" usually take up their quarters. Under the south wall of this pleasant hostelry, the mighty river—like a boy let loose from school—laughs, leaps, and tumbles, and within less than fifty yards of the door are the falls of which such honourable mention is made by "The Angler in Ireland," as the scene of his most killing days. Whilst the boat was being prepared, we strolled to the little bridge, under whose low solitary arch rush the whole surplus waters of the lake. This is the narrowest part of the Erne, which, for the space of ten or twelve yards, cannot be above twenty feet wide; but the depth of its rocky bed is unknown. Not far from this spot we embarked, and pulled away over the widening water to the lake.

Lough Erne lies almost entirely in Fermanagh, which it loves so well, as to traverse the county from end to end. Passing diagonally through its whole length, it offers a greater extent of internal navigation than any other of the Irish lakes. Even many of the larger streams which empty themselves into it, are used by the flat-bottomed boats of the country for two or three miles of their course. Moving tranquilly over the bosom of the lake, we confessed few scenes could be more lovely. Of course, it cannot be compared for a moment with Killarney ; yet here, perhaps, imagination has greater room to weave her pleasant spells. Winding amidst mountains, not a tenth part of it can be seen at once ; each fresh reach as it opens produces something unlike that which preceded it—here a cluster of islets, mere fantastic rocks—there some sweet and quiet spot covered with emerald turf, gay with flowers, and dotted with sheep—now a rich flat completely hidden by a growth of luxuriant timber ; then an island farm, a little world in itself, with its patch of grain. tethered cow, and shaggy goat.

In these matter of fact days the spirit of romance, banished from every other corner of the empire, seems here to have found a congenial resting-place in the bosoms of the people, whence it peeps out in a thousand ways—in a passionate love of old places, old names, and old burial grounds—and the stranger seated in his "cot" is even yet *occasionally* startled from his reverie as the

Loud " Wul-wulleh " warns his distant ear.

The next reach, perhaps, shows him a funeral procession gliding over the calm water, and the long thrilling howl breaks louder on his ear as the corpse is borne along, to be laid in kindred dust, side by side with the bones of those, whose actions and whose memories are so "dangerously dear" to the heart of the Irish peasant.

That part of Lough Erne south-east of Inniskillen is called the upper, and that towards Beleek the lower lake. The former is narrow, full of islands, rather shallow, not exceeding fifty feet in any part ; whilst the latter is a much finer sheet of water, having in some places a depth of from 200 to 230 feet ; but this, however, in common with other lakes, is varied and irregular. The shores on the southern side are bold and romantic, stretching further than the eye can follow—in alternate moor, moss, and mountain—till they join the extensive highland ranges of Cavan and Leitrim. In winter the west winds are so violent as to render the navigation of the lake a source of great danger, but to-day they slept as if they would never wake again, and many a beautiful cutter yacht, with all sails spread, hardly owned the influence of the light and fitful air.

This huge lake has been called the Windermere of Ireland; and of all the wrongs inflicted by the Saxon on this much-complaining land, *this* is about the greatest and most tangible. Windermere, indeed! Well, the love of country is praiseworthy, but not when it makes a man tell fibs. Possibly the comparison was meant as a compliment; we hope so, and must pardon the infatuation, for the sake of the intention. Lough Erne does not offer one dull or uninteresting view. Round its whole shores beauty reigns everywhere; slopes, the fairest and greenest, rise from its margin; finely wooded promontories stretch far into its bosom, forming calm inlets and peaceful bays; the islands are unrivalled in loveliness, and number about one hundred and eighty.

At its eastern end stands Devenish, known far and wide for its ruins and graceful round tower, the most perfect in the kingdom. This mysterious edifice seems as fresh as the day in which unknown hands laid the last stone. Over each loophole or window, immediately under the cornice, rests a fine sculptured head. How many centuries have these silent watchers looked out on the inconstant world around? The iron horse snorts near, and noble mansions have risen, owned by a new race. How lonely the grey old seers must feel; there is nothing to remind them of the far-off time when they were young, By day they are silent; under the starry sky, which is also unchanged, do they hold converse on what was, what is, and is to be. If Mr. Home would throw one of these old gentlemen into a clairvoyant state, and make him tell us all he knew, I should perhaps believe there was something in his science after all.

It is too bad to leave my party so long. Here I am at the east end of Lough Erne, whilst my friends are at the opposite extremity. Well, I must once more take an oar, and tug that savage old Colonel, who is growling like an ancient "grizzly," to the ground. He tells me the various races in this watery realm do not live on amicable terms; that the trout stand on their gentility, and will not associate with the bream; that the perch fall out with the roach, and the pike are universally detested. Yet my old friend troubles not himself about these intestine divisions, but is eagerly selecting the best of our tackle, with such haste that I occasionally hear him asking John to extract a hook from his jacket, or beseeching Willie to take "that confounded barb" out of his finger. In the construction of these trolling traces we have made allowance for "jack," the trebles being tied on six inches of fine gimp—and—there goes the Colonel's first venture.

Having resolved on giving a public dinner, we issued a general invitation, and by a liberal *carte* hope to please all. Over the stern twirls a delicate roach and an artificial minnow; from either quarter revolves a colliogh and a small spoon; and, grace being said, we wait patiently for the expected guests.

"Hullo! you there," bawled the Colonel, whose line from the headway of the boat was running at a rate which soon threatened to bring it to an end. "Stop—back—why the deuce don't you back? Back as hard as you can!" The fulfilment of these orders restored to my friend much of his cordage and more of his temper. Something heavy was on the rod, but whether salmon, trout, or pike was uncertain. Presently we caught sight of the overhanging brows and sinister aspect of the latter, who was satisfactorily disposed of shortly after. Next the spoon came into favour, and ladled out perch after perch with great celerity. Then the fickle goddess again sat in the stern sheets, and gave the veteran another stout pike of 8lb., and a trout of 3lb.; and so we fished and chatted till the soldier protested it was high time for tiffin, when we pulled in for a piece of lawny turf, where kindly nature had already pitched a marquee for our use, which by a careless observer might have been mistaken for a sycamore. No picnic can be a success without a fire; ours soon smouldered, and gradually arrived at cooking order. Fillets were cut from the best pike; our trout had the honour of a spit to himself; and a 2lb. perch was given up to the Colonel. How scientifically he conducted each stage in the delicate operation! First, some wood cinders were placed on a flat stone, and the fish laid thereon; next, the upper surface was dotted all over with small morsels of butter; then cayenne was liberally dusted over the whole; and a trifle of salt, with *just a suspicion* of flour, brought the dish to its culminating point. What a first course it was! Oh, ye sons of luxury, who, after a muttered grace (for the sake of the children), sit down to anathematise the soup, growl at the fishmonger, swear at the butcher, vow vengeance on your poulterer, and consign your particular cook to a place hotter than the kitchen fire—had you *but* been with us at our cheerful meal, would you have sneered at our grateful acceptance of so many good things? Probably you would.

Our party consisted of an old man, a gentle lady, a poor angler, and four or five humble followers, whose united dinner costume could not have been worth a pound. Would you have liked the company? I fear your magnificence would have despised our simplicity; your wisdom, our folly; so we are better without you, and may proceed with our meal without fear of criticism. Our crockery was not what it ought to have been. The hosts were only allowed a willow-pattern plate each; but the comfort of the company was carefully attended to—every man having a good supply of those necessary articles, green in colour, beautiful in shape, and bearing a strong likeness to the shining leaves of the *Rumex aquaticus*. After fish came a fore-quarter of kid, a hind one of lamb, a couple of chickens, tongue, and two mighty tarts, which, being disposed of, the party drank and were merry. The poor angler before mentioned brewed a pint of coffee for his own special use, while John placed two bottles of Bass's India ale within a convenient distance of his master, who, lighting a cigar about five inches long by three in circumference, resigned himself to calm contemplation. Near us were several grassy earthworks known as *raths*, or Danish camps; the latter name very probably a misnomer, as they are found in numberless places where those northern rovers are believed never to have penetrated. It is therefore more natural to suppose they were thrown up by each clan round their wigwams, as a defence against any sudden attack from an enemy. Such forts are met with all over the island, near the coast, far from the sea, in valleys and on hills, and were, in all probability, the strongholds of barbarians whose lives were passed either in carrying off other people's goods or defending their own.

All sublunary things will come to an end if we have but patience, and so at last did the Colonel's cigar; but the sun was now shining in his might, and the lake glowed like a sheet of molten silver. A council of war being summoned, returned a unanimous verdict that nothing could be done except with ground bait. The Colonel here came out strong, and spoke something in this wise : The first great object of fishing was to take fish; if they would behave in a gentlemanly way, and feed on the surface, well; but if they refused what was offered to them on the top, try the bottom. The second important design of angling, he continued, was to produce health. Now, what tended so much to nervous and physical integrity as a cheerful frame of mind? and what was more calculated to make a man at peace with himself and the world around, than success? If they won't take fly or troll, give them the worm. These opinions being adopted by acclamation, all hands set eagerly to work—hazel wands were cut and trimmed, and bait collected; whilst Willie opened a rural kind of "store," and gave out gut, bad hooks, wax, and split shot, to the ship's company. Keeping near the shore, in six or seven feet of water, half a dozen sections of cork—once the property of Messrs. Bass or Guinness—soon dotted the surface of the lake, for a moment or two lay motionless, and then commenced dipping and diving in quick succession. The perch were our first guests; then came in a bream shaped like a pair of bellows, and nearly as large as one of the fancy articles often seen hanging in a lady's drawing-room; then some little trout, bright as if they had dined on a sunbeam. Hitherto the Colonel had not exchanged a single shot with the enemy; but now he was fiercely attacked. With the point of his light trout-rod bent to the butt, the gallant veteran resisted all the assaults of his foe. Tug, tug, tug! What can it be? John, who had been peering into the water, averred that though the creature was kicking up a great dust at the bottom, he caught a glimpse of something at least three feet long. My friend opined it was a red salmon, or the devil. Little by little he neared the surface, and lo! 'twas a huge eel, which I netted, and showed some little common sense by cutting the gut before turning him loose amongst the feet of the company. What a rookrawn he produced—racing hither and thither—playing all manner of slippery tricks, gliding between the legs of one, and through the hands of another, gallantly refusing to yield, though surrounded by foes. The crew were in despair. John crossed himself devoutly. A certain little lady and the dear old commander, standing on a beam, were nearly capsized in the confusion, which at length happily terminated by one of the boatmen jamming the desperado against a timber, and decapitating him. After this, grog was served out to the entire ship's company, who again went to work with fresh energy; nor did they cease till the poor sun, sick of our world, plunged desperately into the ocean.

That night the well of the car was filled with the spoils, which consisted of seven or eight pike, a stone or two of rough fish, and over all—laid out in state—was the great eel, which must have been very flavoury, if the taste bore any ratio to the smell. The day had been delightful—metaphorically and almost literally without a cloud, and the Colonel warmly pressed us to join him in another expedition to Lough Erne and also in one to Lough Melvin. But the rosy month of June was fast passing away, and I, already due on the Moy, was compelled to decline what it would have given me so much pleasure to accept.

During my too short sojourn of three weeks, the sport had been excellent—not so much, however, in point of numbers as with respect to weight. True, we had worked hard, often making

> The night joint labourer with the day;

had our disappointments, blank days, and accidents; but then we had twenty-eight fish to show, amongst which were only two small ones, of 6lb. and 8lb. respectively. In no other river in Ireland could salmon so uniformly fine have been secured by the rod, nor do I know any other station where so much could have been done during so adverse a season. The great and *comparatively* unvarying volume of water—the heavy runs—the large and constant supply of fresh fish, all contributed to this happy consummation. During a somewhat long acquaintance with the Erne, my three best days (in point of number) produced only nine, six, and five salmon, and with the first even of these very moderate figures, the fly, I am sorry to confess, had little to do. If a friend will pardon me for expressing my feeling and experience in his words : " I would rather kill a salmon at the Bank of Ireland or the Grass Yard, than in any other throw which dwells in my memory. The Erne is, for its length, as varied and delightful a river as I know, and contains every variety of cast. Good fishing, great perseverance, with perhaps the least dash of luck in the world, are required to succeed well on it. Great bags are seldom made, but the *quality* of the sport, when you can get it, is A 1." Thus writes Mr. Francis Francis. Every word is true, just, and discriminating.

Kind hands were shaken—we earnestly hope, not for the last time—the luggage was packed, and early on the following morning we rolled over the long bridge ; cast a lingering look at the pool, where many a widening ring reminded us of happy hours and former triumphs, and, passing through the Purt, were soon speeding towards the pretty seaside village of Bundoran, on our westward course.

CHAPTER XXIV.

Ballysidere—Its Fishery and Fishing.

June 30.

How soon the present glides down into the past. How rapidly our periodical literature grows old, changes its name, becomes condensed, and takes rank as history. Even the condition of our rivers prior to the late Act—a thing of yesterday—is already being forgotten ; and how little is known of earlier legislation, designed for the common good; or of the long course of suicidal evasions of those laws which reduced our rivers to the brink of ruin. But this is a hackneyed theme; those evil days are past, and are now matter of history, so we will lay the volume on the shelf, whence hereafter it may be taken, dusty, discoloured, and worm-eaten, to furnish subjects for congratulation to those who live in happier times, when our waters yield their increase, and salmon shall be sold for threepence a pound. When that period arrives, men whose present labours are now lightly regarded, will be held up as public benefactors, whose philanthropy and wisdom entitle them to the grateful remembrance of posterity.

Half a century ago angling for salmon was so little practised that few persons, except those resident in favoured localities, knew anything about it; and, only forty years since rod fishing was held in such small account that our Acts contained *no clause whatever* for its regulation. In fact, there is as much fashion in recreation as there is in dress, and angling at present is undoubtedly the newest mode. Twenty years ago boys were content with football, marbles, rounders, or cricket; and when they went to Cambridge or the sister university, boating was so "exigant" that it became *the* passion. But *now*, contemporaneously with the first suit, comes home the first outfit for the juvenile disciple of Old Izaak, who shoulders his basket, and, on half-holidays, goes as regularly to the nearest water as did the youth of an earlier generation to the cricket field or the tennis court. What would one of these ardent young spirits say, if he knew that when *his* father was engaged at a solemn game of leapfrog, the law took so little care of the interests of upper proprietors that the salmon harvest was reaped only at the mouths of rivers; that such rights were alone deemed worthy of protection; and that a fresh fish on the higher spawning grounds was almost as much a *rara avis* as a bustard now is on Salisbury Plain? Probably "my old governor has been," he would remark, "paying two and nine per pound all his life, and it sarves him right." That is one way to speak of the subject. Another is, that having neglected or squandered our substance, we must endure the penalty. Happily punishment has produced repentance, and repentance newness of life. Let us, however, remember that good resolutions are *nil* without a patient continuance in well doing.

About four miles beyond the town of Sligo the great western road runs through the village and close to the river of Ballysidere, and along this route our party posted gaily early in the morning of the last day of June. I had often passed this pretty stream, and always regretted my inability to spend a few hours on its banks; now, however, with time at my disposal, I looked forward with eager anticipation to a day on an untried water. But over and above the charm of wandering over ground previously unknown was another source of interest, the fishery itself, which may be considered an illustration of what fish cultivation can effect.

Eleven years since Ballysidere could hardly be said to have had an existence as a fishery. A few salmon and trout scramble over the falls and reach the spawning grounds, to form a nucleus on which skill and enterprise were soon about to act. In 1854 or 1855 ladders were erected, and now mark the results. During the first season 18 fish were taken; in the following year 203; and, as the excellent manager said, "every subsequent one grew better and better." By the 29th of June, 1863—a very early date, be it observed—522 fish were on the books, and by the 3rd of July, 1865— with four or five of the best weeks yet to come—the numbers were 1482. Thus a fishery has been created in a period not exceeding eleven or twelve years. Here, indeed, is a bright example of what can be effected; an example which should be held up for the encouragement of all who possess water rights. Were such proprietors animated only by commercial views, what golden realities are before them; but if influenced by higher considerations, what benefactors, might they not become to the age in which they live. I have spoken of Ballysidere merely as a fishery, as a light set on a hill, which *ought* not to be hid; so trust the present owner will forgive me, and pardon the unauthorised liberty which has been taken with his property, for the sake of the spirit that prompted the remarks.

During the present campaign we have not made the acquaintance of a single white trout. The season is still early, and a month must yet elapse before they make their appearance in the great majority of our streams, but here—partly deceived by our own enthusiasm—we were induced to believe they had arrived long since. Probably every reader knows that as there are spring and summer salmon, so also are there spring and summer trout, which last occupy to each other exactly the same relations as exist between the spring fish and the grilse. As few rivers *at present* hold early salmon, so also few contain early trout, though the latter, however, extend over a wider range than the former. The excellence, beauty, strength, and courage of these creatures render them special favourites with all anglers, and it was the hope of enjoying a morning in their society that chiefly made me so anxious to visit Ballysidere; not, however, that my expectations were limited to these, as I knew there were always plenty of grilse in the water after the first fresh in June. If I add that the terms for angling are extremely moderate—half-a-crown for a single venture, or one pound per month, together with a fish each day, I think my duty to the public has been done handsomely, and that I may now go my way in peace.*

The Ballysidere (formed by the union of the Awinmore and the Arrow, which unite near the town of Collooney), after leaping over a succession of limestone ledges, thunders in a beautiful cascade into the west-south-west corner of Sligo Bay. Our first glance at the water showed us that it was neither high nor low. A light northeast breeze just curled the surface, and ever and anon a great fleecy cloud passed over the sun, making altogether a very pleasant combination. The selection of flies could not occupy much time, as our entire stock—tied on the previous night—only consisted of five; three diminutive articles for the "springers"—we expected, but did not find—and two very small ones for grilse. Mounting our favourite black palmer, as dropper, we looped on the trail, whose prominent

---

* The river, together with a pretty cottage, is now, I *believe*, to be let to one or two rods. Terms, 100*l.* per annum.

features were undyed seal's fur and jungle cock wing, and with these we made a preliminary cast in a state of mind any anointed king " under the canopy " might have envied.

I know not how it is, but the first day on a new water always seems a success. Perhaps we are more than usually disposed to be pleased, perhaps we work harder; but however this may be, fortune soon smiled upon us.

"There he was, you didn't see him," quietly observed my companion, who, standing close to my left shoulder, watched the water with his usual gravity, whilst his careless master was gazing upwards at a heavy woolpack, speculating how long it would be ere the soft white mass must cross the sun.

"What was it; did you catch a glimpse of him?"

"Maybe 'twas a trout, may be a shy fish; but we'll change the trail anyhow. It wor a very small break, but mortal quick."

In a moment the second fly was on, and the edge of the cloud just touched the sun as the line dropped lightly on the stream a few yards above the spot where the stranger lay; the next cast came fairly over him. There was a slight ripple and a delicious feeling of tension —my fingers tingle even now with the remembrance—a desperate race over the shallow, and such a bound!—oh, who would not be an angler?

"I think he is hooked foul, master, for I seen something black and white, like a jungle cock, a sticking on his side."

Fair or foul, we were in for a race. Our tackle was as light as it could well be, and the employment of force impossible. Now, galloping along with an active fresh-run grilse at the end of your line, is not quite so easy a condition of things as at first sight might appear, for the rod must constantly be maintained in position, and the eyes of the angler ought to be fixed on two different points at one and the same time, which is not a feat easy of execution unless he squints horribly. If his attention be exclusively directed to the water, he is in momentary danger of a grand downfall, which is safe to eventuate in irremediable ruin. If, on the other hand, he neglects the movements of the fish, and is too careful about his own, the wrong-headed party is sure to take the *other* side of some post, boulder, or islet, and so Piscator comes to grief. With Scylla on the right and Charybdis on the left, we endeavoured to steer a middle course; but the ship was not well under command, was running at an awful rate, and, moreover, there were rocks ahead. In plain language, we were all three tearing along as hard as we could. Mr. Grilse led, seemingly as fresh as ever. Rod followed next, puffing and blowing; and Gaff brought up the rear, blown. But the worst remains to be told. There was a stiff fence in the way which must be dealt with in the next half minute, unless the fish turned. To get anything more out of Willie was impossible, as he was doing his best; so, putting on a desperate spurt in order to recover as much of the line as was possible, I dashed at the bank; was too done to reach the crest, came heavily with my chest against the top, and rolled over into the ditch on the other side. Staggering to my feet, sky, earth, and river whirled before my eyes; whilst a doleful voice seemed singing in my ears, "My fut is jammed in a root, not a toe can I stir; sorra take him for a salmon; we'll be run out and broke entirely; oh! worra-worra." Instinctively I stretched out my hand for the butt, and once more took up the running. Fortunately, the pace grew less severe, and in the next pool the fugitive came to a halt. The speed had told, and the tackle, light as it was, now became fully equal to the strength of the exhausted fish. With one shoe on and the other left in the furze, my trusty comrade limped up.

"The toes is off me, and my fut's all in a jelly," as he slipped the steel under the grilse; "but this pays for all. Will I ever find the shoe?"

In the act of falling, the rod had been jerked out of my hand, but luckily dropped on a bush, where it lay with the wheel, clear, but revolving at a fearful rate, till Willie came up and once more set things right. In his hurry to cross, one foot had for the moment become firmly wedged, when fortunately I, in turn, came to the rescue in the nick of time. The poor fellow must have tugged desperately to wrench himself out of the trap, as we found a portion of the stocking still in the leather, from which by main force he had screwed out the imprisoned member.

In a salmon river, where one fish lodges there are sure to be others; so we trudged back to the point from which we started, and worked over the water for the second time.

"That's remarkable nate—un-common illigant," in a pleased soliloquy, as a short stout fish, feeling the steel, executed a perpendicular leap, quivering for an instant high in air. "Thim trouts is fit to do a'most anything. Murther, but he's at it agen." A vigorous fish of this species is, weight for weight, stronger than a salmon, and requires delicate handling—not that I mistrusted the little black palmer, for O'Shaughnessy is always true; yet there was considerable uncertainty as to the "catch" being sufficient. Minute after minute passed, and at length the captive found all his strength barely sufficient to enable him to keep his head under water. Gradually the broad tail worked more and more feebly over the surface. Now he is almost within reach of a gaff that never strikes in vain, and now his race is run.

Laying down the rod, I walked up to my companion who was stooping over the fish with an aspect in which astonishment and mortification were ludicrously blended.

"It arn't one after all, master."

"What *is* it then?" for the speaker stood between me and the prize.

"He's only a grilse."

Imagination within proper limits is doubtless an excellent quality, but ours had been boundless; we expected to find spring trout in the river, and information correctly given, but imperfectly understood, completed the delusion. The error, however, was mine—fancy converted a fallacy into a fact—a well made summer salmon into a spring trout.

Subsequently we learned that this water does not contain these fish, a few small summer trout excepted, which rarely attain a greater weight than three quarters of a pound. Although the renewal of our acquaintance with the white trout, had been thus unexpectedly delayed, we may, whilst on the subject, say a few words about them. In some rivers possessing large head waters these fish attain a considerable size. At Waterville, for example, they are often taken in the cuts in February, weighing 10lb. and 11lb.; and at Delphi, I have *heard*, they are occasionally caught up to the unusual weight of 16lb. Nothing so good as this ever came in my way, and the heaviest I have yet killed did not exceed 8lb.

"Jack's Hole," "The Mill Race," "The Iron Hole," and many another, had all been tried; there was a delicious uncertainty about every cast, and we fished on with unabated spirit. At last we reached a beautiful lodge—the name of which I know not—and presently "stuck" in a grilse, which, being fairly hooked, fought valiantly and died like a gentleman. In five minutes more I was fast on another, and at

The high topgallant of my joy,

when a small silvery voice struck terror to my heart.

"Arrah, Willie, do ye call this dacent behaviour, and the mistress all alone wid herself, bating the two kars and the drivers, waiting in the road for an hour?" Now, mademoiselle was a linguist; at least she spoke what might be called two languages—remarkably pure Saxon and remarkably impure patois; all of which, as contained in the above oration, was of course designed for me, though addressed to my companion. For once in his life that "hereditary bondsman" lost his habitual fear of petticoat tyranny.

"Hist, hist, arn't ye ashamed; going on this way and the master so busy? *We'll no come*—mind I'm telling ye . . . that is, no just at present," as a terrible finger was held up in menace and warning—lower sank his courage under that steady glance. "Well, well, we'll be wid ye directly;" and then, *sotto voce*, "The devil fly away wid ye for a scolding jade."

Retaining a small grilse as provision for the journey, we sent the rest of our take to Mr. Hepburn, the manager, by a sure hand, and bade adieu to the bright and beautiful Arrow. It was the first, but not the last visit, we trust; for I hope soon to shake that worthy man by the hand, and thank him in person for a letter recently received, which does honour alike to the employer and the employed.

We had a long journey before us, and the sun, though still in his splendour, was yet trending low towards the north-west. Nothing could exceed the dreariness and desolation of the country through which we passed. Interminable plains of dark morass stretched on all sides; here and there a black and sluggish stream stagnated in its slow course to the sea. Not a mountain relieved the tameness of the view; it was desolation without grandeur. Now and then on the edge of the swamp appeared a cluster of miserable hovels, without chimney, without window; the walls formed of loose stones rudely piled together, through every chink and cranny of which the smoke stole forth, and the elements held season tickets of admission.

As the cars rattled along through "a town," a posse of meagre curs would rush out, followed by a troop of half-naked, semi-barbarous urchins vociferating in sharp querulous voices, "Penny—give us a penny, your honour—a penny, only a penny beautiful lady—only a penny, your ladyship's honour." The ardour of the dogs soon went out; expecting no remuneration for *their* trouble, the quadrupeds—wisely determining to keep the little flesh they possessed on their bones—slackened their pace and were gradually distanced. But there was no beating the boys. Occasionally the coveted coin was pitched dexterously into the bog, in the hope of escaping during the search. As it flew through the air a universal charge was made at the ditch, and the prize marked down. Then a race, a scramble, and a fierce fight succeeded, and again the whole pack, at a killing pace, were once more in full cry—"A penny, a penny, good gentleman—a penny, a penny, your ladyship's honour." Thus accompanied, we rolled on, the light-limbed urchins easily keeping up with the cars till we reached the next cluster of cabins, where a fresh relay was ready, took up the cry, fought, howled, coaxed, and wheedled till the proximity of the next hamlet drove *them* from our trail, and gave us for a prey to foes as ruthless as the last.

On we sped, past Screen and across the Easkey. Gradually the sun went down, the crimson light faded to a delicate rose tint, and then all was grey. Here and there over the waste a momentary blaze lit up the solitary pane in some mud hut; deeper and deeper grew the twilight; and, ere the lamps of Ballina shone out into the darkness, mistress and maid, master and man, had wended far into the drowsy realms of the Land of Nod.

CHAPTER XXV.

Ballina—The Tideway.

July 7.

BALLINA! What pleasant remembrances will this name summon back, perhaps, to some hard-worked denizen of the metropolis. It may remind him of his short but unforgotten holiday, and, as he sits brain-weary at his desk, may give rise to a train of thought which will cheer him through the day. Reasonable labour is at once man's destiny and his privilege; but toil, whether of mind or body, should be succeeded by reasonable recreation. What does the unceasing pursuit of wealth lead to, even if the pursuer finds strength to run down his game? What, indeed, but vanity and vexation of spirit—youth early lost, the power of receiving enjoyment from innocent trifles forgotten, temper soured, health impaired, gout, and the doctor's bill? Yes, these are some of the Mammon worshippers' bad debts to the world, the flesh, and the devil: time and the arch fiend never repay. Too much of a good thing is good for nothing, and even money may be bought too dear. As a boy I thought so; I think so as a man, and now would rather possess innocence and peace, health, and a light heart, than all the wealth of the world, if its winning destroyed the one or crushed down the other.

The man who cannot be satisfied with his quarters at Ballina must be hard to please. The hotel, within a hundred yards of the water, is large, airy, and comfortable, and is, during the summer at least, well stocked with all that any sportsman need desire. It was not any lack of comfort in the hospitium, therefore, that made me hunt up a lodging before breakfast on the morning after our arrival.

Willie is certainly a treasure, for in an inconceivably short time the affectionate, natty, indefatigable fellow has thrown a wonderful home aspect over our new quarters. The rods are unpacked and hung round the room, the landing-net leans with a jaunty, careless air in one corner, and from another the gaff peeps slily out, as if ready for mischief. Two wretched little tables in the recesses of the windows are already covered with silks, feathers, and dubbing of every hue; the wheels ornament the mantel-piece, and on sundry small brass-headed nails, hammered into the walls with a shameful disregard to the landlady's paper, are hanging casting-lines and pattern-flies. Books and writing materials are disposed in convenient places. A couple of old shawls convert two trunks into ottomans, and altogether there is such an air of snugness about the place that we resolve, *nem. con.*, to remain for a fortnight or three weeks before plunging into the "far west."

A good or bad servant is a heavy item in a man's account of comfort, under any circumstances; but in Ireland, where the wanderer is so frequently thrown on his own resources, such a treasure is invaluable. How different is the domestic of the two countries, even when both are good. The characteristic of one is obedience, of the other affection. The Englishman is civil and attentive, obeying his master's orders to the letter, and nothing more; whilst he receives your wages you receive his attendance; you have bought him, mind and body; but as to his feelings, these are quite another matter; they are not in the bond. But use an Irishman well, treat him with kindness and courtesy, and he becomes a friend, a humble one it is true, yet you have his love. His service has the peculiar charm of seeming a pleasure; he identifies himself with his patron, whose comfort, interest, or honour it is his wish to promote, and determination to defend; but he seldom presumes; your kindness he fully appreciates, but never repays with impertinent familiarity. Call on him night or day, he is ready. There is no moodiness, no cold civility in his duty, but a kindly, cheerful spirit, ready to obey and still more prompt to anticipate your requirements.

The door opened and the original of the sketch entered.

"Well, so you are come back from the fishery?"

"Yes, your honour; I gave your card and note to Mr. Little, and here's his answer." Opening the envelope I found a printed form, with blanks for name and date, granting permission for the entire season, and authorising the angler to retain a fish per day. Generosity like this should be displayed at full length.

"Fishery Office, ———, Ballina, July 1, 1865.—Leave is hereby granted by the trustees to W. P., Esq., to angle in the rivers Moy and Bunree, for salmon and trout, from the present date to the end of the season, it being expressly understood that all fry caught will be carefully returned to the river, and that all salmon taken, with the exception of one each day, will be sent to the fishery as soon after being caught as possible. On behalf of the trustees, to the water-keepers and others who protect the above."

Comparisons will occasionally force themselves into notice; and it was absolutely impossible not to contrast the liberal policy, which placed the most prolific river in Ireland at the disposal of every sportsman, with the niggard spirit prevalent in our own dear churlish island, where, after strong interest made with some game-preserving squire, a sulky permission is at length obtained for a single day's fishing in his despicable trout stream or weedy pond, where the unhappy suppliant is tolerably certain to catch the rheumatism, though by no means sure of a fin. "*Interdictis imminet ager aquis,*" says some author whose name I have forgotten; but, O pleasant remembrances of the free waters of this hospitable land, preserve me ever from the mental malady of longing after such forbidden streams!

The Moy is, in my opinion, the best open water in the three

kingdoms, and as a station Ballina seems built expressly for the purpose ; but before speaking of the summer angling we will pause to say only a few words about the river during the earlier months. The best time for the spring fishing is from the middle of March to May 15, as the river is large, and cannot be relied on at the commencement of the season. Pontoon seldom wants a clean salmon on the opening day, for all early comers rest there before plunging into the wide waters of Lough Conn ; but in the river, too, are some admirable casts, and many a heart will thrill at the mention of Mountfalcon, Coolcronane, Bannifinglas, and Foxford.

For the sake of convenience we will speak of the angling in this neighbourhood under three heads—the tideway, up the river, and Pontoon.

Twice in each day the flood flows to the weirs, and for an hour and a half before and after high water little can be done with the rod. Through the town, on either bank of the river, are handsome quays, similar to those on the Liffey above Carlisle bridge ; but here no barque ever floats larger than the cot of my stout friend Terry Divers, who is now awaiting me at the steps. How well I remember, some dozen years ago, that brawny form standing just on this spot, steadying the boat with his pole, even as he does now, waiting for an eager young Englishman, who, unwilling to waste an instant, cast his line *down* the stream as he stepped on board. Do I forget the strong shove that sent the cot spinning against the current, the dashing rise, the unlucky stroke ? Oh, Terry, Terry, those combined forces moving in the same line were too much for mortal tackle ! How well I remember your ill-concealed disgust of the bereaved Saxon, and the suppressed rage with which you selected another pair of flies ? Have you forgotten the next two salmon which I hooked, played, and lost ? Have you ever paid for the Sunday hat you then tore from your head and trampled under foot as if it had been a thing of nought ? Can I forget your taking my rod *vi et armis* in order to mend our luck, and presently smashing top and second joints in a 10lb. salmon above the arch of the bridge yonder ? No, no, it all comes back as fresh as yesterday. And do not I remember tearing home for another rod, whilst you packed up the wreck; and, spite of disasters, afterwards bringing home seven good fish before breakfast? But enough of the past, for rods are glancing and eager feet are hurrying down to the quay, and the tide has turned an hour ago, so we, too, will get under weigh, pole up to the weirs, and discourse by the way.

Ballina for many years past has been a great favourite with our countrymen, and during the summer probably there are seldom less than ten or twelve English rods always hard at work on the water. But even with this number the Moy is far from being crowded, for from the Flats to Foxford the distance is about twelve miles. No narrow and puny stream is this, but a broad and glorious river, so wide and marvellously full of fish that if a dozen rods were occupied in the tideway alone there would be room for all and sport for each. Fortunately, the upper waters are in as great favour as the lower, and my friend, Pat Hearnes, never wants clients. His dominions, properly speaking, extend from the weirs to Foxford; he is the above-bridge potentate, and will come into notice more correctly in another chapter.

All this time Terry is poling steadily up the stream, whilst we are arranging the casting line. Compared with the gorgeous flies so lately used on the Erne, those of the Moy seem only pretty diminutives, and altogether no tackle can be lighter than that employed here. The rods generally used are slight and pliant; the three yards of single gut, backed by nearly an equal length of fine treble, together with a pair of small flies, give to the angler's outfit more the appearance of trout than salmon tackle; yet with ordinary skill no accidents need be feared, as the bottom is remarkably clear, and wherever a fish may go, a cot can follow.

That vigorous stroke has sent us under the bridge into the pool below the cutts, and what a picture is here for the angler's contemplation. Over the broad weirs and through the gratings comes the foaming rushing river, forming streams and eddies, whilst, near the arches, the water flows more smoothly and with a shallower current. Twenty yards above this point our anchor was dropped, and the first cast delivered. Our position in mid channel gave us full command of the throw, and now to the right and now to the left flew the line, sweeping round till opposite the stern. Dozens of fish were rising, and probably scores were under the flies; but, as Terry said, they seemed to have taken "the pledge" against them. Now, the said Mr. Terry was rather choleric and impatient, and in twenty minutes after our arrival proposed to move on. The advantage of racing from place to place is always, in my opinion, very questionable. "If you are sure of being over salmon, stick to them," was the advice given to me in my nonage, and very good advice I have found it.

Acting on it, the flies were changed, and the compliment at once acknowledged. "He'll come agen, *I* know," mumbled Mr. Willie, with the discarded insect between his lips, whilst his busy fingers were engaged in looping on a violet and grouse. "I'll swear he'll come agen." A cast or two on the opposite side moistened "the change," which by this time was curving gracefully in a series of short darts, right over the head of our new acquaintance. "I know'd it, and if he hasn't got it firm and hard, 'tis a pity." If you wish to see what a salmon can do, give him plenty of room and light tackle. In the present case space was ample, and nothing could well be slighter than the thread which held him; nor was our fast friend at all indisposed to make the best use of his opportunity. Now towards the weir he flies, then dives deep into the eddy, and next rushes back to his home by the bridge. Terry is already shortening the mooring-rope ready to weigh anchor and follow; but it is unnecessary, as the stout fish once more heads up the stream. No laggard is he; up the torrent—across—down again—deep under water—high in air, he rushes, dives, and leaps. Can he find no friend to aid him amongst all his summer-day acquaintance? Must he forego his proposed tour, and no more revisit the haunts of his infancy? Will he never again see his meek-eyed helpmate, who is, perhaps, even now waiting for her spouse in order to spend the honeymoon at their country lodge? I fear not, for who can contend successfully against destiny? Certainly not the graceful creature whose strength, lately so exuberant, has now deserted him, and whose fashionable friends have shunned him in his difficulties. Helpless as a log, slowly he yields to the steady strain of the line. Nearer, nearer, nearer he comes. Silently and softly the gaff sinks under water, ready for the moment when the victim shall pass over the ambushed steel—one single inch more—*habet.*

"He's a tidy little salmon, for the Moy, eh, Terry? Not far off 11lb." Whilst thus giving vent to his opinion, and expressing his satisfaction, my companion grasps "the tidy little one" firmly above the tail with his left hand, and prepares to administer a playful tap over the occiput.

"I wish I'd half a dozen of your brothers and sisters here; I'd serve 'um just so—there." A slight quiver passes over the silvery mass, as it is laid under an oiled coat to keep off the sun. And so this is death! but where is the subtle essence—the divine afflatus called life? Whither has it flown? We had better leave that question to wiser heads, and go on with our work.

Terry was now less anxious to move than before—nay, was positively unwilling to stir, when, a few minutes later, a grilse was hooked and lost; so we again changed the flies, and in about half an hour afterwards killed a pretty summer fish of 5lb.

Slowly dropping down between the bridges, the pole occasionally checking our speed, we cast on either side as we proceeded; but finding the water too shallow, only fished it very lightly, thinking of old times, when this beautiful stretch was *crême de la crême;* and thus we glided on till within a hundred yards of the "tanyard."

"That's what we call a line of battle," remarked Terry, indicating the direction with the handle of his propeller, and, to judge from appearances, the conflict was raging with great spirit. Moored in line, at intervals of about five-and-twenty yards, were four boats, the occupants of the second and last being each pleasantly engaged in a death grapple with a salmon. Wisely determining to join our countrymen against the common foe, we cast anchor at the correct distance above the headmost cot, but ere the stone was on the bottom our next neighbour also boarded a prize. No river, except the Moy, could show a scene like this, five punts close together, and three of these "in *quasi* possession" at the same moment—there goes *our* line, and lo! at the first cast a grilse is hooked. Whilst attending to my own affairs I yet found time to steal a glance at my brethren, who were all masters of the craft—careful men of business who felt time to be capital, and so well did they employ the opportunity that in twenty minutes the last prize was secured. In the "Castle hole" we landed a fourth, and rushing through "the Dock," which it was not thought advisable to try, were soon floating over "the Flats." In this portion of the Moy the proximity to the sea is very apparent, large mud banks unmistakably showing a tidal estuary at three quarters ebb. This part of "the ground" often affords admirable sport, but to-day it did not answer, and left us at leisure to look at the world around. From this part of the tideway rise wooded heights of no great elevation, but considerable beauty. Immediately below, a schooner and brig were dozing on the mud, high and dry; and still farther down the widening river stretched away towards Killala, and threading its path through long sand-banks —whereon lay many a seal—mingled its waters with the Atlantic.

The Moy runs through a flat, uninteresting country; but, with every disposition to praise, it is impossible to say much for the meadows which fringe its banks. They cannot be compared for a moment with the enamelled meads which border the Thames or the Somersetshire Avon, yet are they not flowerless, but can show their Caltha, Menyanthes trifoliata, and Nuphar lutea, with the best; and as for "the lady's smock," so white were the fields that you might have imagined all the feminine linen of the county here spread out to bleach.

On our way home from "the Flats," at the back of the dock, we put on a cast of trout flies, and were so fortunate as to rise two good white trout, one of which we landed, weighing 3lb. The Bunree, a small tributary bearing a high character during the autumn spates, falls into the estuary at this point. Desirous of seeing it, I strolled for some distance along its stony channel, and could easily believe that, with three feet of amber-coloured water filling its bed, and leaping over many a ledge of rock, the little river would deserve all the praise bestowed on it. Bunree never was in condition during any of my visits, so from personal experience I am unable to offer any opinion concerning its merits, though I believe that, if taken in time and tune, it would "discourse most excellent music."

After this we took one more out of the "Castle pool," and with this ended our sport for the day; no great matter to speak of in the first week of July in such a stream as the Moy, but enough to show that even an exceptional season like the present can afford occupation for the rod.

To chronicle minutely the events of the five following days would be an ungrateful task. The one recorded was neither the best nor the worst of the series; but feeding the mental appetite is a nice operation. Give too little, and it becomes cross; give too much and it falls sick. Oh, believe me, the task is delicate, and requires tact. Fortunately, in this class of dietetics we have one golden rule for our guidance: never continue the employment of any one kind of pabulum *usque ad nauseam*. In pursuance, therefore, of this maxim, we will conclude with a description of our doings on this river one July day, when the water *was*, as it always *should be*, in first-rate order.

Once upon a time, after spending a month on the Erne, I arrived here in the middle of such rain as is seldom seen in July. Meadows were flooded, fords impassable, bridges damaged, and the Moy in such a state as had not been seen in summer for many years. My diary shall tell the rest.

"Will the water never be in order! Without doubt there are many things more agreeable than sauntering up and down a wretched country town for a whole week. I have learned by rote the title-page of every volume in the window of the circulating library, and could cry, over the High-street, the address of every uncalled for letter at the office. I can tell the exact number of buns the baker speculates in daily. I have counted as many as ninety-one beggars, ere stopping from mere weariness, and shall remember to my dying day the exact pattern of the red shawl in which the Belles of Ballina delight. I have paid fifty-four visits to the river, to measure the abatement of its waters; can minutely describe every shade it assumed during that time, from Indian ink to half and half; and have nearly worried Terry to death with interrogations concerning the hour on which we shall be able to commence operations. There was some consolation in this, as Mr. Divers had the villany to charge thirty shillings per week for himself and an execrable leaky cot, which he averred to be 'the most illigant boat in the county.'

"Willie, in his department, has not been idle—whispered consultations between him and Terry have been going on every day, and various councils have been held to decide on the merits of a shade or the attractions of a feather. If success is to be commensurate with wisdom in debate and skill in execution, ours will be marvellous."

Here I must pause; only, however to finish the tale in the following chapter.

CHAPTER XXVI.

Ballina—The Scribe doth a Tale unfold—Up the River, with manifold Reminiscences of "Down the Water," illustrative of what may be done on the Moy under favourable Circumstances—Hypothesis.

July 11.

AT half-past three a.m. on Monday, the 9th of July, A.D. one—I like to be particular in such matters—my companion and myself sallied forth into the High street of Ballina. Rods were glancing in all directions, hurrying towards the scene of action; nobs and snobs, noblemen and gentlemen, tinkers and tailors, soldiers and sailors, were on the alert. Every order in "the capital of the west" appeared to have sent a representative. The justice and the priest, the doctor and the lawyer, hurried along the grand route. It was a high day—a general holiday—and business, if the good town ever had any, which I never could discover—for once was left to take care of itself. A hundred yards brought us to the river; boats were on the move, proceeding to favourite points; but we looked in vain for our man, Tom Nameless. "Where on earth can that fellow be?" The point at which we struck the stream was the upper bridge, where, moored about five-and-twenty yards above the arches, was a well-known Saxon professor, Mr. G——, who, as we came up, struck at a fish, whose keenness said plainly, "Wait an instant, and I'll be at you again," and so it proved, for the next time the flies curved over him Mr. Salmon showed himself a man of his word. If we were early, our friend was still more matutinal; at any rate this *could* only be number one, but that was bad enough; for in the year one, a man killing a fish in my sight became an enemy for life. Judge, therefore, of the state of my feelings when, looking over the parapet, four silvery creatures, laying side by side, were visible in that cot. Had I seen Mr. Tom about to be hanged by mistake, I think I should not have stepped forward to save him. All down the river rods were bending double.

"Oh, Tom, you incomprehensible scoundrel, what has become of you?"

"Don't you know master, that it's Monday?"

To a well-conditioned man the second morning of the week should offer no greater inducement for breach of faith than the third; but, Tom was a teetotaller, and between mass and midnight were many long hours, which that gentleman employed in sipping an abomination called "cordial." *From the name, it should* have been a mild and wholesome fluid, composed, perhaps, of water, sugar, ginger, saffron, and the like; but then it sadly disagreed with Tom's getting up, nor did it improve his health or personal appearance, for when at last he did arrive, an hour or so behind time, it was with white cheek, blue nose, and steps anything but straight and regular. The forty minutes spent on that bridge seemed like an age, and each fresh fish captured was a new wrong received from the hands of Mr. Nameless. In a mood by no means amiable I commenced casting from the quay, and in the hour and a quarter which elapsed before the tide drove us home, Willie gaffed for his master seven as fine fish as need be. Somewhat mollified by good fortune, it was with comparative equanimity that I noticed Mr. Tom, his face considerably more white and his nose considerably more blue than on ordinary Monday mornings, skulking behind a corner. "Go into your cot—you—you—teetotaller, and if you step out of here till I return—the rest was too majestic for repetition. On such a day,

Man wants but little here below;

so, bolting a cup of tea and pocketing a crust, we were soon once more on the quay, and found Tom at his post, fast asleep. I have always considered my "cordial" friend designedly put himself into this condition, as being the only one likely to secure his not straying off in search of "a drop."

Between the upper and lower bridges—a distance considerably short of a quarter of a mile—six boats besides our own were already anchored in line of battle, waiting for the moment when the ebb should enable them to proceed to business. The tide having fallen sufficiently to allow our commencing operations, we took up a position near the upper viaduct—the only unoccupied spot—and cast one look at the flies, which in another moment were dancing over the dark surface of the Moy.

"Mick's stuck in him," groaned Tom; "*he's* sure to have his share, and something over." Rattle, rattle, went the wheel; anxious to receive a lesson from so famous an artiste, I paused to watch the result. Upright as a statue, and nearly as motionless, with the rod well over his shoulder, stood the man who had sacrificed industry and competence for poverty and pleasure. With steady hand, unflinching eye, and consummate skill, he foiled the wild rage of his struggling victim—baffled him at every turn—and in less than ten minutes, spite Tom's maledictions and malicious wishes, gaffed and lifted into his crazy cot a beautiful and silvery six-pounder. Notwithstanding his rags, how I envied the fellow! Stealing a look at the boats below, an equally mortifying spectacle was to be seen, two of their occupants being engaged in the agreeable task of reducing a pair of refractory subjects to passive obedience. 'Twas too bad. Willie laid aside his pipe, and observed in a stage whisper, that "the master's hand was out." Oh, that tattered disciple of Izaak; positively he *has* another, whilst we have not turned a tail. And now a jubilant shout rose from every boat, each of the six having nearly at the same time hooked a fish. That yell startled even the poor artiste, who in an unguarded moment turned to see what could be the matter. A rattling leap warned him of the error, when too late, for the salmon had departed without leave, carrying off his best fly.

Man is an inquisitive animal, never satisfied without knowing the why and because. What *was* the reason of our failure? Could it be the tackle? Surely no! Was it the incapacity of the angler? Vanity forbade the thought. I once read of an ill-fated being with whom nothing prospered—energy, zeal, honesty, were unavailing, for unlucky Joe was born on a Friday. Was that, too, my natal day? In terror I fumbled for my pocket-book, wherein the event was duly chronicled. No, thanks to time, I am not thus doomed to perpetual misfortune, though I have escaped by a miracle, for I was ushered into the world at half-past eleven on Thursday night.

Tom now did what he should have done long before, and lifting the stone, we dropped down the stream. The truth was, our position had been badly selected, for the shade of the bridge cast a deeper hue on water already sufficiently dark, and satisfactorily accounted for our previous want of success. The beneficial effects of the move were at once apparent; as we drifted within a long cast of the poor disciple, a sporting fish dashed at my fly, and overboard went the anchor. The tackle was good and time precious, so giving the butt, but not sparing an inch of line, I kept a tight rein on him, and in a few minutes got him into the boat. Our neighbour, whom Tom affirmed to be a tinker, was now on his mettle; the flies fell within a foot of each other, though with very different results, for his had been again and again over the water, and mine were novelties. A merry dash at the dropper and a deep dull roll at the trail occurred simultaneously; for a brief space both were on the line. Alas! it was only too brief, and then, as usual in such cases, the lightest hooked broke away, leaving us at leisure to manage the other. This looked like business, but "the tinker" was not to be outdone; reeling up, he lit his pipe, pulled a few dirty bits of paper from the lining of his hat, and at once commenced the construction of a more novel and attractive article.

This was a golden opportunity, nor was it thrown away, for before his task was completed we had secured an additional brace of fish. Unwilling to tarnish our laurels, we once more lifted our anchor, removed from a neighbourhood so dangerous to our reputation, and drifted down towards the tanyard. The rain, which had so long threatened, now came down in a way creditable even to clouds fresh from a trip across the Atlantic, and the big drops pattered so thickly that Tom found occupation in bailing the boat with his shoe.

Our oiled coats were, however, garments of proof. "Work away, your honour, we've an hour yet afore the tide comes." Had the torrent been descending in bucketfuls, instead of drops, we should not have flinched—success and rivalry had so completely warmed us that all the rain which ever fell could not have cooled our ardour. Too soon passed the time, and when the flood warned us to desist, we gained the landing-place with eight salmon and two white trout, each about $1\frac{1}{2}$lb.

Fifteen fish and a brace of trout did not constitute a bad day's sport, yet we grumbled outrageously at an incident that befel us about midday, causing us to waste an hour and a half of invaluable time. The misfortune came on us in this wise: A few yards below the last bridge, I hooked something evidently far beyond the average size. Sailing away majestically, "the individual" quietly sat himself down on the bottom, as if meditating a prolonged interview. Urbane by nature, I treated him with the courtesies usual on such occasions, and kept up a continuous steady strain; but I might just as well have pulled at our mooring stone. There is, however, a limit to politeness, and, exasperated at this dogged and unreasonable behaviour, Tom was directed to pay out rope and stir him up with the pole. Such a forcible argument could not be resisted, so our friend got up and moved off leisurely, only to sit down again almost immediately a few yards farther off. If the "individual" was, through his own misconduct, subjected to this ungentlemanly treatment once, he experienced it twenty times; there was no putting him into a passion; his impassibility was wonderful. If *he* could not be roused, I was growing desperate, for on all sides boats were taking fish, whilst we had one that *would not* be taken. Poling nearly over him, I pulled, and pulled, and pulled. Surely mere mortal matter must weary in time. Ay, but in what length of time? in an hour? in a day? in a week? Certainly not in an hour, for I had laboured for more than that space to make that impression, and had utterly failed in moving him.

"He's a raal sulky villin," observed Willie, whose habitual patience was fast giving way; "may I try, master?"

Too happy to be quit of the business, I handed him the rod. "Pole ahead, Tom." Mr. Nameless did so; and after five or six minutes spent in doing all that man could do, came another order: "Shove astern." This failed likewise. The obstinate party had been tried behind and before, on the right and on the left. "He an't mortal! If he don't move this time, I'd better break, hadn't I?" A nod gave consent. Slowly, steadily, gradually, the strain was increased, but nothing came of it; and with a sigh of relief I saw the tight line at length spring upwards, and we were free. From the numbers killed around us during what may be termed our captivity, I doubt not that but for this accident, we should have added five or six grilse to our score; and had it not been for this untoward event, the day would probably have proved one of the best that ever fell to my lot.

By my side lies an old local newspaper, which speaks of the period which I have endeavoured to sketch. Perhaps the reader might like to see it; if so I will give him a *verbatim et literatim* copy:

ANGLING ON THE MOY.—The piscatory amusement on our river during the present delightful season amply repays the sportsman's toil. Our town since the angling opened has been thronged with sporting gentlemen from England and Scotland, and we rejoice that none of them will leave dissatisfied with their stay. On the whole, it is pleasing to record that the Moy has come round to its usual status as a sporting stream. . . . We have made inquiries relative to the number of salmon killed within the present season on the Moy, and were gratified to learn the following results:—Mr. John Gordon killed 54 fish in ten consecutive days. The highest weekly aggregate we have ever known before this year in Ballina was by Sir Humphrey Davy; when angling here in 1823 he killed 45 salmon. In 1843 Sir Richard Sutton killed 100 fish on this river within a month, Mr. Coke 40 in one week, Mr. Musgrave 165 in six weeks, and Captain Congrave 22 in one day. *This* is decidedly the best year that came since, for Mr. George Pollock took 27 in three days, Mr. Forde 15 in one day, Dr. Peard 15, and Mr. Staunton 11.

As a rider to the above extract, it may not be out of place to remark that I had only arrived a day or two before the paper was published, or perhaps it might have been deemed worthy of record that in twenty-one consecutive days I landed ninety-seven salmon, and about half a score of white trout.

In the former chapter it has been shown what might be done on the Moy in a bad season; in the present, what could be achieved in a good one; and if the angler strikes a balance between these extremes he will have a fair idea of what may be expected during an average June and July.

It was my intention when I set out this morning to have commenced a week "up the river" under the skilful guidance of my friend Pat Hearnes—it was, upon my honour, and if you look at the head of this chapter, you will observe that I made a note to that effect; but, instead of going up, I have been all the time going down. "Now, my dear sir," you will say, "this infirmity of purpose, almost amounting to temporary aberration of intellect, is very reprehensible, and must not occur again; it is deserving of censure, and you must consider yourself reprimanded." "Confiteor, domine, excellentissime." Yet, pray believe me, there was method in the madness.

On the way back I paid a visit to Mr. Little, in his office by the weirs, and whiled away a very pleasant hour in his company. With him was a gentleman—an admirable converser—who amongst other matters took a view of the Fishery Act altogether new to me, and certainly much opposed to my own opinions. In his judgment rivers stocked like the Moy received positive injury from the extended fence time. He observed, "The *direct* loss to the lessees was considerable, from the numbers which escaped during the run of the grilse, and that this loss was by no means compensated by the increased stock presumed to result from the increased number of mother fish." As nearly as I remember, the following was his line of argument. Assuming the Moy to have as large a head of breeding fish as the spawning grounds could accommodate, he conceived that every additional salmon which the present law allows to pass the weirs, instead of adding to the amount of fry, actually diminished it.

"Suppose," said he, "a spawning bed capable of accommodating twenty pairs of working fish, the trenches made, the ova laid down, and the gravel replaced. Now, if others arrive subsequently and commence their labours, the previously deposited ova is rooted up and lost, and the gravel rendered so loose as to be unfit to secure that which was last buried. Thus the first deposit is lost, and the second rendered so insecure as to be carried away almost to a certainty by the winter floods; *ergo*, a surplus stock produces less smolts than a smaller one."

This, to say the least, is plausible; but then it rests on the hypothesis of an *over* stock. Grant this, and the position is unanswerable; but oppose it, and how stands the argument?

Few, I presume, will deny that seventy or eighty years ago the supply in our rivers was far greater than at present. The means of taking them were at that time inferior to those now employed, and the inducement to capture them was not a fourth of what it is in our day; consequently, with a more prolific stock, and inferior methods of stopping them, larger numbers must have made their way to the head waters than can possibly do so *now*. This increased amount of mother fish hatched a greater number of fry than are found at present, as may be assumed from the larger number of adults then secured; yet they were reared from the same beds, which are declared unequal to the support of decreased numbers. But even granting our friend's view to be correct as regards one river, the number of streams with a surplus population is at this time very,

very small, and years must elapse before the great body of the Irish waters will be able to complain of this evil. Till then our glorious Act must produce general benefit; nor may we raise our voice against it, even should a particular locality suffer. When the halcyon days of a universal plethora have arrived, our Act will die, full of glory; yet will it live for ever in history as a monument of the wisdom of those who framed it.

I shall be afraid to face Pat Hearnes to-morrow. What will he say to my breach of faith?

CHAPTER XXVII.

"Up the River"—Pontoon—Unexpected arrival of the Colonel—He discourses in the small hours—A week on Lough Conn—Departure for Galway.

Saturday, July 22.

On a lovely morning in the latter part of July we walked up Millstreet and knocked at the palace gate of his Majesty Pat Hearnes the First. Crowned by acclamation monarch of the Upper water, King Pat may be considered solely in the light of a naval power. His fleet, however, boasts no ironclads; no 12-ton guns threaten to hurl misery and ruin on his rivals; yet are his ships admirably fitted for the warfare they have to wage. An old-world potentate is he, who ignores steam, and, like the uncrowned despots of Tyre and Carthage, puts his trust in the oar. Honest Pat Hearnes! light hearts and bright spirits man your flotilla, whilst

> Youth at the prow and pleasure at the helm

form a crew meet for the summer voyages your barques make. This is for old acquaintance, Pat, and long may you reign and prosper!

From the Weirs to Foxford—a distance of about ten miles—the Moy pursues a devious course; fringed with many a bush, and now and then adorned by a noble tree, the river is, nevertheless, for angling purposes, unimpeded with wood. Nearly through its whole course the banks are low and the water generally level with the meadows, which are advantages difficult to overrate, for if there be anything like an air the stream is sure to receive its due proportion. Long before the passing of the late Act, the upper "ground" was held in high estimation, but since that time it need hardly be said it has improved wonderfully. Taken as a whole, the Moy is deeper above than below the town, and in a dry season would *now* probably offer the best sport.

Having knocked at the palace gates, Pat himself answered the summons, led the way to our cot, and in a few minutes conducted us to the "upper falls and rapids." A light northerly air faintly curled the stream, and gave promise of good things. Our stock of flies, never extensive though always new, at this time consisted only of a pair on the rod, so our *artiste* seated himself on the bottom boards, with numberless envelopes secured under his legs and between his knees, and commenced with great zeal to add to our resources. This plan of fabricating by the river has many advantages, one of the principal being the correct adaptation of size to the height of the water. The industrious workman merely looked up from his task for an instant, as a sharp rise at the dropper caught his practised ear; placed a little extra wax on the silk with which he was fastening off the shoulder, and then went calmly on with his business. Once more he lifted his eyes, when a second refusal, accompanied by a scornful lash of a greenish tail, attracted his attention; this time the horns were being carefully adjusted.

"Wait a minute, my beauty, and I'll be about you. There, master, if that won't suit him he must be uncommon perticler." It was one of the jointed flies, so difficult to tie neatly, but so effective in low and bright water, consisting of five rings of shining floss, each in strong contrast to the other, with a turn or two of ostrich between, of the same hue as the next joint above. A jay shoulder, mixed wing, glittering tail, and long crimson antennæ completed an insect such as no fish, flesh or fowl ever saw *in rerum naturá*.

Removing the rejected pair, we substituted the latest specimen of my companion's handiwork, and without further preliminaries sent it flying across the stream. Hitherto the fish had been hard to please, but this time he was less fastidious, and rushed at it like a hungry dragon. Such a rise is the culminating point of human felicity.

"He's a dead one, I know, Pat," mumbled Mr. Willie, whose lips, at that moment holding a topping and piece of tinsel, were not well adapted for oratorical display. "He's safe any way, and see if I don't roast him. Won't we, master?" Now this form of speech was common with my old friend—first an assertion, and next an interrogation; but, as he usually had his own way, the latter was understood to be a mere matter of form. Now our salmon, whose ultimate destiny had been so satisfactorily settled, though pronounced moribund was remarkably lively, and, after executing five or six summersaults in the neatest fashion, took a desparate race, tore the hook from his jaw, and went on his way rejoicing. The Island, Cruckane, and the Rock were unprofitable speculations; and then came Mullins's Pool. Here the hopes of the would-be cook revived; and when a choice between an eight-pounder, a five, and a four was presented to him, the *chef's* satisfaction knew no bounds. Lynche's Pool gave us another, the Stonewall Cast a fifth, and there seemed every prospect of making a good bag; but soon the wind died away and the sun came out with such scorching brilliancy as blistered both face and hands—that is, *my* countenance and upper extremities, those of my comrades being fireproof.

How grateful was the shade afforded by a small aspen tree, whose broad leaves throbbed and fluttered, though to my heated skin not an air was appreciable. It reminded one of the academic groves we used to read of at school, only there seemed more reality about it. To a lover of nature Mayo is a wild and beautiful county, whose rivers are manifold, whose mountains are lovely and sublime, wrapped in their mantles of purple heath and crowned with diadems of granite, and whose lakes, so capable of utilisation, now only bear on their broad bosoms the peasant's barge or the fisher's boat. If these are all charming, what shall be said for its coast line, from the mouth of the Moy to the head of Killery Harbour, stretching to a length—exclusive of the minor indentations of the shore—of 250 statute miles? Let any tourist consult his travelling map, as I did mine, under the tree, and exult in what it shows him. If he be a sportsman, what wealth does it not promise? If he be a sailor, what safe harbours, noble headlands, and peaceful bays does it not indicate? If a poet, what themes may it not suggest? If a painter, what treasures for his easel? Beautiful Mayo! to me there is something musical in the sound of your name. Sweet are the memories of the bright summers and rainy autumns I have spent on your mountains, lakes, and streams, and delicious are the anticipations of that time when I shall visit you again.

All this while my companions had been collecting dry sticks, stones, and dead grass, and having cooked a fish sufficiently large for the wants of six men, graciously brought me a slice, and forthwith devoured the residue.

The receiver of stolen goods is worse than the thief, says the proverb, and in Mayo we have a fine example of the truth of the axiom. The generosity of our early Norman kings was on a grand scale, especially when they gave away the property of other people; and in their dealings with this county they were more splendidly lavish than usual, for it formed *part* of the grant made by Henry II. to William de Burgho, about the year 1180. The history of the transaction is curious. The new possessor soon made a permanent settlement, for, in the twenty-fourth year of the reign of Henry III., the then king of Connaught made a journey to England to complain of the invasion of his territory by the family of the Burkes. Very little is known of the subsequent proceedings of the settlers, until the period of the great rebellion in 1333, when the William de Burgho of that day was assassinated. Mayo fell away from all subjection to the English law immediately after the murder of the earl, for some of the younger branches of the Burke family, seeing that the entire province of Connaught would be inherited by his infant daughter (who afterwards married Lionel Duke of Clarence, and so gave the

Crown its title to the inheritance in the person of Henry VII.), seized on Galway and Mayo, and, to avoid the consequences of their usurpation, not only cast off all allegiance to the English rule, but renounced their English names and habits, identifying themselves and their followers with the natives. The appellation chosen by Edmund de Burgho, who seized on Mayo, was Mac William Oughter, or "the further," to distinguish his family from Mac William Eighter, or "the hither," who had in like manner usurped Galway. From this time till the reign of Elizabeth the Mac William of the time continued to exercise the authority of an independent potentate. The first step towards a return to old law and manners was in 1575, when the then Mac William, accompanied by the O'Malley, came to Galway and made submission, consenting to pay 250 marks per annum for his fief.

The antiquities of the county are chiefly ecclesiastical. There are round towers at Killala, Turlogh, and Meelick. At Cong are the remains of a splendid abbey, where an archiepiscopal crozier of surpassing beauty was found. This work of art was executed by the command of Turlogh O'Connor, the father of Roderick, the last native king of Ireland, and is now in the possession of the Royal Irish Society. At Moyne and Rosserk are ruins of great interest, and the remains of Ballin-tubber Abbey, seven miles from Ballinrobe, are amongst the most elegant specimens of early architecture in the island.

What a day this has been! From eleven to six not a cloud in the sky nor an air on the earth. The rushes, wading knee-deep in the stream, have kept up a sweet jangling with the passing current, as if sending love and good wishes to their sister weeds far off in the ocean. Thrush and blackbird agreed it was too laborious to sing in that noontide heat, and reserved themselves for the evening concert. Cattle laid panting in the shade, and there carried on a defensive warfare against their winged persecutors; only the swallows and my companions' lips were in full activity. Under our tree, in the long rich grass, I read, wrote, smoked, and meditated; now and then poled into the river, hurriedly went over the cast, and, returning faster than

I went, flung myself once more on the cool sward. Pat discoursed at length concerning the varied charms of Lough Cullen and Lough Conn, of their trout, salmon, pike, and perch, which last he said attained a large size, as in fact they do in all the more extensive Irish waters.

The alders on the western bank were beginning to cast lengthening shadows on the stream, and if anything was to be done, now was the time. Slowly, under Pat's most skilful guidance, we drifted over the pools we had fished in the early part of the day. For an hour we did not move a fin. Gradually the shadows grew longer and the air more cool. At The Island we secured our sixth grilse, and at the Upper Rapids two more were brought to bag, and so ended our first expedition "up the river." . . . . .

Stretched on the sofa, as perfectly at home as if he had been there for a month, was my old friend the Colonel, who, possessing a tenacious memory, had not forgotten my refusal to spend a couple of days with him on Lough Melvin and Lough Erne. Being a good geographer he had a pretty correct idea of the merits and locality of Conn, on which he made up his mind to take an ample revenge for my previous delinquency. At present he was more disposed to be inquisitive than communicative, particularly on the subject of dinner. By the time I had set his mind at rest on this important subject our repast was announced. A crimped salmon and a few small fry caught during the morning at once enlisted his sympathies.

"That fish, so firm, dry, and curdy—I'll trouble you for another slice, and one or two of those pinkeens—all Billingsgate could not match it. I say, Walter, how different from the flabby, unctuous article we get at the clubs for two shillings the pound, in the fond misconception of enjoying a luxury? Glass of sherry, my dear? Another with you, my boy. Well, dinner is a pleasant invention. Kid—did you say kid?" and then, after a reflective pause, "This animal must have fed on nectar and ambrosia."

With the first glass after dinner the old soldier came out in force, rung for Willie, ordered a car at eight on the following morning, stretched out his legs, and made himself up for the evening. Merrily it wore away, and somewhere near the small hours I either heard or dreamed the following anecdote of " sporting extraordinary :"

"Yesterday morning I sauntered from my quarters to the Ballyshannon bridge, there to wait for the mail. Captain Joyce, a remarkably heavy swell—a new arrival since you left—was at work there, and, like other idlers, I halted to look on. At the tail of one of the streams was an ancient Triton, uncommonly wide awake. From time to time he rose to the surface, showed his monstrous bulk, and then deliberately settled himself down in his former position. These proceedings touched the Captain to the quick; fly after fly had been put over him without any good results, and when I arrived he had just selected a tried favourite from his hat, and was in the act of making a final appeal to the astute old party. Amongst other observers of these proceedings was the favourite Newfoundland of the Justice, the terror of all petty larceny rogues, boys, cats, and beggars. The animal had turned out for his usual morning promenade, and was now reposing after his fatigue in the middle of the road, sitting on his tail in a dignified attitude, sagaciously observing all that was going on. A long cast was necessary. The heavy line swept through the air, bagged, drooped, and stuck fast. The awful yell that followed filled the Captain with dismay. Horror-struck at such an untoward event (he was firmly persuaded he had hooked an unfortunate tourist sketching on the parapet) the commander spun round with a speed creditable even to a dancing dervish. 'Blood an ounds!' screeched the mob in an ecstasy of delight, 'hark, hark to the wheel!' It was indeed running at a fearful rate, for the dog was hooked fast, and darting home at full speed. 'Stop him, stop the horrid brute,' roared the perplexed angler, who might as well have attempted a *sotto voce* conversation in a hurricane. Round the corner rushed the affrighted Newfoundlander ; the heavy dragoon's 200yds. were nearly out ; but luck is everything. 'Hurroo, more power to him ; here he comes again, hurroo, hurroo.' The crowd, one and all, appeared seized simultaneously with a mania for practising the skipping-rope ; now over, now here, now there, to avoid the slack line, which was sweeping the dust in a way that would have done Macadam good to have witnessed. Fortunately for the peace of the town the animal was at length captured, found to be more frightened than hurt—for the hook was merely entangled in his curly hide—and sent home to tell his own story to his master. The Justice was irate beyond measure. Instead of flying into an ordinary everyday Christian sort of passion, his heat was absolutely tropical; *his* dignity had been outraged; the bench had been insulted in his person. He stamped like a gentleman qualifying for Bedlam, and swore as many round oaths as would, if properly accounted for, have considerably enriched her Majesty's treasury. The first paroxysm over, he talked about idle and ill-disposed persons obstructing the public roads, threatened to put the Act in force, eulogised Dick Martyn and the Act for the Prevention of Cruelty to Animals, steamed home, thought more coolly over the matter, tied up his dog, to the great joy of the whole population, and for the rest of his days won't he hate flies, rods, and anglers more devoutly than ever?"

With the Colonel punctuality was a virtue and something more, so, in order that his peace of mind might not be disturbed, I enjoined Willie to have the car at the door five minutes before the hour specified by my old friend, and ere the clock struck eight we were clear of the town.

The driving was on the most approved Hibernian principle—a principle, by the way, I never understood correctly, but which in practice may be reduced to two heads—level ground, pace moderate; down hill, awful. There was a sufficient proportion of incline to display our driver's skill to considerable advantage, and make me feel anything but comfortable under his guidance. "Thank goodness!" I ejaculated, "here's the last descent." As we gained the brow, signs of the coming event became evident. The driver shook himself more firmly into his seat, and carefully deposited the pipe in his waistcoat pocket. The horse, too, pricked up his ears, and stepped out more briskly; he also was getting ready. With a whoop and a shout the game animal started off at a gallop, and the light vehicle bounded and flew over the stones, rolling heavily from windward to leeward like a ship in a gale of wind. Fortunately we reached the bottom in safety, when I duly registered a vow that, if not dead lame, I would ride up and walk *down* all hills that might lay in my course hereafter through "the Far West."

Lakes always possess one advantage over rivers—namely, a greater liability to feel the influence of wind, and it must be calm indeed if a sheet of water large as Lough Conn is not in good angling trim for an hour or two during the day. When we left Ballina there was a nice westerly air; when we reached our destination the whole lake sparkled with ten thousand tiny wavelets laughing and breaking in the morning sun. So favourable an opportunity was not to be lost, and, with Pat as pilot and Willie at the sculls, we were almost immediately on the ground.

"I say, Walter, no poaching; that's my property," remarked the Colonel, jerking his fly from the centre of a dull, deep eddy. "Back a stroke or two, Willie, and we'll come over him again with something new." True fell the line, and at the fourth cast he came again.

"I seen him that time, sir. He's a raal ould spring fish, as red as a brick. Thim is sad deluders, always a-saying sweet things, but niver meaning ony thing. There's no getting the likes of him to the church door. He's too old to be caught."

"We'll try, Master Willie. Back her again. Very ancient birds are sometimes taken with chaff, you know."

The rising fly once more fell near him. "There's luck in odd numbers," says Rory O'More. I almost *felt* the sharp steel cut into his gristly jaw. With a hand so perfect as that of my old friend over him, his doom was sealed; it was only a question of time, so, quite at ease as to the ultimate result, I went on with *my* work. It was a likely hour, and in a few minutes I too was "in a salmon." No sooner was the deed done than the enormity of the misdemeanor struck me in all its force. I ought to have reeled up, and so have given my companion fair play. Now there was no help for it but to break, or kill my fish out of hand. Shortening the line I gave him the butt, keeping up a strain so severe that the light grilse rolled over and over on the surface, beating the water into a sheet of foam. Ere a minute elapsed, Pat got a chance, slipped the gaff into his side, and all danger of a foul was over. The veteran cast a grim look at the offending party. "I forgive you this time, but mind you don't do it again." Meanwhile the wrathful angler was doing his part manfully with a heavy antagonist, who was tugging away far below the surface with a steady perseverance which deserved a better fate. More and more languid grew his efforts, and in less than half an hour he lay on the water like a log, and was presently gaffed in very workmanlike style by a gentleman whose name need not be recorded. As Willie's practised eye had remarked, he proved an early spring fish, very red, and not in the condition he had been some five months before; nevertheless, Salter's balance declared that the Colonel's prize weighed nearly 15lb. The breeze held up till noon, by which time we had secured six grilse besides the commander's "old bird." The alteration in the weather necessitated a change in our mode of fishing; the flies were laid aside and the trolling tackle produced. My old companion selected a small trout and an artificial minnow, whilst I thought myself fortunate in the possession of the tail of an eel and a *light* spoon that *could* spin. Pat had on the previous day declared the quantity of perch to be prodigious, and so we found it. Gliding along the north-west shore, we were kept constantly at work by this beautiful fish, every now and then getting a good one from $2\frac{1}{2}$lb. to $3\frac{1}{2}$lb.

As we passed along, the scenery assumed so wild and desolate a character as well to merit the appellation of sublime. From its western shore Mount Nephin rose abruptly, towering to the height of 2646ft. whilst on either side, peak above peak, all purple and gold, melted away in the distance, here affording a last resting place for the rays of the sinking sun, and there lying sombre and dark in shadow. Like most of the Connaught mountains their sides were checkered with mighty masses of granite, standing out in high relief from the blossoming heather and the deeper foliage of the pines.

When within a few hundred yards of the low bridge whose single arch spans the short and narrow channel which connects the lower with the upper lake, I was summoned back to the realities of life by a simultaneous shout from the Colonel and Pat. A powerful fish had dashed at the troll, and his strength, exerted in a direction opposed to the course of the boat, had already dragged three parts of the rod under water. To seize the butt and check our speed were matters of course. Pat protested we were "in" another salmon, whilst Willie, whose fingers had suffered severely during the morning savagely affirmed "'twas only a pike, bad cess to him!" A bold dash from the surface removed all doubts by showing us the best trout we had seen during the day. Eight or ten minutes brought him well under command, and soon he was our own. So short and stout was this laker, that I should never have believed him $6\frac{1}{2}$lb. had not the scales attested the fact.

In the morning Lough Conn seemed smiling in all the brightness of eternal youth. Now, as we rolled away, it looked cold, grey, and sombre, as the mist curled over it, and the mountain shadows fell deeper and darker over its dreary length. That bad old man, the Colonel, received a severe jobation for keeping dinner waiting for two mortal hours; priding himself on his punctuality and politeness, the veteran was sadly crestfallen, and did not recover his spirits till Madame, in a neat post-prandial oration, proposed his health, and wished him success during the week equal to that which had crowned the day. Her desire was fulfilled, and even the bloodthirsty commander was so well satisfied that he determined to remain. On the morning of our departure Pat and Terry were in attendance, tucked up the ladies in the first style of art, wished us a pleasant journey and an early meeting, and then, with their "God speed your honour!" sounding in our ears and finding an echo in our hearts, we trotted up the street, and were soon bowling along the road in the direction of Galway.

CHAPTER XXVIII.

Galway.

July 29.

As the reader will probably spend two or three weeks with us in the wilds of Galway, he will not enjoy his trip in that secluded and semi-civilised region less if he learns something of the physical character and antiquities of the county. The dimensions are about 164 miles in length from east to west, by 52 in breadth from north to south; the extent of coast, which is very irregular, has been estimated at 400 miles, whilst landwards the Shannon and the Suck shut it out from the rest of Christendom. The area, according to the Ordnance survey, consists of cultivated land, 955,922 acres; unprofitable bog and mountain, 476,957 acres; and water something less than 100,000 acres.

With the exception of a spur of the Slieve Boughta mountains, running from the borders of Clare, and a similar extension of the Burrin range, the whole of that part of Galway west of Lough Corrib—a tract of nearly the same extent as Tipperary—is comparatively flat, and, although to a great degree incumbered with bog, is yet generally productive. The whole district west of Lough Corrib and Lough Mask is known as Connemara; and what memories and pleasant anticipations does the name recall! To anyone blessed with a sense of the beautiful, how charming is that uncultivated, half-peopled, and semi-barbarous land, with its endless low swells of swamp and moorland—a lake in every low expanse, and a river in every glen. Latterly this region has attracted much attention by its capabilities of improvement, as well as by the charms of its scenery. The bay of Galway bounds it on the south, the Atlantic on the west, and a deep inlet of the sea, called the Killery Harbour, separates it on the north from the mountainous district of Murrisk, in Mayo. From the head of Lough Corrib on the east, to Adris

Head on the west, this district extends forty English miles; and from the head of Killery Harbour on the north, to the bay of Galway on the south, thirty miles.

This wild tract reaches its greatest altitude in the range known as the Twelve Pins of Bunnabola. This mountain group rises abruptly from a table-land of moderate elevation, and forms a picture few can behold without emotion. By night or day, in storm or sunshine, this glorious band, whether clad in thin misty mantles or spreading their purple breasts to the autumn sun, are equally beautiful; elemental changes sweep over them like emotions over some face we love to look on, ever varying but never marring its loveliness. Round their bases are numerous lakes, of which the chief are Lough Ina; the upper and lower lakes of Ballinahinch—skirting their southern slopes—and Kylemore, away to the northwest. Although the whole of this tract is generally known as Connemara, it is properly divided into three districts, that portion lying between the head of the Killeries and Lough Corrib being termed "Joyce's Country;" that to the south of the Pins, Jar Connaught, or Western Connaught; and the remainder, extending westward from Bunnabola to the Atlantic, constituting Connemara proper. Nothing of this extensive tract is known to the general mass of tourists, who follow each other like a string of wild ducks along the high road from Galway to Clifden, and from Clifden to Westport; and yet to my mind the whole world offers nothing more solitary, nothing more interesting. If this be so to the ordinary tourist, what must a ramble in such a region afford to the angler? All the charms of solitude and novelty are his, and I know few feelings more intense than those which spring up in a man's breast as he stands for the first time by some unknown mountain lake or brawling river, and, out of sight of humanity, prepares for a day after his own heart. For my part I soon grow sick of the world.; a little goes a great way with me; it is a dish spiced with condiments all too stimulating for my appetite; the rivalries, the meannesses, the petty jealousies, and the dirty tricks do not suit me—they bring on dyspepsia. In the mountains I never had a fit of indigestion in my life. At present I am labouring under a severe attack, and oh, *how* I long to be there!

Galway is a world in itself—wild, picturesque, and exquisitely beautiful. Forty years since large portions of the country were as inaccessible as when the De Burghos ruled. Without roads, without inns, it was as little known to Britain as Borneo is at the present day. Prior to 1813 the only roads west of Galway were a narrow coast line to Costillo Bay, and a central road by Oughterard to Ballinahinch. These ran over rocks and bogs in so unskilful a manner as to be scarcely passable for any sort of carriage, and the only other means of communication through the district were narrow bridle paths, difficult for horsemen in the summer, and quite impracticable in the winter. On the coast in particular, beyond the Costillo, there was nothing better than a footpath. By the improvements, begun in 1822, a complete line is now carried round the district. A coast road has been formed which touches the heads of all the chief inlets from Costillo to the Killeries, where it joins an inland line through the heart of the Joyce's Country to the head of Lough Corrib, and thence across the central plain of Jar Connaught to the southern coast of Costillo Bay. This in a measure opened the country, and attracted so much attention to Connemara that, in all probability, it will at no distant date become the scene of mercantile and agricultural speculations.

Such was the impassable state of the coast about thirty-six years ago, for the road—commenced in 1822, could hardly have been finished under eight years—and now the beautiful district from Spiddel to the Killeries forms for the traveller the choicest part of his Irish tour. As his car rolls along he sees a boundless expanse of ocean—harbours that for number and security no similar extent of shore in the world can show—glorious mountains, countless lakes, and seagirt islands, even yet as primitive as any Sinbad of the nineteenth century is likely to discover in the North or South Pacific. Clifden is comparatively a new town, having been called into existence by the energy of the proprietor, Mr. D'Arcy, in 1821; and Roundstone, the port from which the beautiful green marble of Ballinahinch is shipped, has within the last few years grown rapidly into importance. In 1854 the Law Life Assurance Society became possessed of the Connemara property, on which they had previously advanced money by way of loan to the amount of 160,000*l*. From the chairman's report for 1864, it appeared that the property paid 4 per cent., and that since the auditing of the accounts the fisheries *alone* had risen 3000*l*. in annual value. All that this vast district required was money to develop its resources. Henceforth this will not be wanting, and the estate that broke poor Dick Martyn's heart will probably prove one of the brightest jewels in the crown of this Crœsus of societies.

Galway is rich in antiquities. At Ballygaddy, Kilbannon, Meelick, and Ardrahan, there are round towers. Cromlechs and stone circles are of frequent occurrence.

Of the numerous remains of religious houses throughout Galway, the ruined Abbey Knockmoy is the most interesting. It was founded in 1189 by Cathal O'Conner, surnamed " The Red Hand," in consequence of a victory obtained by him over the English under Almeric St. Lawrence. Above the tomb of the founder are some curious fresco paintings of great interest, as exhibiting the costume of the native Irish. The Phrygian cap, represented as worn by several of the figures, will some day attract the attention of antiquaries. Knockmoy well deserves a visit for its architecture, which indicates considerable advancement in the arts amongst its founders. The Raths of the early inhabitants and the ruined strongholds of the Anglo-Norman lords are also numerous.

Every street in the quaint old town of Galway is a page of romance. It is impossible to pass carved arches leading into the courtyards of great gaunt-looking houses, without being irresistibly reminded that each has a history. These places, now so mournfully silent in all the dignity of decayed gentility, once knew better days —when the Don brought Bilboa blades, Cordova leather, port and canary to the good merchants. What they could have done with all these things is a mystery. That they drank a good deal of the wine is highly probable, and that, being pugnacious, they used the weapons, is also likely; but what they did with the general cargoes I cannot imagine. The country is a thousand times more rich now than it was then; and where the merchants found customers, or how the customers found money—oh! I give it up; 'tis worse than the Pons Asinorum. The railway hotel, which occupies one side of the principal square, is perhaps the largest in Ireland, Killarney excepted. Here, in 1859, only seven short years ago, poor Leech penned some of his amusing sketches. "He saw," he says, "whilst lionising the town, a great deal that was very amusing, and a great deal that was very dirty." He saw traces of Spanish architecture in quaint gateways and quadrangular courts; he saw Lynch's Castle, and found its grotesque carving very curious; he saw the house in Dead Man's Lane, where lived Fitz-Stephen, Warden of Galway; he saw warehouses without ware; he saw and greatly admired Queen's College; he saw chapels and nunneries, whence the Angelus bell sounded as he passed; and, above all, he saw the "Claddagh." About this dirty suburb pages have been written; it is simply the fishermen's quarter, consisting of poor, ruinous cabins, "with walls of mud and stone, and for the most part, windowless, the floors damp and dirty, and the roof a mass of rotten straw and weeds." "As to the origin of these Claddagh people, I am not sufficiently 'up' in ethnology to state with analytical exactness the details of their descent, but I imagine them to be one-third Irish, one-third Arabian, and the other Zingaro or Spanish gipsy. I thought I recognised in the old lady an Ojibbeway chief who frightened me a good deal in my childhood, but she had lost the expression of ferocity, and I was, perhaps mistaken."

In this work the reader has rarely been troubled with quotations. Personally I abhor them, and should certainly avoid the society of my best friend if he had a predilection for inflicting bad Latin and worse Greek on a trusting comrade. Yet in this chapter I have not only quoted from the sparkling pages of Leech, but have been picking and stealing from the heavy wisdom of the Ordnance survey. The fact is, I do not like the task before me, and for once in my life avoid the river like an insane dog. Internally, no mortal is more fond of the cold element; externally, I hold the application of tepid water to the surface of the human body, not only agreeable, but useful in the highest degree; but to put my foot voluntarily into *hot* water is what I do *not* like.

Well, once on a time "the angling" here was admirable, from the tideway to the weirs, and from the weirs to the lake. In the spring the fishing is chiefly confined to that portion of the water between the salmon steps and the Goal-bridge, but occasionally, if the river becomes low, a few good casts are to be found by wading between the bridge and the cribs.

Now this portion of the water would afford admirable angling to the sportsman, did not a most ungentlemanly custom of stroke-hauling prevail. This pot-hunting work is so exasperating that the gentlest disciple of Izaak would raise his voice against it. Before setting out from Ballina I had a pretty good notion of the peculiar mode in which "*sport*" is conducted at Galway; but Galway lay in my route, as I wished to see the various club and private waters between that point and the Errive; so I comforted myself with the knowledge that, if unbearable, we could order a car at any moment, and leave the "*sportsmen*" to pursue their avocations in peace. "I was there in March," wrote a friend to whom I applied for information, "and saw amongst other iniquities, one spring fish weighing 27lb. hooked in the vent and hauled out in *three* minutes. About the middle of April a strong north-west wind blew back the water on the lake and left the fish nearly dry, when the stroke-hauling became so bad that I could stand it no longer." On this subject we will hear another witness. "You ask how we are getting on in this place of ill-fame; we are now drawing near the end of June, and the continued dry weather has affected us so much, that from the salmon steps to the bridge there is hardly water to cover the fish; the fly is, of course, out of the question, so I work the tideway in a boat about the distillery wall, and have the pleasure of seeing that 'real sportsman,' Mr. G——, stroke-hauling; no doubt he is an adept, as he takes from thirty to forty per day, and sometimes breaks two or three rods—another point of excellence

—for you are aware the art consists in dragging each fish out neck and heels by main force. At this time the tackle in fashion consisted of from four to six large hooks tied on a hemp line, with which the water is raked from end to end. I do not hesitate to say it is useless for a fair sportsman to attempt to fish here under existing circumstances."

Thus wrote as honest an English gentleman and as good an angler as need be. It may be easily imagined, therefore, I went to bed in the railway hotel with small intention of heeding the seducing voices of the early cocks in the "quaint old Spanish town." The musical sound of the clock in the fine church tower in the square chanted matins at four; at five it seemed to say, "I am afraid you can't be well;" at six its warning tones, I fear, fell on drowsy senses; but when the next admonitions of my gentle monitor met my ears, I hopped out of bed and took an airing at the window. There lay the square in the full blaze of the summer's sun; the brave and industrious girls of the Claddagh were vending their fish; a poor scholar, with a few tattered volumes under his arm, loitered by the railings, eyeing the cannon, and perhaps admiring the flowers; and a Bianconi, piled high with tourists' luggage, was preparing for its westward journey. In fact the world was awake, and what excuse had I for sleeping? Dressing *that* morning was a slow operation; breakfast was more slow, and the leading article of the *Galway Mirror* was the slowest of all. At length there was no further reason for delay. Willie had been in and out of the room at least twenty times. Mademoiselle placed pipe-case, pouch, and fly-book in my hat, and laid it on the table. It was clear I was expected to go out.

The river, although a beautiful piece of water, is but short, and on it I found many persons angling after the mode prevalent in Galway. Whether that admirable sportsman Mr. G—— was amongst the number I did not stop to inquire; but, taking a boat, paddled about, hoping to find some indifferent cast where we might be allowed to spend an hour or two in peace. Dodging hither and thither, sometimes fishing after a "sportsman" who had raked the water from end to end, pricking and lacerating six or seven grilse for every one dragged out—sometimes casting into doubtful little runs and eddies, where it was just *possible* a fish might be found—we worked on till we could endure it no longer. In many lands, and during many years, I have seen as much fishing as most men, but I am bound to say that at Galway I beheld something *new*. I cannot say I liked it, and must observe that, had one of those sportsmen pursued his pastime in such fashion elsewhere, he would have run considerable risk of being taken up for poaching; nor will I deny that in my opinion he would have richly earned a month at the treadmill. There is no accounting for taste, but in common honesty let no such performers again send the results of their angling for publication to any of our sporting journals. Of course, if a man enjoys the rare privilege of hooking salmon by the tail instead of by the head, he may use his opportunity; but let him call his achievement by its right name, and say, "I have murdered so many, but in fair fight I have vanquished none." Notwithstanding the heavy odds against us, in one sense we were unusually fortunate, killing every fish that showed at the fly; true it is we had but six rises—five from white trout and one by a grilse; but it was some comfort in our disquiet to have done all that could be done. After a somewhat early dinner, it yet wanted between four and five hours to sundown. To lionise the place was impossible, for that had been done already in a former visit; to face Mr. G—— and his friends again was not to be thought of; so, after due deliberation, it was determined to take boat and paddle over the neck of the lake between the town and Sir Thomas Blake's. Once on a time this stretch of water offered admirable salmon angling, but for some years past it has not given a fish to the rod. Unless the bottom had been changed by the deposition of new matter, or some considerable alteration had taken place in the depth of the water, I never knew fish desert lodges which had been used from time immemorial. I was unable to ascertain that either of these agencies had been in operation here, and yet it was as certain that the space between the back of the cribs and Sir Thomas Blake's mansion contained excellent salmon casts not long since, as that at present it does not hold a rising fish. Our hopes, therefore, were limited to the capture of a dish of trout. Happily, these anticipations were realised, and we enjoyed a pleasant, if we did not spend a very profitable, evening on Lough Corrib.

This lake offers noble trolling for trout at an earlier season; occasionally fish of great weight are to be taken. I never tried it, but was informed that one of $27\frac{1}{2}$lb. had been killed by the rod, though the exact date of the capture seemed uncertain. This, of course, was one of the great prizes sometimes drawn in life's lottery, yet I have reason to believe that lakers of 10lb. or 12lb. may with some little perseverance, be secured. Many of my friends who have made Oughterard their head quarters in April and May, have spoken well of their success. In such an inland sea as Lough Corrib patient angling must eventuate in great results, and the same thing may be said of all other large lakes in the island. The high estimation in which certain stations are held is often due more to their greater accessibility than their greater deserts. Impatience is one common fault amongst anglers, and a tendency to follow in the beaten track is another; but I am persuaded that if gentlemen inquired carefully and consulted their travelling maps diligently, they would often obtain far better and cheaper angling than by overcrowding some few spots to the neglect of others as good, if not better. Such at least has been my experience.

This dreary chapter and this dreary day at Galway are closing together. One has been sufficient, I cannot stand another, and shall to-morrow commence a ramble over some of the private and club waters, of which so many are to be found, in this delicious wilderness of Connemara.

CHAPTER XXIX.

Spiddal — Costello — Screebe — Furnace — Kilkerran Bay — Birterbury Bay — Roundstone — Ballinahinch — Clifden — View from Urrisbeg.

August 3.

POST TENEBRAS LUX—health after sickness, joy after sorrow, day after night, are each in their way delightful, and doubly so from the mere force of contrast. Yesterday I wrought on an uncongenial theme, and at an occupation for the first time in my life distasteful; but the page has been written, the work is over, and now Galway seems to wear a new aspect, as we drive through the streets to gain the beautiful road which, coasting along the western shores of the bay, skirting fiords, and winding among mountains, at length strikes the Killeries, and brings the tourist to the banks of the Errive.

Through the almost uninhabited solitudes of Jar-Connaught flow three small streams of exceeding goodness, the Spiddal, the Costello, and the Screebe; farther to the west we find the Ballinahinch fishery, Kylemore, and others; and at the edge of the county, where it touches Mayo, we have Delphi and the Errive.

Now the majority of these are club waters, and the remainder annually let to one or more rods. It may not be out of place, therefore, as we pass to visit these waters and say a few words on the physical character, piscatorial merits, and market value of each. A charming drive of ten miles along a coast road of marvellous beauty brought us to the little village of Spiddal, through which the stream hurries, and at once plunges into the sea. Over the whole country it seemed as if the sky had been raining granite boulders from the Deluge to the present day, so thickly were they spread over hill and valley, whilst in the bed of the Spiddal they lay in masses of every size and form. The comfortable lodge belonging to "the fishery" stands on a lawn that slopes down to the river, on the opposite bank of which rests the village, whilst between the lodge and the church runs the road to Costello, crossing the river at its mouth. The view of Galway Bay from the house is very fine, nor need the stranger fear bodily starvation whilst banqueting on the beautiful, for in the village he will find good bread, butter, mutton, eggs, and fowls; and what more can a sportsman desire? The length of the Spiddal is about twelve miles, but until very recently a waterfall, situated about three miles from the sea, barred the farther progress of the fish, and so practically reduced the river to a fourth of that extent. Now, however, a passage has been made which gives the salmon free access to the head waters, and the benefit of the extended franchise is already beginning to be felt. The water is well preserved, as the proprietor told me he employs eight keepers—a very strong staff considering the length of the property to be watched. The stream of which we are speaking resembles in its physical peculiarities the Costello, Screebe, Furnace, and one or two others on the coast, all of which possess an importance far beyond their extent. Considered as *rivers*, they would rank very low, being in fact little more than mountain brooks of eight or ten miles from the source to the sea, their high character being derived from a chain of small lakes which offer unrivalled white trout angling and salmon fishing of no mean quality. The scenery on the banks of the Spiddal is very lovely. As I saw it, there was a crystal stream fretting and murmuring at the mighty granite blocks that offered a hindrance to its passage; blooming heather, pleasant woods, and three miles from the sea a waterfall of exceeding beauty; then came a lake of considerable extent, then another stretch of rivulet, then another smaller lake, and so on to the source. In wet weather the best angling will be found on the river; in dry seasons on the lakes; the fish are fine, the salmon running from 5lb. to 18lb., the white trout from 1lb. to 6lb. Four or five of the former and a dozen of the latter would be a fair day's sport on the Spiddal; the proprietor, however, assured me that as many as eleven salmon had been killed in one day by a single rod. Many of the casts are very large and deep, as the Blue Pool, House, Weir, Wood, and Waterfall pools. The river, though *very* low, was singularly tempting, and had there been a fresh I should have desired nothing better than a day or two on its banks; but there was no chance of such a thing, so I could only hope for better fortune on some future occasion. The rent of house and angling is 100*l*. per annum; and what a holiday station for any overworked dweller in our great and busy cities! Why a turn on the lawn, the music of the waterfall, the purple moorland, the sparkling ocean, the profound quiet, and the delicious air, would be agents more potent for the restoration of health than all the tonics in the pharmacopœia; and had I one foot in the grave I should deem that a three months' sojourn in such an angler's paradise would restore me to pristine vigour of brain and body.

We have yet another ten miles before us, so we roll along by the winding waters of the noble Bay of Galway, drawing nearer and nearer to the Isles of Arran, which stretch their sheltering arms across its mouth, and form a haven where the navies of the world might ride, but where now a few small coasters lie at anchor, with an occasional ship from the Baltic with deals, or a rakish Greek brig with corn or meal. Then the road bends suddenly to the west, and we are speeding along the shores of Costello Bay, at the head of which is the far-famed river of the same name—a river which, including its lakes, does not, I should imagine, possess a greater length than nine or ten miles. Hardly any water in Britain (or elsewhere probably) of the same extent, has any sporting reputation at all. I never knew a single member of the club, nor did I ever hear any exact details of their sport; doubtless they have a capital thing, and, like wise men, enjoy their good fortune, and say as little about it as may be. The reticence of the club is admirable; we hear occasionally spirit-stirring accounts from the Thurso, the Erne, the Spey, or the Moy, but from the Costello "never a word." The rent of this little fishery—about 250*l*. per annum—speaks its excellence; and as I stood looking at the lodge, glistening in the evening sunshine, I could not but envy the possessors of such treasures. The situation of the house is perfect, close to the stream, and within a hundred yards of the sea, and whilst looking inland up the course of the river, we confessed we had seldom seen a wilder or more enchanting view. Like the Spiddal, the Costello requires rain to bring it up to concert pitch; and failing this the club are always able to fall back on the lakes.

At the head of a deep inlet called Kilkerran Bay two small rivers fall into the sea—the Screebe and the Furnace. These are new candidates for fame, and will probably within a few years equal, if they do not surpass, their older rivals. The Screebe has a course as long as either of the rivers I have recently described, and, moreover, has one peculiarity which distinguishes it from every other stream with which I am acquainted, for so close is the lower lake to the beach that at spring tides the fish are carried directly into it, and if disposed can at once ascend to three others. This is an incalculable advantage, as it makes the small river entirely independent of rain. These waters falling into the sea near each other are naturally in the hands of the same lessees. I cannot, however, do better than tell my story in the words of the able and energetic manager:

"The Screebe fishery is located north-west of Galway. You pass its head waters twenty-two miles from that town, on the Clifden-road, at a place called the Cross-roads. From the source it runs about ten miles due west through a number of lakes, and then falls into the head of Kilkerran Bay. The Furnace is a small stream running through several good lakes south-west of the Screebe, and falls into the same bay near the mouth of that river. It contains both salmon and sea-trout, but is a late stream, the fish not coming up before the first summer flood. As regards the sport to be had in these lakes (for it is chiefly lake fishing), I consider it is not to be equalled in Ireland, or I may say *will* not be in another year or two. The present lessees have only had it one year, and up to that time the fishery had not been cared for, except to kill every fish possible for the market. The spawning ground on this fishery was hardly enough to breed as many fish as would keep the otters, cranes, and cormorants which lived on it; but the spawning ground has been now increased tenfold; thirteen otters have been killed, and above one hundred cranes. A full-grown otter can eat 365 salmon at ten pounds each in one year, provided he dine off salmon every day, and a crane can swallow fifty or so of smolts for breakfast. As these have been destroyed, and as there was no netting last, and will be none in the coming, season, I anticipate seeing the best sport ever witnessed in Ireland. Last season I *saw* one of the lessees kill forty-two sea-trout and two salmon with his own rod in one day. The sea-trout are in abundance and afford excellent sport. The fishing opens on the 1st of February and closes on the last day of October, but I cannot say there is good sport before June, and July is still better. Although the fish come into the lakes at any time, I never saw many up before June, but as they increase I have no doubt they will come earlier, and then May will become a good month. I propagated in this river last season nearly 400,000 salmon, and, all being well, shall put down a million ova next spawning-time. The accommodation for gentlemen will be first-rate. A new house has been built, which will be opened on the 1st of May. There are seven bedrooms besides dining and drawing-rooms; it has been built expressly for the comfort of anglers. It stands at the head of a sea lough, five miles from the Cross-roads, and within a quarter of a mile of some of the best fishing. As regards the board, I expect it will be very moderate. The scenery round the lakes of the Screebe is very picturesque, though there is not as much wood in the neighbourhood as would make a skewer. You see nothing but water, bog, rock, and hills."

The laws laid down for the guidance of the infant states are so excellent I make no apology for giving them *in extenso:*

1. The price of each ticket for a single rod to be three guineas a week, this sum to include the use of boats and of a furnished lodge at Screebe.
2. Anglers may keep the fish they catch, except when otherwise stated in the rules.
3. No cross-line fishing or snatching allowed.
4. No gaffs allowed; landing-nets will be provided with the boats.
5. All spent fish to be returned to the water.
6. Water bailiffs to be always employed as boatmen, and paid 1s. 6d. per day each.

7. No boats allowed on the water except those provided by the lessees or their manager.

8. Gentlemen shall not permit their attendants to angle.

9. All licences to be taken out in the Galway district; they may be obtained at Galway, Oughterard, Glendalough, Deeradda Lodge, Carna, Spiddal, Currafin, Tuam, and of Mr. Thomas Cornely, at the lodge.

10. Season tickets only will be transferable.

11. Any ticket holder violating any of the above rules to forfeit his ticket.

On the westernmost arm of Kilkerran Bay is a stream smaller than either of those yet named—probably less than half their size—yet it is the outlet and connecting link between two or three small lakes, and beyond question would afford good fishing for white trout in the autumn. It appears, however, from want of accommodation to be absolutely inaccessible, except from points too remote to make it of any value.

At the head of Birterbury Bay is a similar little river, which, like the preceding, will doubtless soon be cultivated, and at small cost give large returns. Yonder is Roundstone Bay, at the head of which stands a thriving village of the same name, destined some day—when the science and enterprise, the engineering and agricultural skill of the nineteenth century are brought to bear on the latent resources of Connemara—to play an important part in the import and export trade of the district. Here poor Dick Martyn, in the hope of redeeming his sinking fortunes, founded the village of Roundstone, perhaps with a portion of the 160,000*l*. advanced by the Law Life Assurance Company on his family estate. I wonder whether any of the happy careless spirits who now haunt Ballinahinch with "a ticket" for a week, fortnight, or month, ever pause to reflect on the awful mutation in "the master's" fortunes, or the broken heart of the last of his race? It matters not, for both are now beyond the reach of human sympathy or human selfishness.

As a club water Ballinahinch is too well known to need any remarks from me. It has so long been extensively frequented, that it will be better to employ the space which yet remains in speaking of other stations of less note. Connemara offers the best white trout fishing in Ireland. From the Spiddal all round the extensive sea-board of Jar-Connaught to the head of the Killeries, this beautiful fish abounds, and, in my opinion, forms the raw material from which the best sport is produced. In this lovely district of course there are salmon; but if the numbers of trout be taken into consideration, I think it will be admitted that they form *par excellence the* fishing of Connemara. The lakes round Ballinahinch are justly celebrated for the sport they afford. I never fished them, but hope shortly to do so.

The road to Clifden skirts the "Lake Country," seen to such romantic perfection from the summit of Urrisbeg mountain. It is a wild, solitary, and almost uninhabited tract, with here and there a cabin dotting the vast flat. Innumerable pools, lakes, and water-holes light up the heathery waste, some of the large sheets of water bearing many a lovely islet, whose woody drapery—the dark and sombre yew—seems quite in harmony with the mournful loveliness of all around. In the great family of towns Clifden ranks as a mere baby. Five-and-forty years ago, history tells us, there was not a house, where now there is a town, not made up of a mere collection of hovels, but with three or four fair streets, decked with many good shops; altogether it forms a sort of sanctuary in the desert. It was too late to push on to Kylemore, and the divine beauty of the evening, showed, past all doubt, that we were quite as well in Clifden. Even my angling insanity could draw no picture of opportunity wasted, so with a heart at ease I strolled towards "the castle," down the banks of a narrow and beautiful inlet. The tide was full and so calm that the rugged shores seemed to grow beneath the water. Beyond the narrow entrance the broad breast of the Atlantic lay so peaceful that it seemed hard to believe it could ever be disturbed by stormy passions. Rounding one of the headlands of the bay, Clifden Castle came into view. In the house there was nothing remarkable, but for situation it was unrivalled. Behind are mountains, wood, and lakes; in front a noble lawn stretches down to the beautiful land-locked bay, whilst to the right the eye ranges over the glorious ocean until it mingles with the dim and far-off horizon.

Whilst watching all this loveliness the sun sank into the sea, and presently a deep rosy flush rose higher and higher till it reached the zenith, when it began to descend towards the south-east. Can that portend rain? Every sign in heaven, earth, and air said No. Then it *must* be for *wind;* and the sun, which has just sunk to rest, must rise very early to-morrow if he wishes to see me before I have measured half the distance to Kylemore.

For the last three or four days we have been following the coast line which bounds Connemara, and have in that time shown the reader "bits" of this fair land; but before leaving it, if he desires to obtain a bird's-eye of the whole, let him come with me to the summit of Urrisbeg, and see as glorious a panorama as ever was spread out to call forth man's adoration and fill his heart with gladness. The rough mountain path has long been lost, and now we wander on over a carpet of heather spangled with a thousand flowers, from slope to slope, till we gain the highest point. Southwards the whole coast lies spread out before us, with its innumerable bays and deep fiords sleeping in the sunshine; whilst dense volumes of white smoke from the kelp-burners' kilns spread a silvery veil over sea and land. Looking northwards towards Urrismore the eye wanders far and wide over a vast level district nearly uninhabited, almost uncultivated, and dotted with well nigh three hundred lakes, whilst at our feet blooms in rare luxuriance the Menziesia polifolia, many a saxifrage, and the deep purple stars of the Gentiana autumnalis, with a hundred more common but not less beautiful plants.

How such a picture stirs the blood and gives fresh vigour to brain and limb! Such a view once seen becomes engraven for ever on the memory, and will visit us many a day hence, when once more in the busy world, to cheer us in sorrow and give us new strength for fresh toil.

CHAPTER XXX.

Early Morning—Up before the Sun—Autumn—The Evening fulfils its Promise—A Breeze—Journey to Kylemore—A Day on the Lake—Doings for the Week—Leenane—The Killeries—Delphi—The Errive—Drive to Westport—The Reek, and what we saw there—On to Newport.

August 18.

THE world was asleep when we trotted out of Clifden. A few stars still lingered in the cool grey sky, winking wearily after their long watch; the valleys, the brown moorlands, and the bases of the Twelve Pins were all in their white night-robes; the horse seemed walking in his sleep; the driver snored audibly, and two of our party were thinking profoundly with their eyes shut; all was in harmony with nature, for nature slept. Oh, give me the morning, the fresh, beautiful morning—the infancy of the day! There is a hopefulness about it that no other portion of the twenty-four hours possesses, for there is yet a long stretch ere noon. *Then* how soon the sun begins to decline; little by little the shadows lengthen; twilight deepens into night; another day is gone, and we are so much nearer to the inevitable hour. But now we think not of night, for the morn is in its prime. Away up in the clear sky the Twelve Pins lift their immortal heads, and look down on us creatures of an hour with quiet majesty. An old cock grouse is chattering drowsily to himself of the fun he hopes to have with his wife and family; perhaps he is laying out his plans for the day, thinking where the richest bilberries grow, or meditating what mountain watercourse affords the longest and most blooming ling for their midday siesta. The small rough cattle have not yet risen to breakfast; only the restless sheep and goats are up and working for their daily bread, whilst an angler, equally restless—no doubt to the secret disgust of *his* wife and family—is padding through the mountains a full half hour before the sun will show his face and bid the world "good morrow." To my mind the scenery between

Clifden and the Killeries is the finest in the island. The road, now climbing a spur of the hills, reveals a thousand charms of earth and ocean, and anon rounding a quiet inlet, or coasting along the shores of a lake, gives us a peep up some lonely ravine into the deeper recesses of the mountains, at this season clad in the gorgeous flora of autumn. When we started on our wanderings, winter lay heavy on the dead earth; and now spring and summer are past—can it be so; for in my heart it is still spring. Have two-thirds of the year of liberty slipped away?—has it passed with the spring buds and summer flowers? Yes, the golden stars of the bog asphodel, and the bilberry with its delicate bloom, preach of the fading year. Well, *carpe diem*, we must do the best with the days that remain!

With the red sunrise comes the first faint flutter of the breeze. Presently the mountain gorges take up their song; dark masses of cloud float swiftly over the sky, thronging and thickening; in short there is half a gale from the westward—so wake up, oh driver! and push on with all speed for Kylemore, for I want some breakfast, and hunger still more on such a day as this to feel the rod in my fingers, and hear the wheel give out a yell of triumph over the first victim.

What a *beau ideal* of a station is this. From its proximity to the water and its distance from all other dwellings, the angler has to deal with the inmates of the *house* and none others; but on Irish lakes generally there is little fear of overcrowding, and on none less than Kylemore. True it is, for a day or part of a day there may be an eruption of tourists, who jump off their cars, rush to the lake, and hurry on elsewhere with the first light of the next morning; but nineteen times out of twenty the sportsman remaining at the inn for a week or month will generally have the water to himself, at least during the earlier part of the day. Although not by any means first-class in point of size, it yet contains room for four or five rods, even if those who hold them be ever so jealous and unsociable. Probably Lough Currane and Lough Melvin are as heavily fished as any of the Irish waters, and on them, certainly in July and August,

I have more than once wished my next neighbour "farther;" but, as a rule, an angler's sport is never materially injured from the too close proximity of unwelcome neighbours. As we drove along the shores of this solitary lake to the inn our impatience augmented with every step. The water was dark with wind and clouds, and the miniature rollers broke on the beach with a sullen plash, that made breakfast a botheration and delay intolerable. The gracious Duncan (his throne is vacant now) handed mistress and maid from the car, and received in the same breath a contradictory order for instant boat and immediate breakfast. "There was plenty of time," he said, "lashins of it; the wind would last till midnight any way, perhaps for a week, and gintlemen must eat; he'd see about a boat." On that occasion only, I brewed the social beverage; poured it out a moment afterwards; swallowed a cup of hot straw-coloured water, two or three degrees below the boiling point, pocketed a piece of bread, and rushed frantically out, to find Duncan the Good spelling over the address, and regarding with a puzzled aspect the innumerable railway labels which by this time were nearly as good as an outside cover, and formed, in fact, a sort of supplementary cuticle to my portmanteau. Leaning against the wall was a tall thin peasant, with a bilious countenance, in close conversation with a little round redfaced man, obviously the brewer in ordinary to all the illicit stills yet to be found in the mountains. These gentlemen, seeing a car drive along at such an unusual hour, had come up on speculation, and, in fact, were "just the boys" Duncan wanted—at least, so he said. In another minute the boat's keel grated over the pebbles, when the long man seizing the sculls paddled us off over the wavelets, every crest of which was whitened by the sweeping breeze that hurried over them. Such a day made success a certainty. All was in readiness when the bilious man squared the boat to let her drive fairly over the throw, and the instant he lay on his oars, away flew the flies (a mixed cast for trout and salmon) into the heaving waters. Every foot, nay every inch, the line traversed was so hopeful that I expected to see a broad tail or silvery side flash up each instant. Another, and another cast. "Kylemore can't be as good as I thought." A horrible quarter of an hour succeeded, during which a despondency, as unreasonable as the previous high pitch of my expectations had been extravagant, settled down on me. Ten minutes more, and then the usual hopeful patience once again had full possession of me. It is always a good plan to change the tackle in doubtful cases, for it largely increases the chance of success by keeping hope alive; so two fresh trout-flies, larger and brighter, were substituted in place of the discarded insects, and a dark green fur body with crimson tips, smoky blue hackle, jay shoulder and jungle-cock wing, occupied the post of honour. What glorious rises even small fish make on such a day. Had I not hooked him, I should have sworn the two-pound trout tugging at the end of my line had been a salmon. Another and another followed at short intervals. Then there was a magnificent rise at the little dropper, and the stout fish, shooting past our stern, steamed right away in the wind's eye. A breeze so heavy as that which now prevailed, always creates a difficulty, by preventing the angler measuring with any precision the strain on the tackle, or, which is the same thing, the pressure kept on the fish. The full force of this was now felt, and whether I was pulling to the value of eight ounces or two pounds, I could by no means divine. Unconsciously, perhaps, remembering the fineness of the finger's length of gut on which the dropper was tied, I was probably nearer the former than the latter weight, so we got on slowly though surely. After all, it was only a question of time. Running my eyes along the shore whilst mechanically keeping up a steady strain on the still powerful salmon, I observed Willie seated on a stone, patiently waiting the end of the struggle, which came to a conclusion about twenty minutes afterwards by the red-faced brewer gaffing with timid deliberation a short, well-made fish of 12lb. This painfully protracted process made me welcome my faithful follower warmly, who, however, looked a little indignant at having been left behind, as he pulled a quart bottle from the basket. "The mistress bid me give you your tea, and this piece of bread and butter, as you've had none the morn. There's nothing so bad as being in too big a hurry." Whether this was part of the message, or an original remark, I *thought it best* not to inquire; but as my friend hated all irregular doings, and in especial such as involved the loss of breakfast, I conjectured it was a mild rebuke for unnecessarily tampering with my digestion.

As we pulled against the gale I could not but admire the solitary and savage scenery around the lake, where "hills peep o'er hills, and Alps on Alps arise;" but soon we were on the same cast we had left, in order to take in our passenger, and in a few minutes afterwards were fast in another good fish. When about half done, and sailing soberly along some five feet below the surface, the dropper skimming most invitingly over the wavelets, a fine trout rose and took it. This at the moment was a huge delight, but presently the danger became too real to be agreeable. Occasionally, like an ill-assorted pair, they pulled opposite ways; there was no keeping that last person steady; a more volatile individual I never saw—sometimes above, sometimes below his fellow-prisoner: frequently behind, but worse than all, more often before the exhausted salmon. How the hook held so long was a wonder, but the parting moment drew near. After a short race the trout made a bound over the water, tore the hook from the jaw of the silvery log to which he was tied, and at the same time obtained a fixed point, which enabled *him* to snap the light thread which held him. How the rogues must have laughed over our discomfiture. Short time was wasted in lamentation, and before two minutes were passed damages were repaired, and "the firm" was once more in full work. This was the last disaster of the day; henceforward all "went merry as a marriage bell," and when evening settled down, our spoils might have set Mr. Groves up for a day's business. We had five salmon, a dozen and a half of white trout, and above a score of the coloured residents of the lake, not one of which, by the way, exceeded 15oz. or 18oz. Some of the trout were fine, one weighing over 5lb., and another above 4lb.; and of the salmon, the largest was the twelve-pounder which inaugurated the sport of the day.

Too happy and too excited to sleep, I heard the fierce wind rave through the mountains with unspeakable delight; and if for a moment I dozed off, it was only to dream of fresh victories. About one the rain drove furiously against the windows, and filled up the measure of my joy. With three hours for sleep before me—I now felt sure of the weather—I sank into that dreamless oblivion which yields such perfect rest. No alarum was needed to rouse me, and at half-past-four, on descending the stairs, I found Willie, Jack, Joyce, and the bilious man ready for a start. It has been before observed that "early fishing" is seldom productive, and that the best portion of the day for sport is from ten a.m. to three p.m.; on *certain* waters, however, I have often done *very* well about seven o'clock, particularly at Lismore, the bridge of Ballyshannon, and the pool on the beach at Waterville; perhaps also Kylemore should be added to the list. From half-past four to within a few minutes of the favourable hour referred to, we only rose a few small lakers, but presently afterwards the fun waxed fast and furious, and by eight we had two salmon and seven white trout in the basket.

Feeling the necessity of food, we beached the boat and walked up to the house, where, standing by the door, was a Saxon brother of the rod, who, like ourselves, was staying at the inn. A more persevering performer *after* breakfast I have rarely seen, but early rising was his abomination; if he ever felt disposed to make a vow against what Prince Hal calls "bed pressing," I am disposed to think he meditated doing so that morning, when Jack Joyce and the bilious party carried the well-stocked pannier past him into the kitchen. There is a sort of malicious triumph that at such moments will make itself felt, and I ushered our countryman in the *salon* shortly after with increased stature and a dignity not always usual with me. The meal was not a long one, yet *that* three-quarters of an hour sufficed to change the aspect of the day, and converted storm into calm, clouds into sunshine, and hope into despondency; then I felt repaid for the scores and scores of times I had risen for weeks together with the sun, and received little for my labour.

It would have been vain even to hope for such another grand break in the uniform glorious weather which so pre-eminently distinguished this summer; still, we fished with great perseverance, always remaining on the lake whenever a chance existed, and strolling over the noble mountains on impracticable days. Our subsequent sport never came up to. or even near. that first recorded; but we generally got a salmon, sometimes two, with more or less trout, and on the whole were abundantly satisfied with our doings in this very exceptional season. That Kylemore is an excellent station from July to October, there can be no doubt. We must not say, " better cannot be found ;" still, let there be the amount of wind and clouds usual in ordinary years, and we maintain that few anglers will leave this wild lake dissatisfied with their entertainment. As the car bore us along its shores on the afternoon of our departure, I felt no small regret at leaving a place where I had been so happy. With what wonderful minuteness memory traced out every spot where victory smiled or disaster attended me. I remember them now with perfect exactness, and fancy that when *they* are forgotten there will be few things I shall be able to recall at will.

The sun was sinking behind the mountains of Murrisk as we drove up to the snug and unpretending hospitium at Leenane, near the head of the Killeries. This beautiful inlet, of which so much has been written, is a narrow and deep fiord running far inland. and bounded on either side through its whole length by a lofty range, as wild and picturesque as any to be found in the island. It is nearly a mile in width, and though the hills rise sheer from the water's edge, yet they fall off here and there, and discover wild glens, savage ravines, and many a more distant peak beyond. On the north-west bank lies Delphi, hid in the wilderness of Murrisk, not only the most secluded corner of Mayo, but probably the most sequestered district in the three kingdoms, for the tourist rarely invades it, and the wandering angler could find no accommodation there. Everybody has heard of Delphi as an admirable station ; but, like the Costello, few except the lessees know anything about it. Several times in passing Leenane I vowed to cross the harbour and view this mysterious *elysium piscatorum*, but something always occurred to prevent the fulfilment of the vow, and when at length

P

it was accomplished no words of mine can describe it half so well as Inglis has done years ago :—

> A short half-hour sufficed to put me across, and stepping ashore in a little cove opposite to a wide mountain hollow I followed the path which was pointed out to me. About a mile from the shore I reached the entrance to the mountain hollow, and another mile into the heart of it brought me to the neighbourhood of Delphi. The lodge itself is not any way remarkable, but its situation is. It lies in a deep recess among the mountains, which rise lofty and abrupt on all sides excepting one, where there is a little lake, along whose margin winds the road to the house. The immediate neighbourhood of the house is well wooded, and abundance of sweet-smelling flowers made an odorous atmosphere around. It is certainly a tranquil and singular spot."

Inglis was no angler, or he could not have dismissed "the little lake near the house" with so slight a notice, for, unless I make a great mistake, it offers about the best white trout fishing in the kingdom. The river below is rather more than two miles in length, and in high water affords admirable sport. In the lodge an anchorite might find himself comfortable in the matter of solitude. Hemmed in on one side by the deep and dark water of the fiord, and on the other, shut out from the world by miles and miles of mountain and swamp, the proprietors enjoy the most undisturbed piscatorial domain to be found within the four seas of Britain. Knowing none of the dwellers in this happy land, nor having any letters of introduction, my power of obtaining trustworthy information was so small that I contented myself with looking at river and lakes, and imagining the glorious spawning-beds lying far off in many a solitary valley among the pathless mountains of Murrisk. Eight or ten years ago this fishery was said to hold the finest white trout in Ireland, and I have *heard* of their being taken here up to the extraordinary weight of 16lb. Since that time no doubt the stock has improved—most of the waters in the island have advanced in different degrees, certainly few, if any, have retrograded; and Delphi, which retained such a reputation in the darkest days of the Irish rivers, ought *now* to be good indeed.

The Errive, a stream without any lacustrine head, after a considerable course falls into the head of the Killeries. The lodge belonging to the river is one of the most comfortable in Ireland, and its situation is excellent. Placed at the mouth of the Errive, it enjoys a noble view down the inlet, and is alike suited to command fresh-water angling, boating, or sea-fishing. This river is now in the market. I knew it when rented by a most amiable and warm-hearted nobleman, who, with his accustomed kindness, made me free of the water. As ill-luck would have it, I was then returning from a month's inimitable angling, and a month's nearly absolute starvation, in the wildest nook of Mayo, during which time I endured great toil coupled with constant wet, and the upshot was that, on the second morning of my sojourn at Leenane, I was so ill that I could hardly stand, and was glad to make the best of my way to Galway and lay up for three or four days.

It was a long drive between Leenane and Westport, over a tolerably level track, rich in wild flowers, and boasting some of the most gigantic boulders I ever saw, under whose shelter the Menziesia polifolia attained its maximum of size and beauty. But though the journey was long we got it over at an early hour, by dint of starting in what Mr. Willie profanely called to his too confiding mistress "the middle of the night." Still this very matutinal start enabled us, after having deposited bag and baggage at the hotel, to be clear of the last cabin of Westport, on our way to the Reek, soon after noon. I am not one to jest at sincerity, or smile in affected pity at those who worship our common Father in a different form or with another tongue. It was in no such idle spirit that we stood on the summit of Croagh Patrick, gazing alternately on the labyrinth of mountains and lakes which make up Murrisk, the hundred isles which deck Clew Bay, or the crowd of devotees performing their devotions on this great "high place." Some were prostrate in silent adoration; others knelt at the various stations round the stony cairns; all performed their rounds on bare feet, a few on bare knees. But there was one person, a priest, who enlisted my sympathy amazingly. When I first noticed him he was limping slowly and painfully round one of "the stations," carrying his shoes and stockings in either hand, whilst his trousers were tucked up in the vain hope of cooling his blistered and bleeding feet. The poor father was evidently an admirer of nature, for slung over his broad shoulders was a large old-fashioned glass, which soon brought us into the most friendly relations. "Maybe the lady would like to look at the say and the islands beyant? Ah! well; *perhaps you would* like it." offering me the rejected telescope, and adjusting his own particular focus with great care; in fact, the worthy divine was dying for a chat, and an excuse to pause on the stony road to repentance. I found him the most kindly and simple of human beings. He informed me he had left his cure for a few days' change, and fancied that the air, scenery, and devotional exercises on the summit of the Reek were likely to produce an equally sanitary effect on body and soul. In half an hour we became great friends. "Ask him to dinner," whispered Madame, who was evidently much taken with him. On inquiry, I found that his religious duties would be over in half an hour, and that his way lay through Westport, so I plucked up courage and begged the favour of his company; this he kindly promised, and I am bound to say I have seldom spent a more pleasant evening. The day had been a long one, but was not yet over. After we had seen the good priest mount his car and trot slowly away, we started for Newport, whither Willie—under the special care of his sister—had been sent on some hours previously to obtain a lodging which we once before occupied when fishing this district. A quarter of a mile outside the little town, which poor Maxwell calls "the *ultima thule* of civilised Europe," I found my faithful comrade seated on a turf bank patiently waiting my arrival.

"Where have you left Mary?"

"Up in the big house, sir."

"What house? Have you not taken the one we had before?"

"No. The new curate has took it for six months certain;" and then, in a stage whisper to his mistress, "the drawing-room, mum, is as big as a church and as empty as a barn," and Mary says, "you'll be lost in it intirely."

CHAPTER XXXI.

The Big House—Head-quarters at Newport—Advantages of our Position in Wet and Dry Weather—Newport River—Burrishoole, Tyrena—Pleasant Dreams—Michael O'Leary's Board—Early Start—An Inn amongst the Mountains—Breakfast—A Day after my own Heart, the Dawn of which is only shown in the present Chapter.

September 8.

COULD Dominie Sampson have been ushered into our new quarters, doubtless his first exclamation would have been "Prodigious!" On a table near the fire flickered a pair of wretched candles, making darkness visible; in the grate a smouldering pile of peat emitted a cloud of smoke, together with a faint light, so faint indeed that the whole of the great room, except the portion immediately round the hearth, was as dark as the sky in a starless, moonless night. A score of Fenians might have been lurking in the shadowy corners. I felt all the depressing influence of the mysterious and the unknown. A vague sense of uneasiness was creeping over me; I tried to shake it off, and lit a pipe by my own fireside; but the huge rusty bars seemed never to have heard of the sweet charities of home, and the rude but spirited carving below the mantel-piece looked so strange and weird in the uncertain light that I began to feel in very uncanny company. In fact, I was fast getting into a highly nervous state. Anything was better than being hagridden in this fashion, so, seizing one of the candles, I set off on a journey of exploration. Holding the "dip" high above my head, I was able to see that a handsome cornice ran round the walls, and that the centre of the ceiling was ornamented with a rich and beautiful design, a portion of which had fallen, perhaps in the midst of some wild revel. On the floor were three or four tattered pieces of carpet, in strong contrast to each other as regarded pattern and colour, whilst the furniture consisted of a few chairs, and a table so diminutive that it showed like a fragment of wreck floating on the wide sea. Altogether there was an air of mournful grandeur and ruined magnificence about the place which was quite oppressive. It seemed haunted by the ghosts of former occupants. The night air, sighing through chink and rathole, sounded like the wailings of too late repentance for riot and misrule. The rooms on the ground floor formed a shop, wherein, resting against the counter, was the proprietor of the mansion, the most melancholy man that ever kept a store. Whether he was on the eve of bankruptcy, whether he was the last of the race who had revelled there, or whether he was doing penance on earth for the sins of his forefathers, I never inquired, for the poor fellow's case was evidently beyond the reach of my art. What that shop contained I never could learn, and the townspeople apparently knew as little as I did, for, during a sojourn of three weeks, I did not hear of a single customer darkening his door. In fact, "the store" was a mystery, for no man could have decided with certainty to what class it belonged. On a long range of dusty shelves reposed eight or ten large bottles and jars, which gave the establishment something the appearance of a chemist's gone to seed. Manifold little drawers, too, were there, labelled "pepper," "mustard," "sugar," but "all was seeming, nought was truth," for bottles and jars were empty, and the spice depôt was filled with rusty nails, broken china, a prodigious number of damaged corkscrews, and all sorts of odds and ends. It was clear the owner was neither grocer, druggist, nor ironmonger, and observation left the mystery more mysterious still. In short, it was the ghost of a shop; everything therein was airy and impalpable, and the proprietor of the empty jars, paper bags, and crazy shelves seemed like a ticket-of-leave man from the silent shores of the river Styx.

In the Newport district the best fishing is *absolutely* dependent on rain. When we left Kylemore, Admiral Fitzroy's glass showed signs of a coming change, and the crystals floating still higher in the fluid at Leenane caused our hurried march from that pleasant hostelry. Still the sky was blue, the mountain tops clear, the wind as unsympathising as it had been of late, and now, as I looked out of my great desolate chamber and saw an unclouded arch, " all throbbing and panting with stars," I felt that even my friend Fitz had proved faithless.

As a "head centre" Newport offers capital autumn quarters. Close to the town flows a little river, with many good deep pools and a fair stock of fish. A short distance to the westward the road crosses a long bridge, through whose arches flow the surplus waters of Burrishoole Lake, where angling can always be enjoyed—of course irrespective of rain—and a few miles farther brings the tourist to Tyrena, which needs description. Some seasons since Colonel Gore, to whom the district at that time belonged, most kindly gave me permission to fish the water. I reached it late in the season, during a week of incessant rain, and enjoyed such sport as ever after placed Tyrena in my most affectionate remembrances. This brook, from its source half way up the mountain side to its debouchment into Clew Bay, cannot exceed, if it reaches, a length of three miles. It flows through probably the wettest moss in Ireland, yet with twelve hours' fine weather its bed becomes dry, a few black boggy holes excepted. But in Mayo, happily, the sky is much given to weeping, when the morasses, always saturated, instantly begin to overflow, pouring into the watercourses a black deluge, and in an hour or two afterwards the torrent is *full* of splendid white trout. Not only is this mountain rill an angling wonder, but it is one of the most instructive in the country. Fancy a stream of only three miles! Why, there are thousands of despised brooks in the three kingdoms of thrice this length which are absolutely valueless, all of which are, however, capable of being made equal to Tyrena. If a man has but water he *can* have fish, as surely as a cottager possessed of a few square yards of ground can grow cabbages. But this is not quite the place to discuss or enforce fish culture, more especially as it has just been done far better than I can hope to do it; so I will recapitulate the advantages of Newport as an autumn quarter for anyone blessed, as I was, in the possession of angling powers, and then go to rest. If the weather be fine the sportsman has Burrishoole. During the fall of a fresh, and some days afterwards, the Beltra is sure to yield sport, and in wet weather there is the best brook of its size in the kingdom to be found at Tyrena.

Except my landlord, a more melancholy gentleman than myself that night never laid his head on the pillow; nevertheless, worn out with a long and rather laborious day, I soon fell asleep. After a while Queen Mab drove her dreamy chariot through my brain. I was in an auction mart, and constrained by some mysterious influence to bid frantically for every lot. Nine gorgeous parrot cages were knocked down to me. A tenement in Bow Street next became mine, under a penalty of 100*l*. per annum if I failed to reside therein seven months in each year. Then I was made the happy possessor of a cradle and four children's cots. How wretched I felt. Parrots were my aversion; an enforced residence in Bow Street was an abomination; and what had I to do with babies? I could not have held, far less have nursed, one to save my life. But another lot is up. Hark at that remorseless "Going, going, gone!" With that light rap the nightmare agony reached its climax, and I awoke. What can that noise be? There was a sound as if twenty thousand hammers were beating the uncomplaining earth. Intelligence slowly returned. Can it be? Yes; now I recognise the well-known sound. It is—it is—a perfect deluge of rain. Eagerly I struck a light; only three a.m. How the torrent poured and poured. There was not an air; nothing but one dull and incessant thud—thud—thud. If I lit one match in the next hour and a half, I lit ten. At last the long hand stood at six, and the short hand midway between four and five; and then, springing out of bed, I dressed at full speed, hurried down stairs, and so out into the dawn and the rain. Not a soul was stirring; the ducks and I had the whole of the steep street to ourselves. The Beltra, so pellucid last evening, was now dark and turbid, and two rival torrents were leaping and foaming down either side of the street. But rain is a fisherman's fine weather; trusty boots and an oiled coat formed garments of proof; and I was as much at ease under the pitiless pelting as my web-footed companions. No Irish village wants either horse or car, yet now I looked in vain for an announcement of these desirable things. As usual, the blessing sought lay close to my door, and had been overlooked. On my return I found it. Near our palace was a narrow court or passage, at the end of which was a car standing on end, with the shafts in the air, getting the unaccustomed luxury of a good wash. Nearer inspection showed me a small board, nearly a foot square, of a flaming yellow, with some extraordinary obsolete vehicle painted thereon, attached to which was the picture of a wonderful animal belonging to a species now extinct.

A few steps brought me to the house. "Tommy, Tommy O'Boyle! Hollo, Tommy O'Boyle!" A portentous snore was the only reply. Bow-wow-wow was the answer to a few hearty kicks on the door.

"Nick, ye villan, lave the pigs alone."

Kick—kick—kick, bow-wow-wow, performed in true classic strophe and antistrophe, at last awoke the owner of the patent safety vehicle. Nick's invocation, joined with my own, had been somewhat potent, and Mr. O'Boyle suddenly appeared in a suit of primitive buff, tastefully overlaid with a white tunic, called by the vulgar a shirt. On the advent of his master, Nick kindly pardoned my too early call, and, being a dog of practical mind, improved the occasion by making a light and cheap breakfast by licking the grease off my boots.

"Could I go at once to Tyrena?"

"Is it a kar yer honour 'll be wanting this fine mornin'?" observed Mr. O'Boyle, with a pleasant smile.

"Of course. What else can I want?"

"I'm thinking it's to Pat's yer goin'. Fait, I'll be wid ye immadiately."

"The coachman" was as good as his word, and by the time I had roused up my servant he drove to the door and we were off.

Mile after mile we sped on towards Tyrena over barren wastes. The peat bog through which we moved, with its blackened surface and dark piles of dried fuel, heaped in immense mounds and cast in every variety of form and size, bore a fanciful resemblance to a city consumed by fire. Everything looked charred. It seemed as if the element had done its work effectually, leaving nothing but discoloured walls and blasted earth. The scene grew more and more wild as we advanced; bleak and sterile mountains without a trace of cultivation; dark valleys and tracts of morass dripping from the recent rains; whilst from every hollow, rivulets blackened with bog-water dashed across the road and threatened to stop our farther progress. Below lay Clew Bay, with its many islets decking the sparkling waters. Beyond rose the Reek, its lofty cone catching the light clouds as they drifted from the ocean. Far in the distance towered the highland ranges of Connemara, with the twelve pins of Bunabola, and the bold cliffs of Clare Island; whilst before us stretched the Atlantic, rolling onwards to the beach with a long and measured swell.

> Making sweet music on the lonely shore.

"Here's the place," observed our driver, pulling up suddenly before a cabin situated on the edge of the bog at a little distance from the road. "Here's the hotel, and the best, too, any way from this to Belturbet."

Now, Belturbet lay some thirty-two miles off, and in declaring Pat's the best *hospitium* within that space, Mr. O'Boyle for once spoke the truth, for it was the only one.

Leaning against the door was a slight active peasant, with a round bullet-shaped head, close curling hair, and eyes as quick and wandering as ever shone in human orbits. If Pat be not the most restless spirit in creation, there is no reliance to be placed on eyes.

Well aware, from the rapid rise and fall of the waters of Tyrena, that if we expected sport we must remain on the ground and take advantage of every shower, we decided on securing such accommodation as Pat's domicile afforded. The exterior of the cottage certainly did not promise much. The kitchen was a fair sample of those usually found in the better class of Mayo farmhouses; on the lime-ash floor children were playing and pigs sleeping; moreover, there were ducks, geese, and fowls, two cats, an outdoor farm boy, and the hostess, all waiting for their common breakfast—a few stone of potatoes—which were successfully progressing under the superintendence of a very pretty girl, daughter to the said hostess. The state room was placed on the left of the common apartment, and, in the opinion of the good people of this primitive district, was furnished with every luxury man could desire. It contained a bed, table, two chairs, and a three-legged stool, all admirably uniform in colour—bed, bedding, floor, chairs, and table, being of a dull chocolate hue from the accumulated dirt of years. One would have conceived from their appearance that water was as scarce and valuable a commodity in this locality, as in the great desert of Sahara. It seemed impossible to remain, and I hinted as much to Willie, who, with a cool unconcerned air, desperately provoking at such a time, was trying to look through the dirty windows.

"Lave it to me, sir," was his reply. "When you and Pat come back from taking a walk up the river, see if breakfast an't ready and iverything snug and comfortable."

With all reliance on the speaker's versatile genius, I had little hope of his being able to fulfil his promise.

The little river was in a terrible taking from the rain—foaming, fretting, chafing, and leaping over rocks and stones, hurling along huge fragments of turf, and behaving altogether in a very turbulent and headstrong manner. It was, moreover, nearly as black as ink, and had I been put on my oath I should with a quiet conscience have sworn it would be impracticable for the next two days. Pat was, however, of a different opinion, and employed himself as we walked along in setting up various hydrometers of a primitive construction, consisting of a series of twigs placed in the sand at the edge of the stream.

As far as the eye could range not even a hut was in sight. Before us the Morne Tomas mountains formed a glorious amphitheatre, and from Carrig-a-Binniogh (the loftiest of the group) rose the stream whose course we were following. Midway up its side the brook had its source, was instantly joined by a hundred little rills, and soon in considerable volume rushed down its sides with a voice of thunder and in a robe of snow. From this point to the sea its whole length did not exceed three miles. As we returned, Pat's divining rods gave the welcome assurance that the water had attained for the present its utmost limits. It had ceased to rise, and in an hour would be in order.

If Pat hardly knew his own house, it was no wonder I failed to recognise it. The hostess appeared to have yielded absolute submission to the Saxon; to have calmly resigned her sceptre, relinquished the cares of state, and retired for ever from the turmoil of public life. I can hardly help laughing now at the aspect of affairs on our return. The spirit of reform was in full activity, and the innovations in Mrs. M'Hale's dominions were alarming. Willie, in a huge pair of fishing-boots, was paddling over the streaming floors, steering his way successfully through an intricate mass of buckets, tubs, and boxes of sand; trotting from one part of the room to the other, all the while encouraging, exhorting, and directing the labours of half a dozen old ladies, who, under the unusual stimulus of a shilling a head, were working with praiseworthy industry. Beds, bedsteads, and bedding had vanished. Whether the colony which inhabited those ancient settlements had transported themselves and their homes to a quieter shore I never inquired, having no doubt of the physical capacity of those industrious insects to have walked off with the furniture at any moment. Chairs, tables, and stools were enjoying the unwonted luxury of a bath in a little lake beside the house, waiting patiently till the ladies had leisure to shampoo them. Floors were rapidly assuming their pristine whiteness, windows were cleaned, doors washed, walls swept, and in a corner was a pile of blooming heath, a couch for a king. There had not been such a demand for labour in the district in the memory of man. Mrs. M'Hale stood by the fire in a state of such utter bewilderment as to be wholly incapable of giving assistance or framing a remonstrance, staring in dull astonishment as each of her chattels walked in or out of the establishment, or presented itself to her wondering gaze in some new garb. In short, it seemed as if the whole furniture was bent on a masking frolic, and a levée *en masse* collected to deck them out for the fête.

"Bedad, your honour," observed Pat, who had all the while been standing on his own threshold with a puzzled air and a humorous smile on his extraordinary countenance, "Bedad, your honour, next time we clean house you shall have it rint free for a fortnight." The indefatigable steward had forgotten no single point. On a flowery knoll a clean cloth was spread, and the fair Margaret busy in culinary preparations. Oh, the luxurious happiness of that humble meal! A plate of oatmeal porridge, a pile of potatoes, a slice of rye bread, and a cup of delicious coffee, brought by my provident comrade, formed the entire *carte;* but time, place, and circumstances lent a gusto that all the sauces of Lazenby or art of Soyer could not have afforded; and seating myself on the fragrant cushion nature gave, with the sparkling waters of Clew Bay before me, the majesty of Morne Tomas above me, the murmuring river at my feet, I ate, laughed, and drank as if life had no sorrow, and the world no care.

With his pockets full of potatoes just removed from the pot Pat steamed into our breakfast parlour, and, without a word, led the way down the knoll. The stream, dark and turbid, swept furiously through the rustic arches of the bridge which supports the Achill road. About twenty yards above this point the brook turned at a sharp angle, forming a most tempting pool, the eligibility of the spot being further increased by a huge fragment of granite, which broke the current, sending it off in two long rippling lines. All this was seen at a single glance as I stood on the bank, striking the line from the rod, previous to making the first cast. Scarcely had the fly touched the water when a quick dash showed there was game afoot; soon the line was again flying towards the opposite bank; in another second there was an eager rise, and we could just see a heavy trout well hooked shoot off into the boiling torrent. Just then the tail fly swept past the rock, and was instantly taken by a small salmon of seven or eight pounds. The strain of the tackle was tremendous, and the fish, now in full current, were settling bodily towards the bridge; the danger was imminent; in fact, the only chance of success lay in bringing them again within the eddy. Once the object seemed nearly attained, when a heavy lunge of the largest fish again hurried both in the centre of the stream. Inch by inch they neared the bridge. Pat danced before us like a frantic dervish; ten men would have been unable to execute his contradictory orders; and my faithful follower, feeling the case hopeless, was silent. Stones were hurled into the raging flood, and produced as much effect as so many rain drops; in vain we endeavoured to turn every eddy, every stone to our advantage. The leading fish was within a foot of the centre pier. Now for a last effort; the good rod, already bent double, was still further pressed, when a sharp crack announced it had been taxed beyond endurance, at the same instant the fish entered separate arches, the casting line crossed the pier, snapped, and I, like the miller's maid, was left lamenting. Fortunately the catastrophe was not irreparable; an idler was forthwith dispatched to the cabin for a second rod, with which he returned by the time I had extracted a fresh casting line from the book. In a few minutes we were again at work, and at once commenced doing a very pretty business, as will be faithfully shown in the following chapter.

CHAPTER XXXII.

A Day after my own Heart—Dinner by Proxy—The Spoils—Night—
Pat redivivus.

September 16.

PAT led the way through the swamp, pushing on from pool to pool more rapidly than we deemed advisable, certainly far faster than we should have done had we been left to our own guidance in this the deepest morass in the kingdom. Every point at which he paused, however, held a rising fish or two, and as the trout were remarkably fine, the basket suspended by a hayband round his neck soon became heavy.

If satiety be the death of enjoyment, novelty lends it fresh life, and here everything was new. A brook, the width of which hardly exceeded half the length of my rod, a mountain torrent of black water rushing down the glen, and a savage wilderness whose recesses still held a remnant of the original red deer, all helped to heighten the charm; and then Pat was so polite that it was as much as I could do to keep pace with his courtesy. No sooner was a flat lightly fished over *once*, than my obliging attendant relieved me of the rod and trotted on as hard as he could go to the next lodge, which he usually contrived to get half through before I came up. On one of these occasions, having succeeded in catching him, I held out my hand for my property; the usurper did not actually refuse, but said, with a feeling I at once recognised and respected, "Yer honour, I ris him three times, and, Mary, warn't he king of the trouts! The crathur's tin pounds if he's an ounce." And he cast an imploring glance at my face, in hope, perhaps, of finding some trace of brotherly love and charity. I understood the appeal. "Try him again, Pat; he's yours if you get him." I had not seen the fish, nor did I believe him to be anything like the size stated, or my self-denial might have been less heroic, as I watched the impulsive party hurl his fly right at the head of the enemy. How I regretted my rash promise as a magnificent fish flashed under the gaudy lure.

"It must be a salmon, Pat."

"A salmon! No, no! A salmon, yer honour? Don't I know a briddawn when I see one? He's a trout, sir, I'm telling ye."

This was said with considerable asperity. With some difficulty we persuaded Mr. M'Hale to be calm and rest on his oars for a minute, at the expiration of which the line once more flew over the water, and before the fly had sailed a couple of feet, the same fish dashed up and took it. The first desperate leap showed him nearly all that Pat had stated him to be, and the second bound, landing him high and dry on the bank, gave us full opportunity to admire the finest trout that ever died under my rod, though unhappily not by my hand. With a diminutive head, high shoulder, deep side, and a weight of 8½lb., what a beauty he was, and what a warning against making rash promises!

From hag to hag Pat again bounded over the bog, the enormous basket with which he had provided himself bumping against his shoulders in a manner truly perplexing. Now this basket, which had for some time been attracting my attention, was nothing more nor less than a horse-pannier, a machine much in vogue in this cartless country, being in fact the only recognised mode of conveying the crop from the field or the turf from the bog ; as for filling it, that was surely an impossibility; it could hardly, therefore, be said to have been brought out exclusively for use, neither could it exactly be considered ornamental. Had Mr. M'Hale's versatile genius suggested its employment, in order to impress on the minds of two luckless foreigners the famed qualities of the water? or was it only to be considered as an exaggerated allegorical emblem of plenty—a species of piscatorial cornucopia? No matter—look at it how I would, there was comfort in it.

The meeting of the waters was a pretty spot; for a few hundred yards before their junction they ran murmuring on, gradually approaching each other, parted only by a low narrow slip of land, sweet from the breath of the Myrica gale; then, like lovers long parted, they hurried into each other's embrace, rushed joyously over a ledge of rocks, and mingled their waters in a pretty granite basin. Here for a few minutes we were unsuccessful; at the lower end of the pool the water became more shallow, and there a salmon dashed at the fly, but turned short as if disappointed; a second and a third rise followed in rapid succession. "Oh! Terry, Terry, I fear your handiwork is anything but what it should be." On the morning of our leaving Ballina the said Terry had given me parting advice and a parting gift. The gift consisted of a dozen flies, carefully done up in brown paper; the advice was, to hover near Tyrena, and pounce down on the river the moment the weather broke up. Whilst mournfully inspecting Mr. Diver's donation, my meditations were rudely interrupted.

"Don't stand looking at the casting line, yer honour," observed Pat, " but cover him again—there you have him!"

Mr. M'Hale was wrong, however; it was no salmon, though a fair substitute for one, turning out when netted to be a white trout of 5lb. I had now an opportunity of examining, more closely than I had hitherto done, the articles with which Terry had provided us.

"Did ever man see the like," remarked Pat. "I'd not wonder if the maker had caught a rainbow and given you a handful—gold, green, blue, crimson, yellow, violet, and orange," continued he, reading one of the despised articles from tail to shoulder; "divil such a thing ever I see."

In fact, the flies were rather remarkable, and deserve description; so, whilst Pat is extracting the hook from the jaw of the trout, we will examine our stock. Whether shade, shape, or steel be considered, never were twelve more unpromising specimens. The hooks, remarkably fine in the wire, inordinately long in the shank, and very small in the bend, were of a kind sometimes used in trout-fishing for taking full-length likenesses of the palmer family, and, as if such ridiculous implements were not already three times too long, Terry had bedecked each with a topping by way of tail. But the bodies—ah! there lay the core and marrow of my grief; they would have exhausted the patience of a saint, but nearly drove a sinner like myself stark mad, as they lay glittering before me in an endless variety of short joints, composed of the brightest and most opposite coloured floss, relieved here and there with a patch of gold or silver. No hackle shaded these naked beauties, unless a single turn of jay at the head could be considered as a sort of ballet equivalent for the ordinary garb in which salmon flies are wont to appear; and even this poor apology was more than half obscured by the long turkey wing. Strictly speaking, they looked like nothing on the earth or under the water; and though Pat's idea of their resembling so many inch stripes of consolidated rainbow might give some faint notion of their general appearance, to my fancy they seemed more like a group of harlequins with yellow tails and long brown coats. To expect sport with such flies, Pat declared utterly impossible; the book was hastily looked over, and a small orange silk body, grouse hackle, and owl's wing selected as point, whilst a golden olive trout-fly was elected to the office of dropper.

The good effects of the change were soon apparent, and every pool became the scene of a fresh triumph. This was too good to last. The mist which had been lying all the morning in heavy masses on the crest of Carrig-a-Binniogh began now to wear a more threatening aspect; even to an inexperienced eye it looked ominous. Pat knew its import well. "Yer honour's sport is nearly over for the present; there's a lump o' rain about to fall on the mountain, and the flood will be on us afore ye can try the three next pools."

This additional stimulus was not required. The wild glen, the tall mountains, the dark torrent, and the stern and lonely character of the scene all conspired to fill me with enthusiasm. The enjoyment was no longer of that tranquil kind so faithfully depicted by honest Izaak and his follwers; it had grown a fierce and eager passion. But three more pools! Could fate be so cruel? On we dashed to make the most of the brief space which remained. The three pools mentioned by Pat were the most tempting I had seen for the day. No sooner had the fly lit on the water than a small trout under 2lb. marked it for his own, and was soon safely stowed with his kindred in the pannier. He had hardly disturbed the water—away flew the fly, again it was seized, and this time by a larger fish. Bearing heavily on the tackle, I snatched a hurried glance at the mountain which seemed to tower almost immediately above us. The cloud had burst, and its contents were leaping towards the glen in a thousand petty channels, rapidly uniting, and then thundering on with increased speed and volume. Heavier and heavier the line was strained on the struggling captive, till he neared the surface, and was dexterously netted before half his energies were exhausted.

"Hooroo!—hooroo; there's time for another; go it yer honour!"

Suiting the action to the word, my excited companion sped away towards a point some fifty yards ahead. A 5lb. trout floundering in the net, and resisting all Pat's attempts to extract the hook, sadly impeded his frantic efforts to reach the pool before the flood, which could be seen too plainly not a hundred yards above, speeding towards us with ruffled crest and angry voice. Pat still kept the lead by a few strides, intent only on hurrying on, and unmindful of the old saw, "look before you leap," he set his foot on a more than ordinarily soft part of the bog, and at the next bound was fairly planted deep at his waistcoat pocket. Plunging desperately forward, he gained a momentary footing on a tuft of rushes, lost his vantage ground, and rolled helplessly into the quagmire. His fall broke the light gut of the dropper, which was still firm in the jaw of the fish; and the line drifted clear of the net as it fell from Pat's hand. A slight bend to the left afforded firmer footing, and in a second I was at the goal. The flood was filling a pool not twenty yards from the one at which I stood—again and again the fly swept across the surface. "What, not another ere it comes?" Once more the line flew over the lower part of the lodge—a dull ruffle followed. A salmon! a salmon! Huzza! I have him.

On rushed the flood carrying all before it. The strong fish breasted it for a few seconds, but, impeded by the line, shot rapidly round and darted down the torrent like an arrow. To give line was to lose him; for brushwood, rushes, and turf sods were whirling along in wild disorder, thick as leaves in June. The narrow course of the brook, its numerous abrupt turnings, and the luxuriant growth of heath and whin that fringed its banks, made it a work of sufficient difficulty to keep the line clear, short as it was, so I pelted full tilt over bog, rock, and heath as well as I could. Fast and furious grew the race—'twas for life or death. Of Pat I thought not—nay, for the time, forgot that such a person ever existed.

Splash, splash, splash. Can it be the echo of my own steps? Had existence depended on it, I could not have avoided turning nervously in the direction of the sound; and what a sight met my eyes! Minus his hat and boots, the big trout flourished in one hand, and the net brandished in the other, his whole person dripping from the late immersion, and his face a bright Modena tint from the colour of the bog, Pat sped like a gallant knight to the rescue.

Two to one are long odds; the fish could hardly hold his own before, and now my comrade's opportune arrival soon settled the contest. The salmon, utterly exhausted, floundered towards the bank—his hour was come; helpless and motionless he was lifted into the net and borne off by Pat, who had just breath enough to exclaim :

"Quick, quick, yer honour; now for the shelter, any way!"

The rain descended in torrents; the very windows of heaven seemed open. The little river was by no means a pleasant neighbour, but roared and reeled along like a drunkard. As Pat subsequently observed, "She had just taken a drop too much."

In the morning I had been inclined to despise Mr. M'Hale's castle; but now, as I passed over the threshold out of the pelting rain, and beheld a goodly array of three-legged iron pots, odorous of dinner, it rose marvellously in my estimation. In the great chamber a block of bogwood blazed cheerfully, and by its light we were enabled to lay out our drenched tackle, and make some slight preparations for dinner. These were scarcely completed when Willie, with a very broad grin on his brown face, announced that the meal was ready. Throwing the door open, I was horrified to find the kitchen crammed with the entire population of the neighbourhood, and a procession organised to conduct me with all honour to the *salle à manger*. Naturally shy and averse to all public demonstrations, I felt the infliction in full force, but there was now no help for it; in front tripped the fair Margaret, followed by Mrs. Mac, then came the scribe, guarded by Pat, and in this order we passed through the crush-room. Instead of feeling puffed up by this great ovation, I felt more like a man passing from the condemned cell to the drop than an honoured guest being marshalled to the banquet-room. In the apartment stood a prodigious rough deal table, whereon, at long intervals, appeared a boiled trout, a mountain of potatoes, a soddened chicken the size of a young partridge, and an enormous dish of cabbage—each and all of which, doubtless, at some earlier period were in themselves excellent, but in passing through the hands of Margaret and her mamma had acquired a peculiar and uniform flavour not much prized by Saxon palates; in fact, the food, animal and vegetable, had been converted into consolidated peat smoke. To feel thankful for the kind intentions of the ladies was easy; to eat was impossible. How grateful I was to the miserable cur that at this moment rubbed his nose against my knees; in secret I blessed him as my deliverer from a great difficulty. I was expected to consume certain viands, not a morsel of which could be swallowed. My unexpected ally was less nice. Slily, pieces of fish and fowl were slipped into my lap, and as slily consumed. The corpulence attained by that dog during my stay was regarded as quite miraculous.

The phantom dinner at length came to an end, and then Pat pointed to the spoils of the morning. Two salmon of 12lb. and 8lb. held the post of honour, then came Mr. M'Hale's great trout, then a brace, whose united merits were good for ten pounds; next figured the rank and file, in number about twenty-four, of all sizes, from 3lb. to ¾lb. I felt as though I had fared sumptuously. Down fell the heavy rain, making sweet music as it dropped unceasingly from the eaves. One by one the guests departed; gradually the household stole off to mysterious holes and corners. Presently a chorus of snores mingled with the sounds of the mountain storm, yet there sat your scribe polishing off a batch of flies, by the light of a couple of home-made rushlights, dreaming pleasant waking dreams of what the morrow would bring forth. During the remainder of our stay there was rain more or less each night, the sport being proportioned to the amount of water. At the end of the week the weather cleared up and sent us back to Newport, to haunt the Beltra and Burrishoole.

In this and the previous chapter Pat M'Hale has figured as my host. Kind and gentle spirit, I have called you from your bloody shroud in memory of many long-passed happy hours spent in your company. Had not some cowardly murderer's bullet sent you to an untimely grave, you *would* have been my comrade as you once *were*. Doubtless you inhabit realms brighter even than the heathery slopes of Tyrena on a cloudless September noon. Pardon me that I have summoned you back to earth once more to walk the banks and braes that in life you loved so well. But now the spell is broken, and you must depart. The play is over; the curtain is falling. *Vale—Ite missa est.*

CHAPTER XXXIII.

After a lazy Day on the Banks of the Beltra, we become more lazy still ; abandon our Duty in a shameful Manner, and go Sight-seeing to the Island of Achil.

September 20.

THE district surrounding the head of Clew Bay contains the pretty towns of Westport and Newport; the former situated on a small stream running into the south-eastern angle of the inlet, and the latter on the river which discharges the waters of Lough Beltra into its north-eastern corner. Westport is a well-built and handsome town; two of the principal streets are parallel to the river, the borders of which are laid out as a public walk, with rows of trees. Westport House, the residence of the Marquis of Sligo—by far the finest mansion in the county—stands in the immediate vicinity of the town, near the sea. Between the two "ports," the head of Clew Bay is studded over with green pasturable islands, varying in size from a few acres to half a mile or more in length, and in number amounting to 170. The shore along the head of Clew Bay is rich, and worn into numerous peninsulas and low promontories, many of them wooded, which greatly increases their picturesque effect. On one of them stands the residence of Sir William O'Malley, and at Newport, close to the town, is the seat of Sir Richard O'Donnell, proprietor of large tracts in the neighbourhood. The scenery of this district is remarkably striking; the beauty of the bay, with its labyrinth of islands, appears to have been known from an early period, since they are distinguished as the "Fortunate Islands" in an Italian map of the sixteenth century.

The absence of rain for the last twenty-four hours, which reduced the brook at Tyrena to a condition midway between a mountain rill and a mountain road, brought the Beltra into excellent tune, so we will suppose permission asked ; leave obtained ; the great melancholy house left behind ; and Willie and his master padding along the road leading to the bridge; for here, as elsewhere in this kindly land, leave is seldom refused, unless the water should chance to be specially leased for the rod. Compared with Tyrena, where, from the source to the sea, I cannot recall a single bush higher than the bog myrtle, the Beltra may, in its lower pools, be called woody. Here and there a group of ash trees cast a shade over the water, and so far represented timber as to make the angler cautious how he propelled his line. Halting on the bridge we got our machinery into working order and commenced operations. The water was all that could be desired, but the day was by no means favourable ; there was too much sun and too little wind. Nor were the streams on the Beltra of sufficient volume to make an angler independent of calms and cloudless skies. The work of the previous week had been hard, and the sport admirable ; now I was indisposed for exertion, and unreasonable in my expectations. The fact was, experience showed circumstances were against me, and I was too fagged to fight the battle with that spirit and determination which could alone win the day against adverse fortune. Then, again, many of the pools possessed a quiet beauty that required to be sketched, and several flowers presented themselves, which needed dissection and examination under the lens. There was also another impediment to exertion in the shape of a solitary robin, who, unquestionably banished from the company of his fellows for malpractices, took a great fancy to me, and fluttered on from spray to spray as I moved lazily forwards. There never was so loquacious a bird. Did I rest for a moment, he was sure to open his grief ; nor was he satisfied with plain prose, for he put his wrongs into poetry, and chanted the lay so soothingly, that I could not choose but listen. Later in the day this lazy, dreamy, disposition left me ; some of the old energy returned, and, though lost time could not be recalled, I thought myself rewarded to the full of my deservings by the possession of ten white and a few small brown trout.

"Who has not heard of the sufferings of the peasantry of Mayo, where, every three or four years, famine and pestilence do their work? Look at that wretched hovel (there are many such); the roof hardly rises six feet above the level of the moor, and the walls are formed of sods fresh dug from the swamp. It boasts no window; from its floor, reek exhalations from the bog; its 'bent' covered roof is pervious to every shower; and that acre of potatoes forms the sole hope of the miserable inhabitants through the long winter, spring, and early summer. Let the crop fail, as it probably will, and the owner must waste day by day from starvation, till he falls before fever or dysentery. Miserable farming, sour wet lands, and the most uncertain climate in the empire, contribute in this part of Mayo to render a general failure of the crops a matter of frequent occurrence. Then the papers teem with heart-rending details of the inhabitants of an extensive district perishing by hundreds in all the horrors of starvation.

"'Why do they not work?' asks the Englishman. Why? Because there is no work to be had. Can a man support a family from an average of one hundred days' work per annum, at sixpence or eightpence a day? Can six or eight human beings be clothed, fed, and pay house-rent on less than three pounds sterling? The wretched father has but one resource, to till an acre of bog, and ward off death as long as he may; food of the worst description, and in miserably insufficient quantities; constant exposure to wet, rags open to every blast, and all those evils uncheered by one ray of hope to brighten the time of trial and suffering. Soon sickness comes; let its breath be so light as not to shake one petal from the rosy cheek of a well-fed child, it will drag the half-starved sufferer to rest."

The truth of the above extract struck me forcibly as we rolled towards the Sound of Achil; not that the country was exactly as it had been when the sketch was drawn, but because sufficient proofs remained to show how correct the remarks must have been when they were written.

Achil, which during the last quarter of a century has attracted considerable attention from the divine, the philanthropist, and the statesman, was previously less known than the Friendly Isles are at the present day. This lonely district contributes but little towards our speciality, for, as a general rule, its lakes contain (I believe) only small trout; still, we were anxious to see a place about which so much has been said. Crossing the sound we rolled over a tolerably level road, and reached Dugurth (the capital) a little after midday.

The mission buildings were as neat and orderly as when Mr. Nangle presided over the infant colony, and seemed still to exercise a wholesome influence over the place. These pages, however, are not suited to discuss the failure or success of an undertaking, which was here attempted on a scale so large as to comprehend little less than a design of converting the entire Romanist population to Protestantism. That the plan failed is certainly not to be wondered at; each party viewed the matter from a different point of sight, and could by no means attain to a happy unanimity on the question of " names."

But enough of this. There lays Black Sod Bay, with each strand and creek, river and mountain, so lovingly described and immortalised by Maxwell in his " Wild Sports of the West." As my eye ran over the place where his youth was passed, I could not but think of his age—the one so bright the other so sad. There shone the river he loved so well, yonder rose the mountain where the deer fell before " Hennessey's unfailing rifle." I fancied, too, I could distinguish the hut on Carrig-a-Binniogh, where so blithe a party will never more meet; nor should I have been surprised to see Patigo get under way, beat the hooker out of the bay, and, standing in for the anchorage, hail a shore-boat, and land two sportsmen bright and joyous from the possession of youth, health, and strength, for three days' sport over the mountains and morasses of Achil. If ever man was formed for happiness it was Maxwell. Alas! that it must be said, if ever man earned sorrow and laboured after poverty and contempt, it was the gifted author of " Wild Sports." To my thinking, notwithstanding their joyous spirit, truth and sentiment, these sparkling volumes are the most mournful books in existence.

Whilst thus gazing far over mainland and sea, we stood about midway up the steep side of Slieve More, which rose immediately above the village of Dugurth. The poor nag that brought us from Newport, now patiently undergoing a minimum amount of grooming, seemed close to us; the ducks that waddled up the street, the ragged urchins that sprawled in the sand, appeared almost within arm's length; the lichens on the thatch, the curraghs on the beach, the rough fishing gear on the stones, were plainly visible, and gave a living interest to a scene otherwise sufficiently solitary and desolate. The heather on the sea face of Slieve More was exactly as poor Maxwell described it, "short and stunted," yet it made a delicious carpet for our feet as we walked over the finest cliff scenery in Britain.

Below, many a narrow and dangerous path led down to the black and slippery rocks, on which, notwithstanding the profound calm that prevailed, a great green roller would at uncertain intervals break, sweeping over the ledges with irresistible force; yet, in the midst of such seeming danger, many a man and boy sat calmly fishing for lythe, glashens, or cuddings, happily oblivious of the many tales that could be told of those whom some treacherous wave in an unlooked for moment bore from time to eternity.

There was a delicious coolness in the light currents of air playing ever and anon over the side of the mountain, that made fatigue out of the question, so we walked on stoutly, and presently halted above Lough-na-Kerogh; at least such seemed to be the pronunciation to my Saxon ears. There, on a low ledge of rocks, were a pair of ospreys, calmly viewing themselves in the blue and unruffled mirror. So dignified and composed were their motions that we had time to note distinctly their appearance and attitude before they spread their strong wings and sailed away in all the might and majesty of power. It has already been said that Achil presents some of the finest coast scenery in the kingdom; and this, as we continued to ascend, grew more grand and striking till it attained its culminating point at Keel. Here the whole side of the mountain, which seemed to have been rent assunder in some convulsion of nature, constituted a precipice of 2222 feet, springing directly from the water's edge. We stood on the summit looking over the wide ocean, which bore no sail; on turning landward, beheld the island spread out before us; an occasional patch of oats, still green, relieving the monotony of the sterile hills and the black peat bogs. Some small flocks of goats crouched amongst the boulders, or wandered over the nearly naked ledges of rock, and seemed quite in keeping with the scene.

The short twilight of an autumn evening was drawing to a close as we once more entered Dugurth, nor do I ever remember appreciating more fully the comforts of a good inn than I did on that evening. when we discussed a hind quarter of Keel mutton, which, from its exquisite flavour, must have quaffed nectar, or fattened on ambrosia.

Northward from the range of Nephin lies a vast tract of desolate moorlands, bounded on the east by the fertile valley of the Moy, and on the west by the mountains of Tyrawley and Nephin Beg. A nearly parallel ridge divides this district into two portions, the waters of one flowing into Lough Conn, whilst the streams of the other, passing through a gap in the centre of the range from the Owenmore river, fall into the head of Black Sod Bay. This savage wilderness—less known, perhaps, than any other part of Ireland—is of great beauty, and possesses special interest for the sportsman. South of the valley of the Owenmore, the mountain outlines are particularly bold and striking, being broken into lateral defiles, and containing many lakes of surpassing beauty. The chief heights are Slieve Cor, Nephin Beg, and Cush-cum-Curragh, the last rising immediately above the shores of Clew Bay, and, with its offsets, occupying the entire promontory of Corraun Achil, and beyond it towering again in many a bold elevation through Achil proper.

This island is of triangular form and of considerable extent, its three sides being respectively twelve, fourteen, and fifteen miles.

Having swallowed all this geographical knowledge from a stout quarto borrowed from the landlord, the effect, as might naturally be expected, proved powerfully soporific. Instinctively my thoughts turned bedwards, and then flew off at a tangent towards Alphonso

Jones. At first sight it might seem difficult to establish any connection between that gentleman and my dormitory; but the fact is, our very comfortable hospitium some years ago, under a former management, had the great misfortune to get into my friend's black books.

"Oh—aw—so you are going into the west!" he observed one evening during the preceding winter, "'Spose you'll find your way to Achil? Every fellah does. But mind you come to a clear understanding about your bed. You remember, Julia" (to his sposa), "what an awful wow I had about ours?"

"How can you be so absurd?" remarked the lady, with something very like a blush, as she made a rather sudden retreat.

"'Spose I ought not to have talked about it to you before her? Never mind, this is the way it happened. During our honeymoon we visited Achil; everything was delightful; weather, fine; country, beautiful; fare, good; whisky, unexceptionable; and on the morning of our departure I asked for my bill, with a feeling nearly akin to that with which refined minds repay an obligation. Running my eye carelessly over it I remarked, 'There is one little error; you have charged me for two beds.'

"'Ah! yes; yourself and lady.'

"'Gracious heavens! Do you suppose I have quarrelled with my wife?'

"'Oh, dear, no, but two persons require two couches.'

"'That depends,' I remarked, somewhat ruffled. 'It can't apply to me and my Julia; that is, to a man and his wife, who, according to law, gospel, and popular usages, are not plural but singular.'

"'Not in this house, sir; but if you wish it I will consult the principal.'

"'Consult the d——. Hark ye, my friend, you may spare yourself the trouble; there's my card, but if I pay for two beds for one flesh may I be hanged.' So you had better take warning, Walter, and come to an understanding if you don't want a wow."

This was evidently a very sore point with Alphonso; whether it was a fact or fiction, whether it occurred here or elsewhere, I cannot determine, for my friend was a great traveller, and, like some other people, apt to tell his own stories till he believed them.

Even the prospect of being charged for three beds would not have disturbed me, as I opened my window and looked out over the quiet village and the lonely sea. What is an error in an inn bill, or even peculiar opinions touching conjugal privileges, compared with a man's peace of mind?

CHAPTER XXXIV.

Achil—Taken Captive—Western Village—New Style of Trolling—Inn Bill—Tyrena in "The Dry Season"—Father Ned—Perseverance—Erica Mediterranea—Carrig-a-Binniogh—A Quiet Evening—Under the Stars

September 25.

IF any man desires the blessings of health and long life, let him eschew "Parr's pills," avoid suppers, and sleep with his window open. Through that balmy autumn night I was more than half conscious of the solemn strains old Ocean drew from rock and cavern; heard the light rustle of the curtains as they swayed to and fro with the breeze, and felt the exquisite sweetness of the air as it stole laden with mountain fragrance down the sides of Sleive More. To wake with the lark is almost a necessity under such conditions; and those "sweet spirits"—mere specks against the blue sky—were singing the praises of early rising as I strapped the razor on the left palm previous to making some small portion of my countenance visible. At this important crisis there was a sound of tiny feet rushing up the stairs, and in another moment the door was flung open, and two as fine little fellows as ever plagued mamma bounded into the room, without the least regard to the sacredness of the sanctuary so rudely violated.

"Oh, I say," observed a precocious specimen of nine, " pa told me you were sure to be up. You must make me a fly and give me a line—now, won't you? We're going to Keel, you know. Mamma is packing up such a cake, and won't we have a jolly day!"

Any vague ideas previously entertained of personal adornment were of necessity abandoned; the razor fell back into its case, and soon I was doing suit and service at the bidding of the juvenile tyrants who had thus taken forcible possession of me.

One reason for leaving Newport was the pleasure we anticipated from wandering over this wild region; another, a wish to see an old friend who had located himself and family in this Ultima Thule of civilised life. I found him—as men who steadily do their duty always are found—bright and cheerful, without an idle hour or an unsatisfied wish. After a prolonged chat on the previous evening, he proposed to lionise us on the following day over the west or most primitive portion of the island, in order to give us some idea of its condition, before the Saxon, backed by a whole army of good intentions, invaded it.

The young tyrants who surprised me in a defenceless condition, held me in bondage till pater and mater came to the rescue some three hours after, and set me at liberty.

As we drove down the level road which led from Dugurth to Keel, I could not but feel how dreary it was. The tallest green thing to be seen was the Osmunda regalis—the only shrub the bog myrtle. Peat swamps, intersected with watercourses and dotted with innumerable pools of black stagnant water, formed the chief features in the landscape. Here and there patches of potatoes, laid out in the usual lazy beds, with the intervening furrows full of water, or a small inclosure, said to contain oats, relieved the monotony. So disguised, however, was "the farm" with marigolds, polygonum, and divers other natural productions of the soil, that I should scarcely have recognised the crop had I been left to the unassisted exercise of my own genius. As we approached the sea, my philanthropic spirit felt quite revived by the sight of a considerable number of small circular ricks, apparently thatched with more regard to neatness and security than is generally found in regions even better cultivated than Achil. Here at least was corn stored up for the winter. A nearer approach dissipated the illusion, and showed my imaginary "wind mows" to be a cluster of wigwams constituting the town of Keel. Altogether I believe this western village to be unique; in my experience, at least, Britain shows nothing like it. In Africa such town architecture is not uncommon, and any illustrated work on that highly civilised country will show many such settlements on the Zambesi and elsewhere; but misery is no subject for jesting, and ere this I trust that the village of Keel is being rebuilt on a more European plan.

Not far from the beach was a lake, on the shores of which the ladies proceeded to unpack their baskets and make extensive preparations for dinner, pending which the juveniles determined to launch a miniature cutter some two feet in length, and of course the seniors were bound to attend. It was a likely piece of water, and I naturally asked my friend if it held any good fish. On this point he could afford me no information, but suggested that, by way of trial, we should fasten to a hook a diminutive trout Master Harry had previously killed, and with this freight send the cutter forth on a voyage of discovery. After considerable rummaging, four or five old flies and a little waxed thread were discovered in the lining of my hat, and with such materials a sort of trolling trace was manufactured, the topsail halyards making not a bad line. We—*i.e.*, the children large and small—watched the graceful little craft, now close-hauled, then running up into the wind, and anon falling off, till summoned to dinner, when the *Dolphin* sailed quite out of remembrance. Lobsters and kid had vanished, the cake had grown considerably smaller and a stout jar much lighter, when a dismal shout from the boys recalled our attention to the forgotten *Dolphin*. That adventurous craft had, it seemed, performed about half her voyage across the lake, when she suddenly went down, stern foremost, to the great dismay of her owners, causing the cry of despair before-mentioned. Springing up, I was just in time to see the bows, jib, and bowsprit rise suddenly above the water and as suddenly disappear. My friend's conversation had interested me; the boys' startling cry had bewildered me; and for a moment I forgot all about the trolling apparatus fastened to the belaying pin of the main sheet. Soon, however, the stanch little cutter once more came to the surface, made rapid stern way, paused in this unusual mode of progression, filled, forged ahead, and then, obeying some unseen force, was whirled round and round, and once more descended towards the locker of Mr. Davy Jones. The *Dolphin* had indeed got a freight, but whether she would ever come safe to port was quite another question. The storm still raged, though with diminished fury; partial plunges succeeded perfect immersion; slowly and gradually the boat drifted towards the opposite shore, bearing her exhausted prize with her. And now a general race commenced; the ardour of the boys would not be restrained, and by the time we got round the lake and neared the scene of action they were a hundred yards ahead and beyond all control. I was, however, able to see the *Dolphin* on her beam ends in about five inches of water, and could distinguish the form of a heavy fish lying on his side a couple of feet or so to windward, when the leading urchin dashed at his boat and gave a desperate heave. There was a momentary splash, and then the youthful angler received his first lesson, and experienced his first piscatorial disappointment. From the little I saw, I conjectured the fish to be between 11lb. and 12lb., but whether a ferox, salmon, or overgrown brown trout, was beyond my power to decide. That night I asked for my bill, intending an early start on the following morning; and deem it simply an act of justice to declare that *one* dormitory only figured in the account.

It was not yet eight o'clock when the car crawled slowly up the incline from the bridge of Tyrena towards Pat's hospitium. Near the summit was a dark stout figure which we knew well.

"You had better ask Father Ned to dinner," remarked Madame, "and I will send you something out from Newport."

The kind and simple priest was a favourite with us all. Warm, though brief, was the greeting, and, as the carriage rolled on, the good father and myself turned in to seek some breakfast before going to the brook for the last time.

There had been a little rain during the night, sufficient at least to raise my hopes, but, alas! insufficient to move the stream, the bed of which was nearly dry. Still I was bent on trying a few of the dark and stagnant pools that lay about a couple of miles up amongst the mountains, and felt sure of a pleasant day in the priest's company. Now the P. P. of Tyrena was, doubtless, a sound churchman, yet his geological education had been sadly neglected at Maynooth; for, the conversation happening to turn on the Causeway, like a "pragmatical ass" I must needs enter into the doctrine of its igneous origin, and forthwith incurred the censure of the Church.

"Oh, docther dear, it is not that ye mane,"—in the mild and earnest spirit of an apostle condemning some heretical opinion held by a friend and a brother,—" Sure ye know 'twas *built* by the great min in ould ancient times, and, by raison of thim, isn't it called the *Giants*' Causeway to this day? Oh! docther, dear, take a friend's advice, and niver talk about what ye don't understand!"

The propriety of Father Ned's advice struck me forcibly, so I was silent and left the victory in his hands. He was but mortal, and the flush of his triumph shone on him all day. How pleasantly we trudged through the rare Erica Mediterranea, now dropping our single fly on a pool as smooth as a great slab of black marble, and then following the pathless swamp, gradually came nearer the base of Carrig-a-Binniogh. The good father carried the net with as much dignity as if it had been a crosier; spoke of the loneliness of his position; the pleasure of meeting a companion; poured forth his troubles about his flock; and finally proposed we should plant rod and net in the bog and scale the summit of the mountain. To this proposition I willingly assented, and after half an hour's stout walking, stood on the topmost peak. Spread out before us was a sight as lovely as ever filled the heart of man with delight. To the south lay the Reek, the mountain tops of Murrisk, and Clew Bay, gemmed with its many islands; whilst at our feet was an interminable wilderness of heather. To the north stretched Black Sod Bay, and all the wild region, made classic ground by Maxwell. To the west was Achil, and beyond rolled the boundless, sparkling Atlantic. In a narrow pass my companion pointed to some droppings and footprints, which he declared to be those of deer. I fear, however, the race, once so numerous, must now, if not extinct, consist only of a few stragglers. In the chapels of this district, hardly twenty years ago, "the rint" was diligently collected. Now the "Liberator" has long been forgotten, and that household word, his name, is unheard. Such is fame! Who would spend health, peace, or life in the pursuit of such a bubble?

Reluctantly we began the descent—found the rod—and recommenced fishing the eight or ten "water-holes" that the bed of the river contained. Had I been wise I should have passed Tyrena in the morning and been put down at Burrishoole; but the sight of Father Ned decided my movements, and having promised him a fish course, I was bound to get one if possible. Never had sport seemed so utterly hopeless. In the earlier part of the day we had not risen a fish; what chance was there of doing so now? Half inclined to give it up as hopeless, I turned to depart; but the good priest, warm with his walk, had already seated himself for the double purpose of rest and observation. At this juncture some good genius recalled to my memory an angling trick I had as a boy often practised in calm weather. Casting the fly on the broad leaves of an aquatic plant, the line was gently shaken till it dropped off noiselessly and smoothly into the water. This manœuvre had been repeated ten or twelve times without any results, but on the next cast, a capital rise startled me completely. It was the last thing expected, and when I felt a two-pound trout tugging at my line, wonder on my own account, and satisfaction on the score of the good father's first course, had reached their climax. With renewed faith the remaining pools were treated in the same way; and when, finally, eight of these fish—all, with the exception of the first, however, less than 1lb. in weight—were counted out on the heather, I felt disposed to believe the science of angling contained no impossibility.

This must have been one of Father Ned's lucky days, for on entering Mrs. Pat's kitchen my stomach felt a delicious emotion at seeing my honest servant cooking a joint of lamb. From that moment bright visions of an eatable dinner gladdened my inner man, and the contents of the creel were committed to his care without fear of their being larded with turf ash or saturated with peat smoke.

As the shades of evening fell over mountain and moor, the first course appeared. Father Ned blessed the fish, flesh, and fowl, though the latter was *non est*. In sober converse we saw the stars come forth, and ere I bade the simple priest good night, the moon was high in heaven to light two belated travellers along the solitary road.

"I forgot to say, master, that the mistress bade me tell you she hoped you'd be home by half-past nine."

This message was rather superfluous, seeing it was near eleven before our adieux were made, and long past that hour ere I lost sight of Father Ned's dark figure standing on the crest of the hill, as he watched his heretical friend fade slowly away into the darkness.

CHAPTER XXXV.

Donegal—We lodge by the Castle—A Morning Walk to Mount Charles—The River—Strong Run after the Netting Season—The Blacksmith attends our Summons—A ministering Angel—Return in a Deluge, and, the lost One being found, the Bells are set a-ringing!

September 30.

I WONDER whether all jackdaws are as matinal as those which reside in the town of Donegal; if so, I trust no gentleman fond of lying in bed after dawn will lodge as close to a colony of those very early birds as we did. Our situation, however, had some advantages, which shall be duly set forth for the benefit of those who may come after.

Donegal lies at the head of a quiet estuary, decked with grassy shores, each abrupt swell being green as an emerald. At low water the channel is nearly dry, but at the top of the flood the tide flows above the bridge nearly up to the old Castle. Five-sixths of the town lie on the south bank of the Esk, whilst a long, straggling row of buildings on the opposite side, lovingly follows the curvatures of the clear and flashing river. Here, "out of town," stands a house of comfortable aspect belonging to Mrs. S——, with whom, as on two former occasions, we have cast in our lot. Now, small Irish towns are not generally pleasant places in which to dwell. Neither sights, sounds, nor scents are what a traveller would select; so, like prudent people, we preferred the circumference to the centre. By doing so on the present occasion we secured three or four advantages, being within twenty feet of the river, in immediate proximity to the most beautiful ruin in Ireland, on the high road to Lough Esk, and in sweet air from morning till night.

There was, however, one drawback to our felicity. On the opposite side of the stream stood "O'Donnell's Castle," a very charming specimen of a mediæval dwelling-house, sufficiently ruinous to be picturesque, yet sufficiently intelligible to inform us how the great chieftain lived when at home. Never were walls more luxuriantly draped with ivy, and never was such tapestry so thickly studded with jackdaws. Had our lively and garrulous neighbours got out of bed at a reasonable hour I should have made no complaint; had they risen with the sun I might have been silent; but their conduct was far worse than this, for I verily believe they talked in their sleep. During my sojourns on the margin of the Esk I have been up at all hours, and could swear that at such times I invariably heard some members of the colony either mumbling to themselves or holding forth to their friends, the harangue uniformly producing a wild outbreak of popular fury.

A short distance below the bridge stood the ruins of a fine old religious house, commanding a pleasant view down the quiet estuary. Here, on many an "impracticable day," I have sat in the shade reading the names of O'Boyle, M'Swire, or O'Dogherty, impoverished descendants, probably, of the savage chieftains who once did suit and service to the O'Donnell.

Donegal forms the north-western extremity of Ireland, and, taken as a whole, is probably the wildest portion of the island. The entire county is uneven and mountainous, and, with a few small exceptions, is made up of lakes, streams, swamps, rock, and moorland; in fact, it is just the region in which to wind up the latter part of the season. As a general rule, small rivers are late rivers; for the fish, as if warned by traditionary experience, are not easily seduced by early freshes, but hang about the coast till the autumn and winter rains ensure them a safe ascent, time to deposit their ova, and full power to return.

In Donegal generally, the rivers are small and late, but as each spate at this season brings up a good store of fresh salmon and trout, the sportsman's pannier will not contain an undue proportion of red fish or ill-made white trout, and therefore, as we said before, this county is just the place in which to wind up the angling year. We, however, shall not be able to follow the plan here recommended, as we have promised an old friend to kill a fish in his company on Wednesday, the 1st of November, in one of the mountain streams of Kerry—a great favourite of ours, where we have ended many a season triumphantly. We have reached the end of September, and on Monday, when we float on Lough Esk, the results will have to be chronicled under the date of October 2.

The fish have now lost much of their excellence and more of their beauty, and, with rare exceptions, are no longer the strong active creatures they were in July and August. Nature shows, in short, that the protective season should commence; but, though compelled to write this truth, the charm of following a brown and dashing stream over the purple moor seems now greater than when, in breezy March or scorching July, we trolled the lakes, or wandered along the banks of the glorious Erne or prolific Moy. But, alas! mingled with the pleasure comes a feeling of pain, that "the year of liberty" is drawing to a close, and that a time of such exquisite happiness must soon be a portion of the dead past, and no longer a part of the living joyous present. . . . .

Donegal, if the season be wet, makes excellent head-quarters for the autumn. Our rod is never taken to pieces, but stands ready in the yard night and day. Close to the door flows the river, and at any moment, before breakfast or after sunset, the Esk is at our service, and seldom fails to yield us two or three trout. Whether, under favourable circumstances, the river would offer occupation for an entire day I do not know, as it was not in order during any of my visits; nevertheless, the pools round the walls of O'Donnell's Castle were rarely neglected, and for an hour, night and morning, regularly formed part of the day's work. Should the weather be dry, there is always plenty of water in Lough Esk—a lake unsurpassed for beauty—from which the angler will rarely return disappointed. In the event of rain the Inver cannot fail to delight him, and should he possess any power of appreciating grand combinations of rock, heath, and mountain, a day on its banks will, I venture to say, live long in his memory. Thus, in our present bivouac, we are nearly independent of weather—a great matter to a keen sportsman.

In the old-fashioned window sat my patient follower, pulling to pieces the wings of certain used-up insects, in order to collect sufficient fragments of brown mallard to tie a few salmon and white trout flies for the Inver. It was not yet six o'clock, and the rosy east showed that the sun, now sadly given to lying in bed, was only just preparing to rise. "They'll never do, master," remarked the perplexed *artiste*, looking at his small collection; "there an't no more to strip to-morrow, and how will it be for the last month?" This was a poser, for no feather answers so well on mountain streams, and of this particular article we were, unfortunately, fairly cleaned out. We could make a good many things, but we could *not* make what was now wanted. In a desponding frame of mind I walked down stairs into the yard, took the rod from the corner, and, stepping across the road, commenced casting below the Cutts. Presently a soft quacking caught my ear. I could hardly believe my eyes, for there, sailing at the head of a bevy of ducks, were a pair of mallards, in plumage as rich as ever gladdened the sight of a needy angler. Except being a little larger, the markings were identical with those of the wild birds. Who could be the proprietor of such treasures? Boys are plenty in Donegal:

"I say, Patsy, do you know whose ducks those are?"

"Ned Casey's, your honour."

"Would he lend them for a few minutes? I should like to borrow as many as could be got, for threepence apiece; the two in front I mean."

"That's quare now," observed Patsy, scratching his head in a contemplative manner; "borrying drakes! Who ever heard the like? But your honour's will must be done; it's plinty ye'll have;" and then, in a parting soliloquy, "O, Peter! What will he do wid 'em at all, at all?"

Anxious on the score of the flies to be used that day on the Inver, I soon returned, and found my servant had completed three for grilse and half a dozen for white trout, as far as the shoulders. These were duly disposed on a sheet of paper, whilst he rummaged our stock in hope of finding what he needed. In this hunt I joined; envelopes were opened, papers examined, manifold tin boxes searched, but not a mallard could be found. The rain, which had ceased an hour or two before sunrise, showed symptoms of again coming on, whilst the wind sighed and rustled through the poplars below the Castle. "How provoking!"—to my poor follower, who was gloomily re-arranging the disordered bundles; "'twill be a glorious day, and here we are without anything fit to use."

Stepping to the window to make a more correct estimate of the weather, I noticed an unusual number of boys "all in a row," on the low parapet by the river, gazing earnestly at the window. Could the chimney be on fire? But what on earth had each urchin under his arm? I had quite forgotten the liberal order about the drakes, and was now agreeably reminded of it by seeing a green head and yellow bill protruded half a yard or so beyond the line of each borrower's person. "There they are!" cried I, pointing into the road. "By Jove! they really *are* come; run, run, and bring them up one by one." For the first and only time in his life Willie believed his master to be hopelessly insane; the expression of his countenance was a compound of terror, wonder, and distress, as he glanced from the window in the direction of my finger. In another instant he was clattering down stairs, and in the next was pounding up again. Seven first-class animals were rapidly despoiled of the five or six good feathers to be found on each wing, eight others were indignantly rejected, and the moderate sum of 1s. 9d. paid for "the loan" made us rich for the rest of the season. The transaction took wind, and for the rest of my stay waterfowl became a source of anxiety to their owners. The mania for borrowing became universal, nor did a single morning pass in which during breakfast my servant, with a very broad grin, did not report, "Sir, the drakes is come again."

The flies were soon winged, the breakfast dispatched, and in half an hour after my friend's mind was relieved on the score of his master's supposed lunacy, we were trudging along the road towards Mount Charles. The walk was a pleasant one, winding upwards towards the moorland, and affording now a glimpse of the grey ocean, now a clearer view of the brown hills. Passing through the village, we soon reached the descent leading down to the bridge, and, as directed by our kind friend Mr. S——, made straight for the smithy, where we found his trusty ally hammering with might and main on a ploughshare at white heat. Having told our story and craved his aid, the name of our friend proved a tower of strength, and the best guide to the Inver flung away hammer, pincers, and red hot iron, pitched a hat on his head, and marched straight off to the nearest pool.

With an extra foot of brown peat water, a more tempting mountain river than the Inver cannot well be imagined. Many of my readers, I am sure, have such a stream in their memory, now sweeping along in broad shallows, now curling over rocks, and anon resting in a darker pool, the head and tail of which are sure to hold many a bright-eyed salmon and silvery trout. At one such as this my guide paused, and arranged on the casting line a Ballina grilse fly, and for droppers a small fiery brown and golden olive, which in another moment were skimming over the pool. I had made up my mind for a rise at the first throw, and felt proportionately disappointed at not getting one. Never was hour more favourable ; there was a grey sky, a stiff westerly breeze, a smir of rain, and beautiful water. The lodge was rather a long one, and every inch was tried down without the smallest sign of a fish. Bryan, the smith, though near was not visible. I heard the voices of my companions, and was able to detect certain odours indicative of pipes, but that was all. "So this is the way you look after the interests of 'the master's' friends, is it, Mr. B. ? And that fellow, Willie, too. Evil communications corrupt——well, of course they do. National schools ought to teach one hundred proverbs with the catechism." Left to my own devices I tried a claret body, black hackle, and mallard wing with equal want of success, and next mounted a dark olive, which, for all the good it did, might as well have remained unwetted.

Whilst mournfully brooding over the conduct of the deserters, Willie's honest face appeared above a fragment of rock. There was an odd smile on it as he walked up to his master.

"Bryan advised me to tie this, seeing the fust fly failed ; it's a queer article, master ; but he says, when the rig'lar patterns won't do, this one, in high water, often answers uncommon well."

Bryan's "advice" was sufficiently uncommon to justify my giving a sketch of the insect. Here is an attested copy—Gold tag, yellow fur body, gold tinsel and red hackle, with black centre ; two or three fibres of blue macaw for horns and two for tail complete the picture. In hot weather I had often found a large black palmer kill grilse when nothing else would move them, but I did not believe in this "gold spinner," and felt indisposed to waste further care on the lodge, as I had been steadily over it three times. Bryan's faith, however, was unshaken ; he declared there were plenty of fish in it, and that a new fly might do something ; so, walking to the head of the pool, I commenced thrashing it once more. At the second cast a salmon came gallantly at me, previous disappointment was forgotten, and, in my eyes, Bryan was the greatest of modern discoverers.

I think it is Byron who says :

> I care not for new pleasures
> So that the old but hold.

This song has probably been chanted by every son of Adam, and I could not but take up the burden. Here was the last day of September; yet the thrill of delight, as the line tightened under my fingers, was as new and fresh as when the first fish of the season was hooked eight months before in "the scholar's throw" at Lismore. As the brave creature flew round the pool and then dashed down the stream, I felt, whilst steering him clear of difficulties, that no new pleasure could equal the zest of the old. My servant, seeing that his last work of art was likely to command public attention, immediately commenced another, and, giving the gaff to Bryan, hastened on with his work. After a sharp burst our prize turned to bay, and, for a while, fought with stubborn determination. At length, in an evil moment, the poor fellow exposed his side to the action of the stream. Taking advantage of his error I rolled my man over, ran him down the stream, edging the unfortunate nearer and nearer to the shore. The smith's practised eye saw the end was near, and, dashing before me, stepped lightly on a slippery and projecting point, and in a manner worthy his fame, gave the *coup de grace* to a thirteen-pound salmon, on whose side the slightest tinge of copper was apparent. Once more—hopefully this time—we stood at the head of the pool, and were again successful; and before we left it, two grilse and a fine trout were added to the bag, attesting the goodness of the river, the excellence of the "queer article," and the *advantages of perseverance.*

Netting had ceased for some weeks, and a large supply had accumulated in the river. There was, therefore, on a day so favourable, no lack of sport, and our affairs prospered till after two o'clock, when a sudden and unexpected fall in all descriptions of stock took place. For the last hour the storms of rain had come down more heavily, and those disagreeable wet stains on stones previously dry—which you and I know so well—began to make themselves too visible. The river was rising—there was no longer any possibility of doubting it; and, what was worse, the fish had ceased rising too; but with seven salmon and nine trout in the bag, and the sun likely to continue above the horizon till 5.40, retreat was out of the question. The rain might cease, in which case the river would soon fall, and perhaps give us a splendid half-hour before dark; at any rate it was a chance worth waiting for, and one we were little likely to throw away. Bryan, however, thought the prospect hopeless, and was, moreover, tortured with visions of cold iron that should have been glowing, and damaged ploughshares that long since ought to have been mended. His potatoes were growing cool in the pot by the whitening embers; excitement was over; the future promised little, and conscience, taking advantage of the opportunity, was reproving his late abandonment of duty for the flowery path of pleasure. As I knew the river pretty well from former visits, there was no excuse for keeping even so able a guide as Bryan; with many thanks, therefore, for his services, and an appointment for the coming Tuesday, I saw him scutter over the bog like a wild duck, and soon disappear in the mist.

Three—four o'clock—the water has attained its maximum. Half-past four—a quarter of an inch lower. Five—heavy shower; river rising. All this weary while my sober companion had been sitting under the very insufficient shelter of a bank, vainly trying to save a wetting. To say he was like Patience on a monument would have been a similitude most disparaging, for poor Patience, if left too long on her silent seat, is apt to grow green and melancholy with mildew and rough weather; but that dear brown face was as calm and bright as ever.

A few minutes more and twilight began to fall, when preparations were hastily made for departure. "Do you know the way back to the road *in the dark*, master? I think it's somewhere over there," observed Patience, pointing with the butt of the rod vaguely along the south-eastern horizon. Alas! I did *not*, and my heart sank within me; but what was the use of confessing my ignorance to one equally ignorant? With a stout assumption of superior knowledge, with a feeble "all right," and an invitation to "come along," we struck into the swamp, whilst the darkness rapidly settled down, making doubt more than doubtful.

"Holloa! stop; holloa! there." What a delight to hear a voice besides our own. Facing quickly round we saw a horseman struggling through the bog, and presently recognised the brave, kindly face of Father T——. "At what hour do you expect to reach Glenties?" he said, laughing, "for it seems you are going there. Bryan told me you were out, and that he had not seen you leave the river. Knowing what a stubborn heretic you are, I expected you would wait to the last, and perhaps come to grief in the darkness, so I rode up to look after you. Give me the bag; we have not a minute to lose; take hold of a stirrup leather, and Barney, may be, he'll pull us all through."

Cold, drenched to the skin, weary, and half famished, I held on, sinking midway to the knees in the wet moss at every step. The good steed showed himself worthy of his charitable master, and after half an hour's floundering brought us to a high bank, outside which lay the high road to Mount Charles.

The long, single street of the village was reached at last. Here and there a solitary "dip" made darkness visible in some huckster's window, and, oh! how I rejoiced when that good Christian Father T—— flung open the door of his hospitable dwelling, and sent the bright firelight streaming across the dark and reeking road. My friend's charity was of ample measure. "Do as you would be done by" was his rule of action, and all he had to give he gave. Bread and cheese were at once set before the famished wayfarers. Next a bottle of sherrry was produced, and dexterously decapitated by a single blow. A full tumbler of the generous fluid was filled for each of his guests, and a scant modicum taken by the host. But his real kindness did not end here. "No, no," he said, "no sitting. You are too wet for that. Another glass, take my horse, and get home as fast as you can." Declining his offer of the horse, I swallowed a bumper, and was soon trudging down hill towards Donegal. Dear and worthy Father, should this ever meet your eye, pray believe I still hold a grateful remembrance of your kindness, and hope yet to stand once more by your side on the banks of the Inver.

It was a darkness that might be felt, whilst the rain poured down in torrents as we toiled along. For every drop that fell on my devoted head, a corresponding quantity flowed over the top of my boots. We were perfectly wet through—regularly saturated—so there was no need to hurry. An hour's pounding through the slush brought us to the banks of the Esk. A little figure stood in the doorway, and peered out into the gloom. "Oh! master, dear, we thought you were kilt entirely." The words were few and the voice low, yet they reached loving ears far away. A door was hastily flung open, and light feet flew down the stairs. "Oh! Walter, is that you? You horrid fellow, you will some day frighten me to death! Run, Mary, for hot water! Dry clothes are by the fire. Don't stand in the passage as if it was a summer's day. You are making the place in a flood. Dinner was ordered for seven, and now it is near ten. I shall ring the bell in a few minutes."

Do you remember, dear one, that happy meal—the cozy pipe —the nocturnal chat?—how I drank the health of a friend whose last letter was dated not a hundred miles from Eaton-square, and how *you* vowed that amongst the many good Christians who walk this fair world of ours, none could compare with Father T——?

CHAPTER XXXVI.

Donegal—Lough Esk—A Journey through the Wilderness.

October 6.

THE males of a family either are, or, for the maintenance of domestic doctrine and discipline, are assumed by Materfamilias to be, sadly troublesome delinquents, and this evil reputation, which begins with childhood, continues to old age.

The knight and his squire were quite unable to see the iniquity of coming home four hours or so too late on Saturday night. True, the weather was such as no respectable dog would have been abroad in if he could have helped it; but that was our misfortune, not our fault. *We* did not make the rain or the darkness; in fact, would gladly have dispensed with them, and considered it very hard lines to be held responsible for what we neither desired nor could prevent. It is with no wish to raise our virtue to an undue height that I say we, the poor ill-used masculines, behaved nobly. I drank half a bottle of *vin de grêve* (by desire) to obviate the evil effects of so much rain water, and, as the quality was good, finished the remainder (also by desire) as a prophylactic against aches and pains in general; likewise at night a stiff tumbler of whisky punch screaming hot (again by particular request) as a diaphoretic; and what could man do more? These sacrifices, though acceptable, were inefficient. The health of her Majesty and her prime minister had received a severe shock; even the tranquillising influence of the Rev. Dr. O'Callaghan's evening sermon failed to produce perfect repose in the minds of these unhappy females. Our sins required further expiation—we were delinquents still. On the following morning, whilst passing through the yard for my rod, Mademoiselle accosted me.

"Is it to Lough Esk you'll be going after breakfast, master?"

"Yes. Why do you ask?"

"I'd like to know, that's all. It will be hot like yesterday, I'm thinking. Willie says it won't be good for the fishing."

The weather had again become fine, and we were about to enjoy a little longer the last days of Indian summer—a season so beautiful in the highlands of Donegal. The mist lay heavy on the river, and, moved by a faint air blowing up the estuary, curled in a thousand graceful wreaths, slowly sailing upwards till lost in the blue above.

Doubly beautiful looked the ivied ruins of the castle; weird and spectral the aspens showed on the low parapet under its walls; whilst an occasional yellow leaf dropped silently into the water, eloquently reminding us that summer was over and winter at hand.

A few steps carried me across the road to the shingles, where I at once set to work for my family. The fish were neither large nor numerous, yet a decent one was presently dragged on shore, rapped on the head, and laid on the stones which served as a larder. Before breakfast time the industrious workman, having provided for the immediate wants of his household, was doubtful as to the propriety of once more trying the last stream down again for his own special amusement, when the question was settled for him.

"I can only find three, master," said a very demure little maiden, arranging the trio more symmetrically on a dish. Mary had come, as usual, to carry home what was wanted for present use, and whilst we hunted among the stones for a brace of small sea-trout which she had overlooked, that spoiled "young person" took up the conversation where it had been left an hour before.

"Willie says it won't be a good day for sport. We shan't have many more like it this year, and I'm sure the mistress would like to go on the lake."

I saw what was expected, and resolved to do it handsomely. "There," placing the missing fish beside their companions in misfortune, "now, you have all. Run away home. I'll see what can be done."

The proposition was favourably received; Micky Doolan's car was ordered, and soon bore us towards a low-wooded point, where the stream, gliding under a rustic bridge, breaks away from one of the most beautiful mountain tarns in the kingdom.

Lough Esk, a gem of the first water, lies in the midst of heathery hills, which, at its northern extremity, seem actually to drop into it, whilst the winding western shore is flat and richly wooded. Leaving her Majesty and lady-in-waiting for a time under the charge of that gentleman-usher Mr. Doolan, we embarked, just as that individual, having unharnessed his nag and tethered him to a sapling, lifted a hamper on his shoulders, and stood prompt to obey their orders. Small in size, this lake has few rivals in loveliness, but, lying out of the track usually followed by wandering anglers, is little known to the sporting public. That it afforded good white trout-fishing I knew from a friend who resides on its shores; and from my knowledge of the gentleman who owns the principal part of the land adjacent, I *believe* no angler will apply in vain for permission. It would be difficult to imagine a day more unfavourable. The dark purple water was smooth as a mighty sheet of glass, and so perfectly were mountain, rock, and tree reflected in the mirror that Scott's beautiful lines might have been written here some still autumn day long ago, to paint what we saw:

> Reflected in the crystal pool
> Headland and bank lay fair and cool,
> The weather-tinted rock and tower,
> Each drooping tree, each fairy flower,
> So true, so soft, the mirror gave.
> As if there lay beneath the wave,
> Secure from trouble, toil, and care,
> A world, than earthly world more fair.

"If you don't try, you can't succeed," is a maxim peculiarly applicable to the brethren of the rod. We were paddling carelessly along the western shore, crossing little bays and skirting miniature headlands, the ground all the while looking very likely: but there was a hopelessness about the day that induced a laziness in painful contrast with our usual energy. Were we, too, falling into the sear and yellow leaf? Notwithstanding our extreme deliberation, a phantom minnow and kill-devil were at length twirling far astern, and lolling in the stern sheets I occasionally caught a momentary glance of the baits as they crossed alternate patches of shade and sunshine. Midway up the lake the boat glided within an oar's length of one of the fairy promontories—a miniature cliff, some six or eight feet high, with broken fragments strewed at its base. Dreamily thinking of some of the great ocean rocks, I had seen in my wanderings, I still continued to watch it, and felt certain a heavy fish ran warily at the minnow, and equally certain that it was a trout of unusual size. Willie, who undoubtedly was paddling in his sleep, when appealed to stoutly protested he had not taken his eyes off the minnow as it passed the point, and as obstinately maintained that not even a "pinkeen" had stirred. I had great faith in his judgment in matters piscatorial, but in the present case, though silenced, I was not convinced, and was as ready as ever to swear, not only that I *had* seen a trout, but had narrowly missed being introduced to the king of the lake. Before reaching the northern side we picked up two or three small things, one of which, a little salmo ferox, was made heartily welcome, because, though insignificant himself, he had unquestionably powerful relations.

That day fly-fishing was a dismal practical joke. The artiste, whose spirits were saddened by misfortune, viewing everything through a very gloomy medium, was tortured with dark forebodings about the dinner, his mistress, Micky Doolan, and "our maid."

It was past twelve o'clock—breakfast had been hurried, and I too began to feel a natural anxiety, which shortly after was much relieved by a thin column of smoke that began to steal up through the trees about half a mile to the southward. Simultaneously lines were reeled up, rods laid over the stern, and three oars being put on (we were glad at last to find something to do), the boat flew swiftly over the glassy water.

With a consciousness of merit, the ladies were graciously mysterious, so of course there was mischief afoot. Micky was all smiles. Two iron crocks were on the embers; one contained potatoes—what else could there be in it? But the other—I hate concealments, especially on the subject of dinner. There was a

s

scent of onions, subtle, provoking, delicious; there was a whole pile of plates; no wonder the party were so long invisible; they must have been foraging half over the country, and had, perhaps, committed a burglary, for Micky's ideas on the question of *meum* and *tuum* were believed to be rather vague. Shall I ever forget the emotion with which I beheld the wooden cover at last removed from crock number one? Shade of immortal Soyer! it contained Irish stew—flavoured to perfection, done to a bubble. That the entire party were not taken ill was a special mercy, and that Messrs. Micky and Willie left the place alive was simply miraculous. The human mind has a fatal tendency to forget the future during present enjoyment. Fully occupied with the savoury mess before me, crock number two had faded out of my mind, nor could I at all understand why Mademoiselle so frequently left the circle and vanished through the bushes in the direction of the fire, and returning, exchanged mirthful and meaning smiles with the queen of the banquet. Clean plates were served out to the astonished guests, and, everything being ready, Micky was ordered to bring in the next course. When the cover was removed a mighty pudding became apparent, and a triumphant shout arose when the first incision revealed apples and bilberries. It was impossible to resist the call, and the health of our entertainer was drunk enthusiastically. Subsequently it appeared that, whilst botanising along the shores, a considerable quantity of these delicious berries had been found. Micky was sworn to secrecy and taken into partnership. " He knew," he said, " where there was an apple-tree about a mile off, also a shop" near to this garden of the Hesperides. These were great tidings; the horse was put to the car, and the adventurous Micky being sent forth on his embassy, returned with a hat full of pippins, a bag of flour, sugar, onions, and a magnificent stock of plates, which timely supplies enabled mistress and maid to achieve the wonders we have recorded. I have been to many grand spreads before and since, but none ever did, or perhaps ever will, come up to that unrivalled banquet at Lough Esk.

Our party was now united, with the exception of Mr. Doolan, whose duty it was to return the crockery and look after the nag. A light easterly air had sprung up, of which we—being on the lee shore—enjoyed the full benefit. It would hardly have blown out a match, yet it raised our spirits, and confidence is near akin to success. Notwithstanding the dinner, I remembered the point past which we were now paddling.

"There, Willie, between those two stones, just where the fly is dropping. *that* was the place where I saw the big trout."

The obstinate party slowly opened his mouth, probably with the intention of stating at length his reasons why my opinion was erroneous, when a tearing rise cut short the proposed oration; he was, however, incorrigible, for I heard him murmur to himself, "Well, I never *did* see the like; but it's no trout anyway, that's one comfort." Whatever it was, the great unknown afforded me full occupation; for, surprised in shallow water, he went off at a pace that promised soon to arrive at the end of the tether. Whether it was the Irish stew, or the whisky, or the pudding, or the surprise, or a little of all combined, it would be difficult to say, but there sat the most accomplished angler in Ireland, with the oar in his hand, vacantly staring, alternately at his mistress, the fast-revolving wheel, and the countenance of his master, who was rapidly waxing very wroth indeed.

"Do you intend to see me run out? I believe you are drunk, sir. Pull; why don't you pull?"

As if suddenly roused to consciousness, the poor fellow glanced for a moment over his shoulder to mark the direction the fish was following, and then bent in earnest to his work. A sharp spurt enabled me to regain a considerable quantity of loose capital, and though the fetter which held Mr. Ferox was nothing stronger than a small-sized trout-hook, still our hopes rose as we got into deeper water and the pace diminished. Twenty minutes of delicious anxiety, and our prize, yielding to pressure, slowly approached the surface. Willie had long abandoned the oar, and, gaff in hand, was peering into the purple water.

"I know'd it," he said at last with dogged deliberation; "I know'd it were *not* a trout."

Now I had made up my mind that it *was*, and this obstinate

perseverance in what I could not but regard as factious opposition, provoked me greatly. However, I held my peace, feeling sure that the hour of my triumph was at hand.

"It's a red salmon, master."

"Are you sure it is not a cod?"

Even as the words came from my lips the line grew suddenly slack, there was a slight plash, and then a dull sound as of a falling body, and hope, doubt, and fear were alike at an end. My companion was correct, and our first prize for the day proved to be a fine fish of nearly 14lb. Somehow I had not associated Lough Esk with salmon, and had limited my expectations to white trout or a ferox or two, so this unusual good fortune put us in the highest spirits. The light air still held up, and was just sufficient to produce the smallest possible curl on the water. We had yet between two and three hours before us; as evening came on, the trout rose well, and when in the dusk we landed at the bridge fifteen of these fish had been added to the bag. They were, however, no longer the stout silvery creatures they had been six weeks before; they, like the year, were passing into the sere and yellow; a darker shade had fallen heavily on each; bodies had become thinner, heads and fins seemed to have grown larger; in fact, they were rapidly getting out of season, and this change was more marked in the lake than on the river.

During the remainder of our stay at Donegal the weather continued too fine for first-rate angling, yet each day was spent either on the Inver or the Lough. On the former, when there happened to be a good breeze, we were able, by the aid of very small black and red palmers, olives, clarets, and fiery browns, to get a few trout; but the full harvest of this lovely mountain river is only to be reaped when the rain-clouds from the Atlantic are brooding over the hills, and when a thousand rivulets are pouring their tribute of brown water into the main channel. On the lake we did better, picking up with the troll many a good ferox, no one of which, however, exceeded 6lb. in weight. Nor did we ever walk home in the gloaming without a fair load of white trout, amply sufficient to justify my praise of the autumn virtues of the loveliest mountain water in the world.

The last morning of our stay has arrived; so has Mr. Doolan; so has the car; and we pause before mounting to take a last look at the bright river sweeping round the old walls of O'Donnell's Castle, and to bid adieu to the restless, noisy jackdaws, whose loquacity, by the way, we had long since graciously pardoned. But the best friends must part; a weary journey lies before us, and it will be dark long ere we crawl over Crotty Bridge, and roll into the courtyard of Lord George Hill's hotel.

The district of the Rosses is separated from the more reclaimed country about Glenties and Ardara on the south by the river Gweebarra, the sandy channel of which is from a mile and a half to a quarter of a mile in breadth throughout the last eight miles of its course, and can only be passed by fording in dry weather. On the whole line of coast from Bloody Foreland to Malin Beg Head there is but one gentleman's seat; this is at Ardara, a village at the head of Loughrosmore Bay, from which there is a pretty good communication—over the heights that stretch from Bluestack to Malin, Beg, Killybeggs, and Donegal. Westward from Ardara the coast again becomes precipitous, being lined with cliffs from 500 to 600 feet in height on the northern side of the great promontory terminated by Malin Beg Head. The loftiest cliffs, however, on the whole line of coast, are those of Slieve League, immediately east of Malin Beg—where the height from the sea to the summit of the shelving rock above, is at one point 1964 feet.

This description, extracted partly from the "Memoirs of the Ordnance Survey," introduces the reader to a vast wilderness of swamp and mountain, glens, lakes, and rivers; but it affords him no aid whereby to feel all the magic of the scene. Passing through Mount Charles, we entered on a track of moorland that appeared endless. Hour after hour the car rolled along the solitary waste, through Ardara, through Glenties, and across the Oanea, now shrunk to half its size.

Wilder grew the landscape as we toiled slowly up the lofty

mountain range which forms the eastern boundary of the Gweebarra, and wilder still as we hurried down the long descent which ends at the police barrack beyond the bridge. Whilst our wearied horse rested we had ample time to admire this most solitary spot. On every side it is shut out from the world by uninhabited wastes; but the glen through which rushes this glorious mountain river is indeed sublime. Running between lofty hills, toiling with innumerable rocks, it frets its way to Gweebarra Bridge, below which it forms a long, deep reach, and then falls into the estuary. As an angling station I have no personal experience of its merits, for though often halting here to bait my horse, I never threw a fly on any of its pools. That it affords admirable grilse and trout fishing in a wet season is, however, indisputable. More than one of my acquaintance have rented it at various times, and I have no reason to believe they were ever dissatisfied with their sport.

The sun was sinking as we walked up the steep road towards Dunglow. Lights were shining in the hospitable house of my old friend at Roshane, as we wended our weary way slowly towards the ford, and when at length the kindly voice of the host, and the sharper tones of his worthy wife, bade us welcome to Gweedore, the night was far spent, and mistress and maid, master and man, were as weary as any four wayfarers in Her Majesty's dominions.

CHAPTER XXXVII.

Gweedore—Poison Glen—Dunlewey Lakes—Arigle—Valley of the Claddy—Angling Regulations—"Waters of the Neighbourhood"—The Middle Lake—A Mountain Storm—Old Dan.

October 13.

IN the most solitary nook of the Rosses, two lofty walls of nearly perpendicular rock hem in a narrowing strip of level swamp, through which flows a small and shallow stream. This pass is the Poison

Glen, the stream, the head water of the Claddy; and happy is he who for the first time stands on the gravelly strand of Dunlewey, to gaze on a picture that may be paralleled but can hardly be surpassed. The little river (if the weather be fine) tinkles over the stones, and is lost in the long lake, from whose margin Arigle, the loftiest mountain in Donegal, rises abruptly. To the east is the dark glen, whilst westward the valley widens and widens till it meets the sea at Bunbeg.

Separated from the upper lake by a short stream (it is barely a hundred yards long) is a second sheet of water of considerable extent, on whose northern bank a large brook debouches. Then there is another connecting river joining another small lake to the chain. From this point the Claddy finally breaks away from all restraint, and after lingering for a short space round the hotel, with scarcely a moment's pause, runs its brief race of prodigal riot to the sea.

Having thus roughly mapped out the scene of our future operations, we will as lightly sketch its sporting qualities. From the latter part of June to the end of the season, the Claddy, after rain, is all that man can desire; yielding salmon, white and brown trout in ample measure. When the water has shrunk, from a continuance of fine weather, the angler will do well to shift his ground and take to the lough, instead of tramping daily over the black and charred peat bog.

At the bottom of the garden, boats belonging to the hotel are always riding at anchor, and one of these will soon bear him to a new field of operations : while, if there be anything like a breeze, the middle lake will not send him home salmonless. Before reaching this point the stranger will pass through a wide and shallow sheet of water, thickly fringed with bulrushes. The pool is not remarkably tempting at first sight ; but only try it with three small flies of any shade or pattern. I did so once, and remained there the entire day, pulling up to windward and then drifting to the lee shore. The number of small but beautifully-shaped trout taken on that occasion I should not like to record ; though I *did* hear subsequently that a certain inquisitive young lady counted as far as one hundred and seventy-six, and then gave up the task in despair.

Separated from the river only by a narrow grass plot, a mountain road, and a kitchen garden, stands the hotel, which well deserves a few grateful words from me. Shall I record that the managers are upright, civil, and obliging; that the house is thoroughly comfortable; that the food is excellent, and the cooking good? All this might indeed be said without fear of contradiction, but yet would leave much untold. Three times it has been my good fortune to visit Gweedore; each time my visit was long and I felt at *home*.

Before me lies a printed form headed "Fishing Regulations for 1866." As the reader may like to see them, I give the paper *verbatim et literatim*.

Terms on which gentlemen staying at the Gweedore Hotel will be permitted to fish in the rivers and lakes belonging to Lord George A. Hill are as follows:

The lakes and that part of Gweedore river which belongs to his lordship may be fished without any charge by persons staying at the hotel, they being required to return all salmon caught to Mr. Cunningham, the manager of Gweedore Hotel, and to pay 4s. per day for boat and two men, and 2s. 6d. a day for boat and one man.

Gentlemen fishing the river Claddy, between the lakes and Bunbeg, to pay by the day, week, month, or season, according to the following rates:

When all salmon caught are either returned to Mr. Cunningham or paid for at market price,

Angler to pay per day		£0	3	6
"	" per week	0	18	0
"	" per month	2	2	0
"	" per season	5	5	0

When angler keeps all salmon caught by him,

He will pay per day		£0	6	6
"	per week	1	16	0
"	per month	4	4	0
"	per season	10	10	0

Gentlemen will be required to deliver all salmon in good order to Mr. Cunningham, and are requested to land as many as possible of the fish with a net instead of with a gaff, as the latter injures the fish very much, and consequently lessens their value.

Gweedore, April, 1866.

About a couple of hundred yards below the house is a bridge, with one high arch, over which runs a road straight across the moorland. Dipping over the shoulder of a hill, it drops rather abruptly into a narrow, boggy valley, through which flows the Gweedore river; and this, like the lakes, is free. The lower half mile is deep and still, but from thence to the Fox's Leap the little stream presents a series of charming pools. Let there be but half an air from the north-north-west, and I know no more pleasant angling than is to be found on that narrow, deep, and dark "lower half" mentioned above.

The journey of the previous day had been severe. During the earlier part of it, master and man padded up the hills for the mere pleasure of the thing, and down, entirely out of consideration for the quadruped; and, as about five-eighths of the road consisted of alternate ascent and descent, it is evident that we walked much and drove little. As night fell the poor horse grew more and more weary, and then we were obliged to use our legs. To add to my troubles, some months previously a new member had been adopted into the family. Jack, an infant at the time, had since become a great cat, and in our various wanderings always insisted on perching on somebody's shoulder. Unfortunately, that spoiled animal usually elected me as bearer in ordinary, and during the present journey rode at least twenty miles on my back from which he would occasionally spring and race over the bog till regularly planted. He was worse than the "old man of the mountain," for that individual did sit quiet, whilst my cat o' mountain was never still for a moment. Once I tried to lose him in a hamlet through which we passed, and wept crocodile tears with Madame on her bereavement, but an hour afterwards was nearly frightened out of my wits by being unexpectedly clasped round the neck from behind. Jack had a good master, and knew it. My back aches even now at the remembrance of the anguish I endured from the claws of that harpy.

Completely done, I went to bed supperless, and awoke, nearly as tired as when I lay down, to see the glorious mountain peaks all around me showing clear and purple against the sky. Standing on the grass plot, one glance at the river warned me to avoid it, but a crisp north-west air whispered a pleasant song about the lake. At this season the angler's day need not begin before ten, and seldom extends much after five, so we strolled slowly back to make the most of Mrs. Cunningham's capital breakfast. Seated at my side of the table, quite unconscious of the pains endured on his account, was that hairy monster Jack, eyeing alternately the milk and a polished metallic cover, from beneath which savoury odours were rising It was a pleasure to see him. Well, well! I must make up my mind to carry him all the days of his life.

Lobster and eggs, cutlet and toast, coffee and tea, are wonderful restoratives; at least, they restored me so completely that an hour afterwards I shouted lustily for Willie and his mate, and was soon moving warily over the shallows towards the middle lake.

Less than half way up its northern shore, a long bar of sand and gravel stretched across the mouth of the mountain river previously mentioned. Here salmon bred in the stream congregate till the late autumn floods tempt them to ascend; and as this season many fish were on the lodge, we expected at this point to find sport. From west to east the bank was tried with a dark cast of flies; from east to west it was flogged with the most sparkling beauties our book contained. The first experiment was a total failure; the second attempt was little better. We *rose* a fish certainly, but that was all. Five times out of six, unless a salmon be *very* stale, if he comes once he will come again; but we could make nothing out of this one. Ten times the flies were changed. We tried him deep, we tried him on the surface; he was attacked from the shore side, from the lake side, from the east, from the west. For one mortal hour that creature stood siege; then the baffled assailants drew off their forces, and very crestfallen they were. Still following the north shore, we presently reached a low reef of dark water-worn rocks, where with renewed hope we recommenced our labours. When about half over the cast a fine fish of 13lb. or 14lb. sailed quietly up to the dropper, but if his mouth was not closed I am much mistaken. Taking exact marks, we rested on our oars for a short time, and came over him again and again; but neither would *he* say a civil word to us, notwithstanding all our efforts to please him, so we left the house promising to call again on our way back.

When we quitted the hotel there was every probability of a fine day, but for the last hour all things seemed to portend a change. Over the dull grey sky countless small dark clouds were flying; mists first floated over the peaks of Arigle, and then lingered there, growing denser and more dense till they rolled in heavy volumes nearly to the base. Then the gusts of wind grew louder and louder, darkening over the surface of the lake. A storm was at hand, and the conduct of our scaly friends was explained. They had long noticed what we, with our boasted superiority, had not been able to see until it was close at hand.

How the big drops danced over the surface! How the wind shrieked and raved through the mountain passes! Presently the dry channels in every little hollow became wet, soon a thousand streams were in motion, and in an incredibly short time after the storm commenced they grew into torrents, and foamed and raged down every glen.

The best cast was before us, for we had reached the short stretch of river which connects the upper with the lower lake. In many places salmon rise well during rain, especially when it is of a character likely to produce a fresh; and now it seemed that Dunlewey was one of these. We had not made half a dozen casts when there was a deep eddying swirl at the dropper, and in an instant all was life and animation. Who cared for the rain? As to our boatman, it was a normal state of existence. My faithful comrade was as contented when wet as he was when dry, and for his master—he never thought about it at all, for the tackle was light, the fish strong and active, and that person had enough to do to attend to his business. The fight was too fierce to last; furious and desperate runs ended in leaps as wild and headlong. Now here, now there, it seemed as if several salmon were continually throwing themselves out of the water, and I could hardly believe such a series of summersaults were delivered by a single individual. Flesh and blood could not stand such goings on; the pace was too good to last, and in less than ten minutes he was in the basket. As quick as possible another and another were hooked, played, and lost; then a fourth fretted his brief hour on the stage and died. Presently there was a lull, not in the storm but in the sport; flies were changed again and again, but in vain; it was time to shift our ground and pay the promised visit to our friend on "the reef."

I think he must have been anxiously expecting us, for no sooner had the flies fallen on the water than he was at them. We had guessed the fish to be 13lb. or 14lb. and were not far from the mark, as when brought to scale he proved a little over the lesser weight.

By this time the water in the boat was surging from side to side with every motion, and the margin of the lake was already deeply coloured by the boggy streams that poured into it. "There may yet be time to send a line of invitation to our early acquaintance of the morning; so turn ahead, boys, at full speed." As we approached, a large patch of black water with a semicircular outline became too visible; but was it *all over* the lodge? That was a question; opinions differed. It reached certainly very near its outer edge, but then the shy customer of the morning also dwelt in that part of the house. Well, here goes—one can but try; and in less time than it takes to record it, the rod was arching over my head, as rods always should. Suddenly remembering how long the business of life had been neglected, our new *attaché* flew towards the shore and dashed headlong up the boiling and discoloured torrent. The whole thing happened in an instant. I could still feel the fish, but I also felt that the line was foul, apparently twisted round one of the countless blocks of granite which filled the bed of the river. No orders were needed; every man saw the danger and the remedy. In twenty strokes the boat's keel grated on the strand, and Piscator, reeling up as hard as he was able, floundered and stumbled up the stream in a line with the impediment. As usual in such cases, the moment the rod came over it the difficulty vanished, and the fish, once more feeling the strain, dashed on towards some stronghold which perhaps then rose clear in his fancy. I dared not give him an inch of line for fear of again getting foul, but rushed madly on over ground that in cool blood I would not have faced for a trifle. One false step would have been equivalent to a broken bone.

"There ain't no getting over this here, master." As my companion remarked, there *was* a difficulty, for the rocks were abrupt, far apart, and slippery as glass. Now came the tug of war. As the fish shot against a strong column of falling water we gave him the butt. For a brief space the forces were balanced and the onward rush stayed; a second more and he was weltering down, still resisting the united action of the rod and the torrent. Willie availed himself of the opportunity, stepped lightly on a nearly submerged stone, and as the salmon rolled past drove the steel home, with just sufficient breath left to exclaim:

"If we hav'nt paid the full price for *you*, 'tis a pity."

All hands had taken in enough water for one day, so, hauling the boat up high and dry, we turned her over on the heather, deposited the oars in the nearest cabin, and set off homewards in such a deluge of rain as rarely descends on man's devoted head.

The fairy web of night and day,

called twilight in vulgar prose, was falling around us, yet we floundered merrily across the spongy bog, and splashed along the road towards the hotel, not distant, but more than half obscured by the mist, the rain, and the growing darkness.

What a wonderful thing is memory! How vividly I now recalled my earliest visit to Gweedore! It seemed but yesterday that my first season was drawing to a close. With the design of getting information for the following year, I had been moving across a country which to me was then a *terra incognita*, and had blundered by chance into Dunfanaghy, to find Horn Head a delight, and M'Swine's gun a perpetual excitement. How keenly I now remembered my first introduction to the Midges, that close, sweltering night when we drove under Muckish, on our way to Lord George's. How vividly the pleasure now came back to me with which, on the following morning, I saw for the first time the river, the mountains, and the glen! Again I seemed walking homewards over the moor in a deluge such as was now falling. It appeared but yesterday that, confused by the storm, I took a wrong turn in the road, and should in due time have found myself once more in Dunfanaghy, had it not been for a little white-haired peasant, spiced with a concentrated essence of peat-smoke 50 per cent. over proof. Poor old Dan! my comrade for many a day afterwards, how I bawled at you, roared at you, spoke slowly, confidentially, soothingly; and how your answer was always the same gentle, patient smile! You never knew that I felt disposed to strangle you, nor how ashamed I was when, in the extremity of your distress, you faltered out, "No Engleesh." Do I forget the five salmon you gaffed for me on the following day in little more than an hour, out of a single pool at the bottom of that boggy inclosure yonder, which was to have been called "Leech Park?" No, of course not; no man ever does forget such things.

It was just such an evening as this, old comrade long dead, that we walked home together. To-morrow I shall think of the reverend locks that streamed from under your old blue bonnet as we sat triumphant on the heathery rock by that round pool. Ah, me! how happy I was! Such joy comes but once. *You* cannot share the sport I hope again to meet there, yet you will be with me, for I shall sit a few minutes where we sat, and dream once more of "the days that are gone."

CHAPTER XXXVIII.

Expectation — The Myrtle Grove — In at the Death — Ruined Cabin — An Impostor — Down to Bunbeg — Gweedore River, and how to get there — Mountain Lake — We set out on a long Journey, but say nothing about it.

October 20.

ALL night long the river sang a pleasant tune; there was not much light or shade in the performance certainly, for it was rather of the street minstrelsy order, which begins fortissimo and tries crescendo; nevertheless it was charming to me, its sole auditor, and might therefore be considered a great success.

It was long before sleep visited my eyelids, and dawn was only just stealing over the world when I awoke. The wind was still gusty, freshening up with every shower; huge masses of cloud drove over the sky, leaving occasional bars of blue, and on the brown and dripping moor sunshine and shade paved the earth with alternate patches of umber and gold. In short, it was a fishing day; nothing was wanting; clouds, wind, and water were just what they should be; they promised a rich harvest, and I longed to reap it.

It was hardly nine when we walked out of the yard towards the bridge, Willie lagging a few steps behind to fix some new device on the casting line. So short was the distance that I was over the bank impatiently waiting on the rocky incline—slippery from the seepings of the bog—before he came up.

At this point the Claddy, rushing through a smooth but deep channel in the rock, formed a pool so tempting that for the life of me I never could pass it without a trial. The lodge, however, did not deserve my partiality, for, though I had often bestowed much time and labour on it, the gains seldom repaid the trouble. On the present occasion we fared no better than in former seasons, so we moved rapidly down the water, making odd casts here and there, to any point that might possibly hold a running fish, and soon came to a spot known amongst our party as the "Myrtle Grove."

Many of our readers will recognise the pool. It lies, perhaps, two or three hundred yards below the bridge, having on its northern bank an unusually luxuriant growth of the Myrica gale. At its neck the river spreads out into a broad and shallow run, which, narrowing as it goes, forms as lovely a stream as ever gladdened an angler's eye, whilst at the bottom it steals away in a swift and smooth shoot. Here many a good brown and white trout, and many and many a salmon, has died. Here we had often arrived light, and gone away loaded, and now, with the surface crisped over with a sharp squall and darkened with a coming shower, we did not doubt that a triumph was at hand.

How well we succeed when hope is high! Light and true flew the line. With what a taking motion the glittering insects darted hither and thither through the brown water! It could hardly have been done better, yet we are within three feet of the end without a rise.

"How dirty and disagreeable!"

The speaker had come up unnoticed. Turning, I saw a very spruce gentleman sadly perplexed about his raiment, picking his way with great care from one tuft of heather to another. Glancing hastily back at the line, I was just in time to see a bright gleam at the very edge of the pool, shooting towards the bottom.

"Oh, dear, what's the matter? I wish you'd look where you are going."

There was little opportunity of asking my new acquaintance what was the cause of his grief, for the fish, on feeling the hook, had dashed straight away and was racing round the turn—through rocks and broken water, at a pace that made delay impossible, and elaborate courtesy a thing not to be thought of. Willie was already thirty yards ahead, doing his utmost, whilst I was getting over the ground, which was wet and broken, as best I might, in momentary fear of a foul. These sharp bursts do not last long—the pace is too good. Little by little the line was gathered in; for longer intervals an olive tail fanned the water, and then a side yellow as burnished gold gleamed for an instant on the surface.

"What is it?" to Gaff, who was panting and labouring, still about twenty yards ahead.

"Should say it's a trout, if—puff—he wasn't—puff, puff—so big."

The fugitive, now in deeper water, turned to bay, but the rod was by this time well over him, at high pressure, and he yielded.

What a group we should have made had some Leech been at hand to sketch us! In the centre a glorious trout, with diminutive head, deep flank, broad shoulders, and a side tinged with the ripe glow of a tropic sunset; over him stooped the reader's old acquaintance, fumbling in his pockets for the weighing machine, whilst, wiping an inflamed countenance and getting choked in an abortive effort to hide his laughter, stood the scribe. I was afraid to say so, but in my inmost soul I wished the gentleman who knelt beside the dying fish in an agony of delight, had a change of raiment; never did man want it more. His patent leathers would never again bear a polish; that waistcoat, lately white as snow, was henceforth and for ever destined to wear a dirty purple hue. As for his Lincoln and Bennett, and superfine frock coat, I shuddered as I looked, yet the wretched man was utterly oblivious of his condition; every faculty was absorbed in the contemplation of the expiring beauty.

"I would'nt have missed this sight for a pound," he said, stroking the vermilion spots for the twentieth time. "I say, you there, you are never going to squeeze it into that basket, are you," to Willie, who, having bent the object of his idolatry head to tail, was about to deposit him in the creel.

"Dear me"—rubbing face, waistcoat, and inexpressibles with a delicate pocket handkerchief till an admirable uniformity of shade was attained—"I must go home and change. Only let me have him, I will take him back without brushing off a scale. What weight did you say? Oh, eight pounds and a half; thank you."

Glad to be rid of such an incumbrance so early in the day, we bade our new acquaintance good-bye and pushed on to the next cast. This was a long narrow reach of deep water, with just such a stream

T

as salmon love. Had there been but one in the lodge he could hardly have helped rising, and to-day few rises were likely to be made in vain ; that break so sharp looks like business. In such a place no fish could have a chance ; there was no need to give line ; from first to last a heavy exhausting strain was on him ; nothing could stand it long. Sharp eyes were on the watch; the gaff was always ready ; the next turn, "Well done, Willie ; not bad for number two."

Resting the water for a few minutes, and changing both drop and trail, we tried it over again, and were so unfortunate as to play and lose a fish at each attempt.

This round pool is the place where, many a day ago, during my first visit, I landed five salmon. It was my opening season, and success had been small. Once only in that happy time three fish had fallen to my rod. Imagine, then, the pride with which I saw *five* ranged side by side. My wildest imaginations were surpassed, and henceforth nothing seemed impossible. "Dan, my poor dead friend, there is not a drop wherewith to toast your memory, so I will e'en sit on this tuft of blooming ling, smoke a meditative pipe, and watch another hand fish your favourite lodge." The daydream was a long one, for when my honest companion woke me up with the inquiry, "Will we go on now, master ? I've put four flies over it," the weight of the creel was increased by the addition of one salmon and two white trout.

The Crotty is smaller than the Inver, but remains longer in order, owing to the size of its lakes ; and during the Lammas floods I know no prettier or more hopeful river on which to while away that magical time. In the north, the flax destroys all autumnal fishing, generally finding its way into the streams in spite of the water-bailiffs during the first week of August; but here, happily, the obnoxious plant does not thrive, and the unpolluted Claddy is as lively and sweet in August and September as most other rivers are in June and July. If the truth must be told, this station is a great favourite with us, not only because it attains its best condition when most other waters are useless, but also for the rare beauty of the neighbourhood, which, though most solitary, possesses all the appliances of civilization.

Inexorable time, which drives us all forwards whether we will or no, warns me to "move on." There, in the midst of that aguish swamp, stand the walls of a cabin long deserted; and, close to the ruin, the river forms a deep pool, which, in the changeful light, seemed black as ink. Willie drew closer to his master, and pointed with the butt end of the gaff to a small wave which, rolling towards either bank, was at the moment breaking against the peaty shore. No explanation was needed; it was plain that a salmon above the average of the water had risen, and equally plain that he was marked out exultingly as an object to be murdered forthwith.

"How big?" in a husky whisper to my companion, who at the moment was rapidly turning over the leaves of our book. "Did you see him?"

"Why, no, master; that is, not exactly, but I *think* I seen the rim of his tail."

"Well, what was he like?"

"Maybe he's fourteen pounds, maybe more."

No unnecessary time was lost, you may be sure. The casting-line was speedily yet carefully examined. Knots and loops were inspected, and a new fly mounted for trail. Already the squall of wind and rain darkened the surface, as the line dropped easily on the water at the neck of the pool. Cast followed cast, and now we were over him—*ay, and into him.*

"The fish feels uncommonly light, Willie."

"Wait a wee, master; he don't know what's the matter yet. He'll grow heavier presently. He's fourteen pounds if he's an ounce."

Round and round his prison flew the captive, now on the point of dashing out of the back door, now meditating an escape by running straight ahead. Still, though active, there seemed nothing in him. My poor companion looked from the bending rod to the tension of the line, and from the line peered vainly into the black water. He seemed puzzled.

"I can't make it out anyhow. I'm sure the salmon as rose wor a big one for the Claddy, and this, whatever he is, ris at the same spot. Oh, worra, worra, it isn't a *fish* at all, at all."

The honest fellow was bending over the stream in order to get a better insight into the difficulty, and now stood at my side with a very crestfallen expression on his brown countenance.

"Bear on him, bear on him! He ar'nt worth nothing; we're only losing time."

A stiff strain solved the mystery, by bringing a 4lb. white trout wallowing to the surface. The river was narrow, and Willie, seizing the opportunity, put the gaff into him. At any other time we should have admired the broad, thick, little fish, which was now unceremoniously knocked on the head and huddled into the basket; but he was in disgrace, having practised shamefully on our credulity by trying to pass himself off as a great person. What was to be done next? Should we show the fly at once to the real Simon Pure, and ask him then and there what he thought of it? or should we wait for a more favourable moment? The squall had passed and the sun was shining, so, without a word of discussion, we moved off to the cast below, in a spirit of unanimity that was quite delightful.

On and on we trudged, taking a trout now and then at rather long intervals. For the last half hour a dark mass had been slowly gathering on the horizon, and now began to mount rapidly towards the zenith. The hour of trial was at hand, so we walked back to be ready to take full advantage of the opportunity. It soon came; the sharp rain fell in a slanting sheet, whilst the little wavelets curled and foamed. One cast above him and one over him—he has it *firm*. Now, Willie, we shall soon see whether you are correct as to weight. What boots it to describe the closing scene! A salmon well hooked in a narrow river cannot escape; he might as well send for a "sea lawyer" and make his will at once. I do not know whether our present patient had set his house in order, but I do know he played his part manfully, kept the great enemy at bay as long as he could, and died only when he could not help it. Though not quite so heavy as had been supposed, the fish proved to be the best I ever landed at Gweedore, weighing a little over 13½lb.

In high glee we bent our course steadily downward, landed another in the wild and rocky lodge some half mile above the Parsonage, and yet another in a brimming pool nearly opposite that snug dwelling of our old friend. Then came a lull in the sport, and pausing a few minutes to look at the fish pass, we came to the village of Bunbeg.

Here stands "the store," a huge *omnium gatherum* kind of shop, started many a year ago by his lordship as a depôt whence his poor tenants might procure all such articles as they could by any possibility require, at little more than cost price. Fame is hard to win, and human praise is the last thing Lord George would desire, but efforts such as his *must* at length succeed; nor can I doubt that even in this world his long patience will reap its reward, and a wild tenantry will yet hail as their great benefactor the man whose long suffering they have so cruelly tried, and whose love they have so vainly laboured to extinguish.

The early autumn evening fell before we had fished half our way home; but we had done our best, as our backs testified, whilst we trudged wearily along the last two miles of road. Did we wish the load lighter? You may swear we did *not*. How well I can still see our host's quiet smile as he surveyed the spoils spread on the floor.

"Eight salmon and eleven trout. Your honour hasn't forgot the way to do it."

"Where is the fish I sent home in the morning? I should like to look at it before the cook has it."

"Do you mean the one the gentleman brought in?"

"Yes, exactly; he kindly offered to take it."

"Why, he ordered it to be *boiled* for his early dinner, before starting for Derry, and the servants finished it. I hope you did not want it."

If ever I catch a curiosity again, see if I part with it on any pretext whatsoever.

Through the night there were heavy dashes of rain, and the Claddy was as high as on the previous day. How tempting it looked as we leaned for a moment over the parapet of the bridge! But there is an irresistible charm in novelty, so we walked a short distance up the road, and then struck across the bog to the right. The moor looked dark and dead; in every crack—between every hummock—water was lying. Ever and anon a snipe sprang at our feet, whilst the soft whistle of the golden plover seemed to say, "Autumn is passing, and winter is at hand." In less than a quarter of an hour we struck into a rough bridle path, half road, half rivulet, and passing some ruinous cabins, soon stood at the head of the inlet where the Gweedore river falls into the sea. For some distance above this point the water is as still, and about half the width of an ordinary canal. Level with its banks, it is readily acted on by any wind from the north-west or south-east, and now, on this breezy, showery day, was in excellent tune. In the first hundred yards two salmon were risen, and one good trout bagged, but the stout gentlemen first mentioned could not be brought to close quarters. Again and again we returned at stated intervals, only to find them perfectly impracticable; so at last, making a virtue of necessity, we bade them good-bye, and went our way.

With such wind and water sport was inevitable, and by the time we reached the leap, we had made an excellent basket of fish, ranging from $\frac{3}{4}$lb. to 4lb. These higher pools, sheltered from the breeze, were less productive than the lower; still, having time to spare, we took the rough and smooth as they came, and fished straight on. Standing at the head of one of these, polished as a sheet of glass, I played the flies quietly across till they reached the side under a low bank of brambles, the dropper rising and falling in a manner as lifelike as I could make it. Which was the most astonished, the 11-pounder who, intending to take possession of a midge, received a sting, or a certain person who "was busily thinking of nothing at all," it is impossible now to ascertain; but I *do* know that in that individual all other feelings were merged in delight at his unexpected good fortune. The prize, however, had yet to be won. Patience, a quick eye, and light hand did something towards the winning, when my gallant squire, seizing his opportunity, rushed manfully into the mêlée and gave the *coup de grace* to our enemy. This brought our affairs to an end on the Gweedore river. For the next five or six days we were faithful to the Claddy; and as the water, though falling still, kept in good trim, we did very well, bringing home each day two or three salmon and more or less white trout.

Taken as a whole, Gweedore Hotel forms an admirable sporting residence from the 20th of June to the end of the season. During the last eight weeks of that time, the gun may be taken into partnership with the rod; but to the sportsman who prefers the angle, I may say, without fear of contradiction, he will find few days in which a salmon may not be taken, either in river or lough; and when this cannot be done, close to the house he will meet with as good *small* brown trout fishing as can be had in the three kingdoms.

There is still one water in the neighbourhood which must be mentioned. On the summit of the lofty mountain, in front of the house, lies a tarn of ten or perhaps fifteen acres in extent (at all events it does not look more), called Lough Na-Brack-Baddy, or the Lake of the Saucy Trout. I never visited it but once, and then during a long spell of impracticable weather. No boat, to my knowledge, ever floated on its surface; yet it holds noble fish, unsurpassed for beauty of form and excellence of flavour. The one whose capture is recorded in the earlier part of this chapter came out of it, and would in due time perhaps have returned, had he not been taken in by your scribe, and subsequently devoured by an unprincipled "mercantile ambassador." Old Dan was never weary of describing its glories, and every word he spoke was true. Give me a Curragh there in May and June, with a few good baits, and a cast of ordinary lake flies, and I should be well content to bide the issue.

Private and confidential: Some day we intend to try it. Should the experiment fall *below* the level of our great expectations, depend on it, my dear Sir, *you* shall immediately receive the fullest information of our exploits.

CHAPTER XXXIX.

Old Ground—The Major discourses about Prawns—Snipe-shooting—Autumn Surf—Old Gun—On the Mountain—Banks of the Cummeragh—My Friend's Yacht—We anchor the Horse, and launch forth on the Lower Lake—Black Trout—Upper Lough—Red Salmon—We leave off in the dusk, and go home in the dark.

October 28.

ONCE more we are journeying over well-known ground. As we roll along the road from Killarney towards Killorglin the Reeks show clear and purple; a stream of sunshine lights up the Gap of Dunloe, and the islands, clad in the gorgeous tints of deepening autumn, invest the lake with unrivalled loveliness.

Summer is dead—buried under the falling leaves. Winter is at hand, and the air has a coolness which makes us wrap our cloaks closer, and meditate a walk up the next hill. Again we pull up at Killorglin, light our pipes, hear the news, and discourse of old comrades. Again we admire the lofty pine-clad hill near Lady Headley's. Against the porch of the hotel leans a solitary rod, reminding us that the season is not yet over, though the dull hue on the moorlands is more suggestive of the gun than the angle. Cahirciveen is as wretched and dismal as ever. By-and-by we run merrily down the long descent which terminates at Inny Bridge, and slowly mounting the opposite hill pass the Butler Arms, with a triumphant whoop from the driver, and soon pull up at the long, low, hospitable cottage of my friend Major D——, whom we had come thus far to visit in fulfilment of a long-standing promise to kill a November salmon.

What a joyous evening we spent in the snug little dining-room! The ladies were not banished, but drew round the sparkling bog deal fire, talked of their mutual experiences, the angelic nature of woman, the iniquity of mankind in general, and, in fact, attained the highest pinnacle of matronly happiness. The Major, whilst scientifically compounding a fourth tumbler, opened his heart and became communicative. He told how in the previous month "his lady fair" required stock for her aquarium, and how, the weather being impracticably fine, he shouldered his landing-net, ordered Patsy to follow with the stable-bucket, and betook himself to the sea-shore at low water. "The first few rock pools did not yield us so much as a 'tittlebat;' but the next scoop under a ledge fringed with pink weed—by Jove, sir"—stirring his glass with dangerous energy, "I had a dozen prawns as long as my finger and thick as my thumb. Hang the aquarium, sir. I worked like a horse, and brought home the bucket half full of these delicious crustaceæ" (he was fond of parading the profound learning to be gained from sixpenny treatises, "about the foreshores and their inhabitants") "and by Jove, sir, didn't Patsy and I stick to business so long as the springs lasted!" When the prawns were discussed we came to matters of more immediate concern. The host declared with his usual energy that fishing was out of the question; there had been a long spell of fine weather, the Inny was nearly dry, and as for the lakes, there had not been a ripple on one of them for a week.

It appeared, however, that my old friend had made ample preparations for our amusement. The morning broke as grey and calm as those which preceded it. The potted crustaceæ were all that could be desired. Men, guns, dogs, game-bags, and ammunition enough to decimate the country, were collected on the little grass plot under the solitary window of our *salle à manger*. Yet still the Major, with feet in his slippers and back to the fire, continued puffing and puffing with a garrulous tranquillity that was maddening. At length the gigantic cheroot came to an end, and the procession getting under way, shaped a course nearly due east, and in less than half an hour reached some small swampy inclosures at the edge of the beautiful curved strand, through the centre of which the Inny cleaves a passage to the sea.

The long ling, with narrow black fissures between the hummucks, was literally full of snipe. The autumn had been unusually dry, and this swamp—the deepest in the neighbourhood—was in high request with the birds. Crossing the bank, we had hardly taken three steps before one sprung at our feet, and was knocked over by my comrade in the first style of art. So numerous were they in this small inclosure that the setters were coupled, and we walked the birds up. During the next three or four hours we could not have fired less than a hundred shots; but whilst my friend performed admirably, I did not kill one out of eight, and felt rejoiced to quit the scene of my disgrace for a walk along the firm dry strand leading to the swampy meadows which border the debouchment of the Inny.

The heavy surf, so common on the Irish coast, at this season, was thundering on the shore. Like charging squadrons the huge rollers rushed on, their long white plumes floating wildly as they hurled themselves headlong on the stubborn sand, thickly strewn with lines and patches of foam. What a picture of a battle field! The gallant onset—the unflinching defence—the shattered ranks—the cumbered ground—and fame enduring as the foam!

Near low water-mark, half buried in the sand, lay a brass cannon of antique workmanship. Heaven only knows how it came there! When the Armada, battered by shot and crippled by tempests, fled along the coast, and some goodly ship went down in the bay, this gun perhaps then sank like lead in that moment of horror, and now, uncovered by the surf, rose to recall the tale of wreck and disaster. As we watched this memento of half forgotten wars, the advancing tide flowed up to it; each wave heaped sand on its head, till it seemed to sink down into the grave. None of the party had ever seen it before, and half a century may elapse ere the spectre again becomes visible to mortal eyes.

Before we separated for the night the Major pointed to a glass of Admiral Fitzroy's. The crystals had risen an inch since morning. "'Twill be a near shave," he said, "but there will be a fresh in the Inny before the month is over."

Cock shooting in the open is one of the most delightful of Irish sports, provided you have a brace of setters that understand their work. It affords constant variety. Now an old grouse rises in a terrible hurry; yet, inveterate grumbler that he is, finds time to complain of our invasion of his rights; then a brown hare glides through the heather; next a snipe with shrill cry and wavering flight rises before Ponto's nose, whilst a flock of golden plovers, with plaintive note and rapid wing, flit past from time to time. From each and all of these mountain races we had taken toll one day as we traversed the heathy range to the westward of Lough Currane. A change was at hand. Lower and lower drooped the clouds—more thick and fast fell the mist. The house at Derrynane—close to its solitary little harbour, where poor Dan O'Connell passed probably the only peaceful days of his busy life, grew less and less distinct, and finally vanished out of sight. The restless ocean lay under "the blanket of the dark," but the drizzle did not extend to the southward; and the Cummeragh, its head waters, and the glorious range of the Iveragh mountains spread out beneath us, gloomy yet clear. For an hour or more we crouched under the lee of a boulder. No change for the better occurred; so, making the best of it, we trudged home through the soaking drizzle.

After prolonged fine weather rain comes on slowly. The following morning, though dull, was dry. No man could predict with certainty how the day would turn out, but the Major was an old campaigner, and always kept an eye to his communications. The commander's arrangements for the day were eminently judicious. If calm, we were to shoot; if breezy, fish; and, as it *was* calm at nine a.m., we collected dogs and guns, together with a couple of bare-legged boys to carry the game, and started for the wide tract of bog and heather which stretched from the head of Lough Currane to the sources of the Cummeragh. We had scarcely reached the ground when the character of the day showed itself unmistakably. The hurly-burly had commenced, and we were in for a westerly gale. Anxiously the Major looked down to the road from time to time as we shot our way towards it, for Willie had been left behind to put the boat on a cart and bring her on, in the event of the wind getting up. It was blowing great guns, and just the weather for making a last successful trial of Larnaena and E-a-li-a-nane.

The binocular was in frequent request. After a more careful survey than usual my friend deposited the instrument in his pocket, and gave a sigh of relief.

"Where did that fellow of yours steal the flag? By Jove, sir, there it is, flying in the stern-sheets of my boat."

On nearer inspection the bunting appeared to belong to no nation in particular, and turned out to be a smart apron of Miss Mary's, purloined for the occasion.

It was near one o'clock when we halted on the margin of the lower lake. The miserable horse was taken from the shafts, tethered to the mooring-rope, and anchored with the boat's kedge. The cart was turned on end, and served as a landmark, to which the dogs were secured, representing the owners of the property. The small chain of lakes we were about to try formed the head of the Waterville fishery, and after the first autumn spates are usually full of fish. We were soon afloat and sculling round the low treeless shores, composed of patches of shingle and peat. Ere long the Major was into something tolerably heavy, but languid as a fine lady; and in three or four minutes one of the boys landed a trout called white, but now black as my boot, and reduced to about half its summer weight. My military friend admired many old things, particularly old wine and whisky, but ancient fish were his abomination. "Right about face, in with him!" was the order. Presently it came to my turn. Then we were engaged simultaneously; but the cry of the ruthless Major was the same, "In with him!" In fact, the inhabitants of the water seemed to have gone into a general mourning. After losing an hour and more we got the boat into the upper lake, and here we succeeded in landing half a score of trout in decent condition. A wilder day I have seldom seen. Larnaena and E-a-li-a-nane—mere mountain pools—were breaking with a sullen plash on their pebbly margins, the low clouds were hurrying along in black and threatening masses, and the dark, overhanging hills looked particularly savage. My companion, however, was bent on getting a salmon, and refused to knock off whilst a chance remained. Premature twilight was coming on over the desolate mountains as we reached the southernmost side of the lake, where a small stream ran murmuringly over the stones. It was now or never.

"There, take it! You have kept us waiting long enough," remarked my comrade, striking so vigorously that I turned my head to see the result, and at the same moment became conscious of an increasing weight on my own rod, and a severe voice at my ear, "There he is! Why *don't* you give him the butt."

How often it happens that perseverance wins the fight at the eleventh hour! He who has done so knows how sweet such triumph is. It made the Major less critical, and the Scribe excellent company. If the truth must be told, the pair of salmon we landed some fifteen minutes after were far from being in condition, for one was black as my hat and the other red as a brick; but the soldier's eyesight suddenly became imperfect. "There, pack them up; 'tis too dark to distinguish colours. We'll decide on the shade to-morrow."

By the time rods and tackle were packed there was little light to spare, and when we reached the lower lake it was dark. As to the exact point at which cart and quadruped were to be found, no two of the party could agree. After a time a dismal howling was heard, which on our nearer approach was exchanged for joyous barking. Even the ill-used horse welcomed us with a subdued neigh.

Whilst the nag was being harnessed, the Major, with increasing irritability, fumbled silently about the wheels of the cart. "What had he lost? Could we assist him?" These and similar politenesses for a time produced no reply. When at length he spoke, loud was the voice and powerful the brogue, and so fierce was the flame of his wrath, that it licked the varnish clean off his courtesy.

"Martin," he said, "it's hanged ye'll be, so sure as my name is Peter Dowd. Look at this. Here's the rope, but where's Ponto, ye thief of the world?"

The missing setter had gnawed his fetters and levanted. This was bad enough; but, unfortunately, I have sometimes an awful inclination to laugh at unseasonable occasions, and the funeral oration, pronounced immediately after by my disconsolate friend, proved irresistible.

"He's gone; the like of him is not to be found under the canopy. I never *will* see him again! Never! Oh, never!"

The poor Major's fury was too great for words, and in solemn silence we jolted on through the rain and the darkness. Once already on this luckless night we had been capsized into the bog, yet the lips of the insulted warrior were hermetically sealed. Once more we were sprawling in the swamp, and then those awful portals were for an instant unclosed.

"The villain will be hanged some day, that's a comfort; but oh, murther! I never will see him gain! Never! Never!"

CHAPTER XL.

The Last Act—The Inny in order—Disinterested Advice—The Major distinguishes himself—Grand Total—Homewards—De mortuis—The wind up—Vale.

THE curtain rises for the last act of our domestic drama. Over the dripping and cheerless mountains raves the boisterous winter wind. The rain ceased at midnight; the glass is getting up, and the Inny, according to my host's prediction, is in condition for this, the closing day of the season. From the energy and industry displayed on the previous evening, the preparations seemed more suitable to the commencement than to the close of a campaign. Two new trebles and twice that number of single casting lines were made, a dozen flies fabricated, and the rod and wheel which had seen so much service were carefully inspected and pronounced in good working order. Exposed to the influence the Major caught the infection, and came down to breakfast with his lower extremities cased in stout boots, instead of the gay embroidered slippers in which on less momentous occasions he was wont to indulge. The short day could ill afford luxurious hours, so my old friend gave up his cheroot, lit a mighty pipe as he crossed the threshold (an example instantly followed by our attendants), and under a strong head of steam, we were soon running down the incline at the bottom of which flows the Inny.

This pretty mountain stream boasts a fair share of heavy spring trout—*perhaps* also a few early salmon, and might, if the freshes were carefully watched, occasionally afford good angling in April and May; but being regularly netted by the proprietor, is of little avail except immediately *after* each spate. When the annual close time commences a good stock soon accumulates; two months had now elapsed since the nets were withdrawn, and the angling—at least as far as numbers went—had reached its culminating point.

The great prolongation of the rod season was no doubt intended as a boon to the upper proprietors; nevertheless, this gain was obtained from the public loss. It was a sort of robbing Peter to pay Paul, and legislation in the endeavour to propitiate extreme interests steered the dangerous middle course which so often brings the good ship *St. Stephen* on the rocks. During the last week of September not one fish in fifty is in a condition fit for the table; and each day of the succeeding month renders a seasonable salmon a greater rarity. After all, the difficulty was to insert the *edge* of the wedge: happily that useful implement is now *in situ*, and only waits a little pressure from without, to be driven home. The current of popular opinion is setting strongly in favour of river reform; even the rinderpest is not an unmixed evil, since by increasing the price of one kind of animal food it has directed men's minds to a source of supply hitherto neglected. But if we hope to raise our waters within any reasonable period to the rank of a national benefit, it can alone be realised by increasing the annual close time. What we want is a sufficient stock, and this can only be obtained by legislation checking, at least for the present, undue consumption. If the net season ended July 25, and the angling season closed September 25, the fisheries would be benefited, the sportsman satisfied, and the upper proprietors possessed of a property worth improving. If these last were certain of having their waters well stocked for a period of two months, artificial propagation—twenty-five times as profitable as the natural method—would pay, and soon become universal. Legislation in the dark ages of our fisheries was eminently one-sided; to be successful it must be impartial. Monopolies do not answer. The time has not yet arrived when the doctrine of share and share alike, as applied to river proprietors, will be tolerated; it must come, however, and *then*, and not till then, will our water farms yield their strength. Some day our streams, from the source to the sea, will represent so many joint-stock companies, with shares in the ratio of ripal rights, bound together for mutual defence and by a common interest. I repeat that this time *will* come, and I can only add, the sooner the better.

"Nice cast that," observed my host, with a due regard to his own interest, pointing to a deep run in a straight line with the bridge. "You try it whilst I move a little higher up."

In this wicked world who can be safe from the arts of designing men? Here was this faithless commander, with fair speeches, beguiling his guest out of the best pool on the Inny. Even so, old friend; but we know the water quite as well as you do, and it will go hard if you do not find a Roland for your Oliver before the day ends.

About two-thirds down the lodge was a deep nick cut in the bank by drainage from the bog, and at this point we obtained the first rise. Instinctively glancing up the stream (whilst stretching out my hand to catch the casting-line, in order to change the trail) I saw one of the Major's imps warily watching a fish his wicked old master was playing with enviable firmness and skill. Did his neighbours covet his ill-gotten gains? I fear they did. Making the best of a bad business, we came over our salmon carefully, and were rewarded with a second rise, and in due time with a third, fourth, fifth, and sixth. More than half an hour had been spent, but not a scale had as yet found its way into our pannier.

"There, he's stuck in a third," remarked my poor companion with the calmness of despair. "It's all right," tossing the casting-line in the air; "try him once more, any way."

One of the honest fellow's peculiarities was a jealous hatred of any man who chanced to kill a fish in his immediate neighbourhood. Such an act always appeared to him as a personal injury, and, like many of the followers of Knox, having a long memory for disagreeables, he usually held a large amount of unpaid debts, which sooner or later he contrived to liquidate.

Stealing involuntary glances at my fortunate neighbour, we once more came over our fish, who this time made a dashing plunge at the dropper, more in sport than earnest; but it is unwise playing with edged tools, and so our shy acquaintance found when the trail sank deep in his flank. Master and man were savage, and the tackle was new. Strong measures were in fashion; and a desperate strain was kept up, and as the salmon wallowed over the surface Willie made a successful dash at him with the gaff. Huddling our first prize into the basket, we proceeded to take vengeance on our treacherous host by keeping ahead and fishing all the best pools we could reach first.

But the veteran was not to be done in this way. As we hurried on, he hung back, placing a longer and longer interval of time between us, thus making the pools we had too lightly fished "as good as new" for himself. Whenever we caught sight of him the wicked old commander seemed always to prosper, and in the opinion of my jealous attendant, must have bagged at least half a score of fish. It really *was* provoking, but do what we would, success still held aloof. If we hooked a salmon, some disaster was sure to attend us. Two had been lost by the mouth giving way, and a third had been knocked off the line when ready for the gaff, by an officious trout taking the other fly; and still the Major's rod seemed to continue in a chronic "state of bend."

Less than two miles above the bridge was a deep pool of considerable extent, having on its western bank a long low rock, and here our sport commenced. The place seemed full of fish; pleasant rivalry had wound us up; everything went like clockwork, and when the soldier came hurriedly over the fence it was to find us still in possession, and on the point of landing our sixth salmon. Notwithstanding the splendour of this closing scene, the Major was still confident of having won the honours of the day.

"I'll bet you a ten-gallon cask of potheen, Rory and I will make the best show. Come, Willie, turn out your creel. What! only six fish and a beggarly half score of trout? Rory, show the gentlemen what we can do."

With a malicious grin that imp slowly drew out one salmon after another, arranging them in order on the turf. Then appeared the trout! What a show they made! Ten of the former, eighteen of the latter. "Ah! you may look," to my follower, who was suspiciously examining their mouths; "every soul of them caught fair. There, pack up the game; the ground is soft; twilight is falling, and we must be on the road before dark."

With a sigh I gave up the rod, and felt as if parting from a friend. For nine months we had been inseparable. In heat and cold, in storm and sunshine, it had been the humble minister of unalloyed happiness, such as I shall probably never more enjoy. In its silence I had not been solitary; it had neither deceived nor betrayed me; and of whom else could I say as much? That night we drank a solemn bumper to the memory of the departed season, and made vain promises for the time to come. No one believed them. Yet they served to cheat us of an hour of sorrow. Another week brought our visit to an end, and made the "Year of Liberty" a thing of the past. Forty-eight hours after I was once more at work amongst the poor, the sick, and the wretched, whose jubilee may commence in a future world, but whose lot can never be bright in the present.

November 10, 1866.—Since the last sentence was written scarce a year has passed, yet in that brief space important events have occurred in our little household. Poor Mary, having sworn "to love, honour, and obey," is now in the tropics fighting the battle of life. The good old Colonel has gone the way of all flesh, and the grass is not yet green on the sod which covers the remains of one who was in infancy my protector, in youth my guide, and in manhood my best friend.

My gentle companion, however, sits near me; her cheek, perhaps, a thought more pale; whilst Willie is drawing the cork from a bottle of hock. The lamps are lit, dessert is on the table, the *ex officio* butler has received his usual glass of wine, and yet lingers about the room.

"Them painters is gone at last, mum. The door looks illegant; the holes where the screws went is stopped up, so that no crathur on earth can see where they wor, and I've buried the brass plate under the sawdust in the binn the master filled this morn. I s'pose it's little we'll be here now, as every year will be a year of liberty; but oh! master, won't we miss poor Mary!"

APPENDIX.

A TOURIST-ANGLER'S GUIDE.

THIS Guide, being a partial epitome of the "Year of Liberty," has been added to the work more for the benefit of the wandering sportsman than for perusal by the general reader, its design being to show the former at a glance the principal lakes and rivers that lie in his route. Before proceeding further, however, it may be advisable to say a few words regarding the arrangement which has been adopted.

Designed rather for strangers than residents, the island has been divided by arbitrary lines into strips or districts, generally extending from one sea-board to another, each division being in direct connection with some great route, leading to Ireland from England, Wales, or Scotland. For example: whilst the line from Holyhead to Kingstown places the angling-tourist at the edge of the great central lake district, that from Bristol to Cork would bring him at once into the south-west division of the county.

The reader must not suppose that *all* the waters in the several districts are here mentioned. Lakes and rivers, ordinarily of inferior sporting quality, are so numerous, that if each were to appear in review before us, a volume, not a chapter, would be required for their illustration. But though these are now passed by in silence, the angler must not imagine they are beneath his notice; on the contrary numbers of the smaller streams on the coast, though unsuitable for stations, occasionally afford admirable sport after rain. The tourist should therefore constantly have an eye to business, and everywhere institute diligent inquiries as to the condition necessary to bring each up to concert pitch. By this means he will frequently in the summer and autumn earn many days which will henceforth and for ever be laid up in the storehouse of memory amongst his treasures,

Having premised thus much, we will start *viâ* Glasgow for Sligo, and, if the reader will draw a line from the latter town to Galway, he will find we have given him the whole of Mayo and a corner of county Sligo as the district in which to make his

First Angling Tour.

Lough Gill lies close to the town of Sligo, and affords good salmon angling in the spring. Permission is given on application. Hotels excellent. Private lodgings can be obtained.

Ballisadare River is about five miles distant, and yields admirable salmon and grilse-fishing from May to the end of the season. The present proprietor has, we hear, built a comfortable sporting-lodge, and proposes to let the angling and house for 100*l*. per annum, a moderate sum if the equivalents are taken into consideration.

The Easkey is well worth a visit in summer or autumn; the Great Western coach-road to Ballina crosses the stream.

The Moy affords the best free angling in the kingdom. In the latter part of April this river will well repay the sportsman, though his journey cost him time and money. At this season he will meet only with salmon, the grilse not arriving until about the 15th of June. Should he wish for more general angling, Lough Conn, whilst holding the king of fish, will afford admirable sport in trolling. The lake abounds with heavy trout, pike, and perch. Pontoon is about an hour's drive from Ballina, and should on no account be neglected. In June the grilse throng into the Moy, and the sport is as good above as below the weirs. The hotel is very comfortable, and private lodgings can be obtained. Should the tourist follow the coast road from this place to Belmullet, he will cross several small streams which, if taken at the fall of a fresh, may afford good white trout fishing in the autumn. Continuing his course along the shores of Black Sod Bay he reaches the debouchment of

The Owenmore River.—A finer looking stream than this can hardly be imagined. It is not, however, as good as it looks. Over netting has for the present, injured the stock to a great extent.

Ballycroy River lies a few miles to the southward, and affords excellent white trout and salmon fishing (*vide* Maxwell's "Wild Sports of the West"). This river is usually let to one or two rods. Extensive grouse moors rise around its head waters. At the head of Chew Bay lies the small town of Newport, which forms admirable head quarters during the summer and autumn. This station commands

The Beltra River, Burrishoole Lake, and Tyrena (a mere mountain stream).—The Beltra affords a little salmon fishing, and fair sport with white trout. This river has been occasionally let to a single rod; leave, however, may generally be obtained. Burrishoole Lake contains plenty of trout, and a fair stock of grilse; whilst Tyrena, in wet weather, yields admirable angling. Following the coast road to Galway, the tourist first reaches

The Errive, which is generally, however, let as a private water, and the same may be said of *Delphi*. A little farther to the west lie the river and connecting lakes of

Ballinahinch.—Here angling can always be obtained on fair terms. All nets are withdrawn, so very superior sport may be expected during the next five years.

The Screebe and Furness.—The chain of lakes constituting this fishery, afford admirable angling for white trout during the autumn; they also contain salmon; close to the best lake is a comfortable lodge fitted up for the reception of tourists; the terms are about three guineas a week per rod.

Costello belongs to a club, and has little interest for the tourist-angler.

The Spiddal is usually let for 100*l.* per annum, and in average seasons is well worth the money.

Galway.—The angling here from April to the end of the season is too well known to require comment. We have now reached the south-west extremity of the line which marks the boundary of our first tour. Passing inland, we come to

Lough Corrib and Lough Mask.—The former affords excellent salmon and trout fishing; the trolling is very good, the best station is Oughterade.

THE SECOND TOUR (*viâ* Glasgow and Londonderry).

This north-north-west division is bounded by the Atlantic, and by a line stretching from Lough Foyle, to the village of Bundoran. A short drive of eight or ten miles brings the tourist to the shores of Lough Swilly, crossing which he arrives at Rathmelton.

Lough Fern (the property of Sir James Stuart), is one of the earliest lakes in the kingdom, which the generous owner places at the disposal of the angler; leave can be obtained through the landlord of the hotel. Two or three spring fish and a basket of trout may safely be calculated upon in any good day during March, April, or May.

The Doe Castle Fishery lies a few miles north of Rathmelton. The river and lake hold very early salmon; the proprietor leases the angling. Terms can be ascertained on application. The grilse and white trout fishing during the summer and autumn are admirable; eight or ten miles to the westward, bring the tourist to Dunfanaghy. A short distance beyond the village stands the union workhouse, near which is a lake affording excellent brown trout, ranging from one to six pounds. There is also another lake not far distant on the road to Doe Castle, said to abound with char. Ten miles to the south-west is

Gweedore.—This fishery, so far as the angler is concerned, consists of a chain of lakes, together with the Crotty and Gweedore rivers. The accommodation at the hotel is all that can be desired. About a moiety of the angling is free to anyone staying in the house, the remainder is let by tickets. Terms can be seen by reference to the chapter on Gweedore. The botanist, the angler, and the artist will be equally delighted by a visit to this district. A drive of two hours enables the traveller to reach

Dunglow, near which is a small stream, draining a chain of lakes. During the autumn spates fair white trout fishing may here be met with, and some of the lakes are said—I believe with truth—to hold large trout. Accommodation by no means luxurious. Ten miles to the south-south-west runs

The Gweebarra River, which is occasionally leased to the rod. If not let, permission may be obtained. Within an easy walk of Gweebarra-bridge are many good lakes; the district is rather inaccessible, but the grilse fishing in the river is excellent should the season be wet. A few miles to the south-west is the village of Glenties, close to which flows

The Oanea River.—Here white trout are plentiful in the autumn; some salmon may also be taken. Accommodation can be obtained at the village Inn. Due south lies Killybegs, and near it the hamlet of Dunkeneely, where is a stream worth trying should the weather be wet. A little beyond,

The Inver River crosses the high road to Donegal. This water is the property of Mr. Sinclair, to whose kindness many a stranger is indebted for a day or two's admirable angling. The Inver is a late river. Three miles farther on is the town of Donegal, through which flows

The Esk.—Lough Esk is its head water. This lake holds plenty of white and brown trout; the fishing is good in August, September, and October; permission can generally be obtained on application. Ten miles to the south lies the town of Ballyshannon.

The Erne affords the finest summer angling in Ireland. The fishing is usually let to about eight rods; for particulars, application should be made to the lessee. Four miles above Ballyshannon is Beleek, which is a good station for Lough Erne, on whose wide waters excellent sport may be had with red trout and pike.

Lough Melvin (good in spring; better in summer) is three miles distant. Scott's hotel at Garrison is the best station from which to fish this lake, which contains salmon, grilse, gillaroo, and the salmo-ferox. The last attains a large size here.

The Drowse drains Lough Melvin, and falls into the sea at

the village of Bundoran. In the spring some salmon may be taken in it, and during the autumn freshes this stream affords capital sport. The tourist has now reached the end of his district; should he return to Derry,

The Swilly may be worth his notice for a few days; whilst by following

The Finn, he may once more find himself at Derry with a full pannier.

THE THIRD TOUR (*via* Stranraer and Larne).

The lines from "the Lakes" *viâ* Morecombe and Fleetwood, will bring tourists from Cumberland, Yorkshire, and Lancashire to Belfast, which commands the district we are about to visit equally well with Larne. The section marked out for our third tour contains the counties of Antrim, Derry, Down, Tyrone and Armagh. In the centre of these lies

Lough Neagh, the most extensive sheet of water in the island, into which the greater part of the rivers of the foregoing counties debouch. During the autumn

The Maine River affords very superior trout fishing, as at that season the great lakers are running up; the same thing may be said in a less degree of many of the affluents of this inland sea. Toome Bridge is probably the best station for Lough Neagh, whilst Randalstown forms comfortable quarters for the Maine River. The fish of this district are probably the heaviest in Ireland.

The Bann, the only outlet of Lough Neagh, is a noble river; the part best suited for salmon-angling is situated two or three miles above Coleraine, and is rented by a club of a dozen members, each of whom has the privilege of taking out a friend. Membership is a thing to be desired, as the sport is good and the terms very moderate.

The Bush flows into the sea close to the Giants' Causeway. This river, however, has little interest for the tourist-angler, being always in private hands; it is at present leased to two rods.

Between Fairhead and Larne are two or three small rivers, the principal of which falls into the sea at Ballycastle, but for sporting purposes they are of little value.

THE FOURTH TOUR (*viâ* Holyhead and Dublin).

The district now to be visited by the angler contains a great chain of lakes, extending with little intermission across the centre of the island, from Mullingar to Sligo, comprising—*Virginia, Belvedere, Dereveragh, Lough Owel, Lough Kay, Lough Garra, Lough Arrow,* and many others. Mullingar commands Belvedere and Lough Owel. The green-drake fishing on these two lakes is excellent.

Dereveragh also is admirable in the May-fly season. Boyle is the best station for Lough Kay, Lough Garra, and Lough Arrow, which are second to none in the kingdom in May and June. It may not be out of place to remark here that all these lakes afford first-class trolling in the summer and autumn, containing, besides trout, heavy pike and perch. I know no more delightful angling tour than might be made by a seriatim visit to the waters just mentioned.

THE FIFTH TOUR (*viâ* Bristol and Waterford).

The angler, by following a line drawn between Waterford and Limerick, commands several salmon stations on the *Suir* and the *Barrow*, nearly all of which can be fished free of charge. The sport to be met with in this wide range is often excellent throughout the season.

The Greater Blackwater, between Lismore and Fermoy, is second to none in the kingdom. Previous to the erection of the Queen's Gap, Lismore formed a charming station during the spring and summer; the best angling, however, is *now* obtained above this point. Some stands are generally to be let; there is a heavy run of spring salmon in the Blackwater. A few hours by rail brings the angler to the shores of the Shannon; nearly all the casts about Castle Connell—by far the best portion of the river—are let at a high figure; the sportsman, however, who follows the course of this noble river, will obtain some of the finest trout-angling to be met with in the island.

THE SIXTH TOUR (*viâ* Bristol and Cork)
Commands the counties of Cork and Kerry. *The River Lee* offers no mean salmon angling in spring and during the summer. Grilse are pretty numerous. All particulars respecting this water can be obtained by application to Mr. Hackett, fishing tackle-maker, Cork. A pleasant run by rail brings us to Killarney, where we have the Upper, Middle, and Lower Lakes—the Laune, the Flesk, and Lough Guttane. The lakes of Killarney are free, and would afford first-rate spring trolling, were it not for the cross lines of the professionals.

The Laune occasionally gives a good day in spring, but is better during the summer and autumn. The trout trolling on

Lough Guttane is often very good. Permission is rarely or never refused to the stranger. Kerry, a sort of angler's paradise, abounds in lakes and rivers. We will proceed to mention some of the principal. A drive of two hours by the mail car conducts the tourist to Lady Headly's Hotel at Rossbeigh. This inn forms excellent head-quarters for

Carra Lake and River, and the Beigh.—The angling on the river is sometimes good in spring; the trolling on the lake in the earlier months bears a high character. The salmon are of good size and the red trout very fine. Part of this water is free, and on the remainder, angling by the day, week, month, or season, can be obtained on very moderate terms.

The Beigh is a little mountain stream close to the hotel, which, during the autumn spates, holds fine white trout.

The Black Stones River is an affluent of Carra Lake, and, during the early months of spring, affords better salmon angling than either the lake or Carra River. It is usually, however, let with the shootings. Ten miles to the south-west is the small town of Cahirciveen, where is a stream that looks very promising in wet weather. I have never fished there, but have heard good accounts of the water.

The Inny flows into Ballinskellig's Bay, and in August, September, and October (should the weather be wet), will afford excellent salmon and white trout fishing. Three miles farther on is

Waterville, where is a capital hotel at the bottom of the village—the "Hartop Arms." Lough Currane is well known for the excellent salmon trolling it affords in spring; here, also, red trout are numerous and fine. During the month of May the salmon rise well to the fly. In July and August the lake is full of white trout, at which season also a few grilse will fall to the share of the angler.

The Cummeragh is an affluent of Lough Currane, connecting it with two small mountain tarns. Towards the close of the season these waters afford good sport.

The Lesser Blackwater (station, "Old Dromore Hotel").—This river is admirable in summer and autumn, but requires rain to bring it to concert pitch. Any angler intending to visit the district should write to the hotel keeper for information, as the angling is occasionally let to a club. At the head of Bantry Bay are two small rivers,

The Owrane and Beal, which afford good angling should the summer be wet.

Following the coast line back to Cork, are several small streams, with which the writer has no personal acquaintance.

We have now conducted the tourist over most of the principal waters in the island; and, in conclusion, have only to wish him health and good sport when he visits them.

www.ingramcontent.com/pod-product-compliance
Lightning Source LLC
Chambersburg PA
CBHW022047230426
43672CB00008B/1095